An Offering of Light
Healing with Jyorei, Natural Agriculture, and Art

An Offering of Light

Healing with Jyorei, Natural Agriculture, and Art

Roy Gibbon & Atsushi Fujimaki
with Gerard Rohlfing

Revised Third Edition

SHUMEI AMERICA PUBLICATIONS

Medical Disclaimer

The information in this book is based on published and unpublished sources. The purpose is for educational and research purposes only and should not be construed as giving medical advice. The authors and publisher do not diagnose, treat, or prescribe. If any readers use the information to solve their own health problems, they are prescribing for themselves, which is their constitutional right, but neither the authors nor the publisher assume any responsibility.

Published by Shumei America Publications
2430 East Colorado Boulevard
Pasadena, California 91107 USA

Revised third edition, 2017

ISBN-13: 978-1-9778-6898-5
ISBN-10: 1-977-86898-3

Cover design and diagrams by Tokiko Jinta
Text design by Atsushi Fujimaki
Illustrations by Yasushi Fujimoto

Printed by CreateSpace

Contents

Chapter

Your ears are useless if you ignore words spoken on the meaning of Light.

—Meishusama (*Poems of Inspiration. Miakarishu1*)

PREFACE

This book is for people, especially Westerners, who wish for a deeper under-standing of the teachings of Mokichi Okada. Known as Meishusama, Mokichi Okada was a spiritual teacher who was active in Japan during the first half of the twentieth century. His life was dedicated to serving humanity through spiritual healing, the arts, and spiritually-based food cultivation.

Quotes from his writings are used liberally throughout this text as we believe they allow his spirit to become more alive for the reader. Because of the abundance of these quotes, this book easily could have been subtitled: Commentaries on the Teachings of Meishusama.

Some readers might already be familiar with the spiritual benefits of Jyorei, and it is natural for them to want to learn more about Meishusama and his teachings after first receiving this blessing. We hope that this book satisfies them. We also hope that members of Shumei currently practicing Jyorei will find this publication revealing.

While writing An Offering of Light, we found that a reappraisal of Meishu-sama's teachings in light of Western culture was needed. So rather than routinely summarizing his teachings, we attempted to clarify and elaborate them using concepts familiar to Westerners, while still remaining true to his message. Therefore, some of his ideas have been paraphrased in terminology more familiar to those in the West.

The scope of Meishusama's writings and transcribed lectures is vast and diverse. He was not a systematic writer and a comprehensive overview of his thoughts does not yet exist. While it is not our intention to present a conclusive study of his ideas, we hope that this publication will offer a glimpse of the underlying unity and integrity of his thoughts. While the book focuses on his most relevant thoughts, some ideas that he only lightly touched upon were thought important enough to explain further. Consequently, the organization of Meishusama's teachings found here is unique to this publication. Meishusama wrote and spoke to people in a variety of ways, depending on his audience and their circumstances, preferring to adapt his ideas to the situation at hand. This is understandable as his purpose was to give spiritual guidance rather than set forth a complete philosophical or theological system. For a deeper perception of his ideas, we encourage readers to study his writings directly.

The best way to validate Meishusama's teachings is through the practice of them. This cannot be done solely by gaining an intellectual grasp of his concepts or by reading this book. His advice must be acted upon. Meishusama felt that to realize his teachings fully, one must live the spiritual practices that he prescribed. As Mokichi Okada affirms about the truth of his own words:

Those who would appreciate the truth of this principle must give and receive Jyorei for a few years in succession. If they do this, they will be able to grasp the profound reality that these words merely hint at.
—Meishusama. (Natural Power. Essential Teachings of Meishusama)

Our hope is that this book will spark a deeper awareness of Meishusama's teachings and thereby benefit all.

ACKNOWLEDGMENTS

The creation of this book was a collaborative effort involving many people. Its inspiration grew out of a leadership-brainstorming session held at the National Center of Shinji Shumeikai of America in Pasadena, California in November of 2001. The project coordinator was Atsushi Fujimaki. The main authors were Roy Gibbon and Atsushi Fujimaki. Gerard Rohlfing wrote the brief biography of Meishusama, and Sensei Koichi Deguchi provided valuable assistance with the chapter concerning Natural Agriculture.

We wish to thank Sensei Eugene Imai, Director of Shumei America, and Sensei Alan Imai, Director of Shumei International Institute, for their guiding vision and assistance. The following people helped us with comments, critiques, and suggestions: Kenji Ban, Rod Barker, George Bedell, William Blake, Sandy Bres, Nova Brown, Carole Buchannon, Bibi Chapman, Adrian Chatman, Robbie Christianson, Alice Cunningham, Elizabeth DeCastro, Tony DeCastro, Marion Deland, Chuck Easter, Sharon Franquemont, Sensei Chisako Fukushima, Anne Gardner, Eric Girolamo, Akira Hashiguchi, Ron Helgesen, Michwel Heril, Djann Hoffman, William Howell, Dr. Diana Jerkins, Olya Kenny, Sandy Kipper, François Kuwata, John Marcus, Steven McCord, The Very Rev. James Parks Morton, Jody Pappas, Annie Pierce, Mike Radice, Lothar Rapior, Don Riedel, Renee Ronnie, Mary Ann Scott, Sheila Shaw, Sensei Cathy Shima, Marty Shimomura, Linda Siegel, Sandra Snyder-Traverso, Chuck Surface, Linda Tan, Elizabeth Torres, Jan Totten, Andrea Vanda and Shigeyuki Yamakata. We also received suggestions, encouragement, and support from numerous other friends, members of Shinji Shumeikai, and the staff of the National Center in Pasadena. For all their kind help we are deeply grateful.

Our special thanks go to Tokiko Jinta for her wonderful diagrams and cover design, and to Yasushi Fujimoto for his excellent illustrations.

Finally, we express our appreciation to Kaicho-Sensei (Ms Hiroko Koyama), President of Shinji Shumeikai, for her continuous support and encouragement. It is because of her recognition of the need for this publication, that we were able to finish this book.

Most importantly, it is with gratitude and joy that we dedicate this book to Meishusama, our source of inspiration, wisdom, and Light.

ABBREVIATIONS

Most of the quotes in this book are taken from three publications by Shumei America Publications: *Essential Teachings of Meishusama, Kannon's Way Teachings of Meishusama,* and *Miakarishu: A Collection of Light* (both translations 1 & 2). Two other publications by Shinji Shumeikai: *Natural Agriculture Teachings of Meishusama* and *A Hundred Teachings of Meishusama* are also used as sources of quotes. (The first book is currently in the process of being translated into English and the second one is out of print. These six titles are abbreviated as follows:

ET: Essential Teachings of Meishusama

HT: A Hundred Teachings of Meishusama

KW: Kannon's Way Teachings of Meishusama

MK1:   Miakarishu (A Collection of Light), first edition

MK2:   Miakarishu (A Collection of Light), second edition

NA: Natural Agriculture Teachings of Meishusama

CHAPTER 1

MEISHUSAMA

Introduction

If we want to establish eternal peace on this earth of ours, we must first eliminate the feelings of stress and discomfort from every individual and replace them with feelings of ease and comfort. Everybody who feels this comfort will loathe war and love peace. This is an indisputable and certain fact.
—*The Three Great Disasters and the Three Lesser Disasters. ET*

A general sense of isolation, meaninglessness, and despair seems to pervade our times. For too many of us, life is full of tension and struggle. Despite all the modern conveniences and mass entertainment available, many of us are still left feeling empty and inwardly impoverished. There is an old saying that "money doesn't buy happiness," and this could also be said for many of the other luxuries of our post-industrial civilization.

Everybody wants happiness, but it is not always so easy to attain. People pursue happiness in many ways—including relationships, entertainment, health, wealth, and status, to name a few. Searching for happiness outwardly may distract us from our inner pain, but does not make us truly happy. Looking deeper into the subject, one might ask, "What exactly is true happiness, and how can we attain it in a meaningful, satisfying, and lasting way?"

Happiness is not a superficial mood or attitude, but is a state of being derived from our spiritual condition and the quality of our soul. It is a sense of joy, satisfaction, and well-being that permeates our life independently of changing circumstances and events. After we have found such happiness, it is quite natural for it to spill over into the various activities and relationships in our lives. Now, instead of looking for happiness, we begin to radiate it wherever we go.

The promotion of this true happiness was the fundamental concern of a man called "Meishusama," an honorary title that means "Master of Light," and by extension is the purpose of this book, as it introduces his teachings and prescribed activities.

Meishusama was born with the name Mokichi Okada in the late nineteenth-century Japan, and rose up from abject poverty to help millions of people attain greater health, happiness, and fulfillment in their lives. After enduring numerous painful illnesses and personal tragedies, as well as unjustified governmental persecution, he eventually emerged as one of the most dynamic spiritual leaders in modern times. Not only did Meishusama receive an invaluable spiritual blessing from God that allowed him to attain personal health and happiness, but he also found ways to share this blessing with people around the world. How was this done? What was his secret, and how is it relevant today, half a century after his passing?

Meishusama was one of the most prolific writers of twentieth century Japan. Beginning in the 1930's, he wrote extensively—creating books as well as magazine and newspaper articles. Many of his lectures were also transcribed into print. He created thousands of Japanese traditional-style poems and left writings on various subjects estimated to comprise over nine thousand pages. His works, which were abundantly produced mostly during the ten years from the end of World War II to his passing in 1955, relate to almost every field of human endeavor. They exemplify his spiritual insight, compassion, knowledge, and down-to-earth pragmatism.

Meishusama's personal will was surrendered to a higher power, the very power that created the universe in all its beauty, variety, and splendor. People have given this power many names, such as God, Allah, the Great Spirit, Brahman, Divine Mother, the One, the Tao, and many others. What is important here was Meishusama's relationship to this divine source and the effect it had on his character and behavior. He was a remarkable person who seemed to deeply affect everyone who came into contact with him. Like many of the great humanitarians of the last century, he worked tirelessly and at great personal sacrifice to serve the society around him. The more he relinquished personal gain, the more he became filled with a profound, luminous energy that he was able to use to alleviate the suffering of others. By simply raising his hand toward someone, he could help that individual feel energized and healed.

Meishusama called this energy "Jyorei," which means "purification of the spirit." Not only was it powerful and profound, but this ability to heal could also be transferred to others. An increasingly large number of people have now dedicated themselves to assisting Meishusama in his mission to heal and transform the world. Through this miraculous power, numerous people from diverse backgrounds have been healed of painful ailments and incurable diseases. These miracles have served to awaken many people to the power of God and have been instrumental in inspiring them to redirect their lives toward serving others.

Many of Meishusama's followers considered him to be a divine manifestation of God in this world. Some saw him as the prophet of an approaching new age of universal salvation. He was graced with highly developed psychic perception and spiritual awareness, which allowed him to see into the spiritual world and then describe what he saw there. He was also able to discern the inner principles and structures of the universe, the spiritual conditions of individuals, and the nature of divinity itself. Miracles followed wherever he went. He was continuously engaged in curing people and inspiring them to awaken to the spiritual dimension in life. Amidst all of this, he still remained a man of easy humor and gentle kindness. Despite great persecution and endless demands on his time, he still managed to enjoy the simple things in life. It was not unusual to find him arranging flowers in his room, gazing at the clouds in the sky, laughing with friends, or catching the latest movie or concert.

His followers included people from all walks of life. Some were shopkeepers, students, farmers, office-workers, and housewives whom he helped to find a new purpose in life and to work for the betterment of humanity.

More and more I give my life to serving people and the world. —God's Love. MK1

Biography

Early Life

The man who in later years would bear the honorary title "Meishusama" (Master of Light) was born Mokichi Okada in a crowded slum area of old Tokyo in 1882. It was during the time of Japan's most drastic modernization, following a long period of feudalism.

As a boy, Mokichi was always pale and sickly, forever coming down with some new ailment. In spite of this, he persevered in his studies and graduated from middle school with outstanding grades and a passion for artistic creation. At age 14, with the dream of becoming an artist, he began a preparatory course at what is now the Tokyo National University of Fine Arts and Music. Amidst the ongoing storm of Westernization, this school was the first to place a special emphasis on the traditional expanse of Japanese and Eastern arts in which Mokichi had a strong interest.

Illness

But his dream was not to be. Barely six months into his new life, he suddenly encountered eye pain and blurry vision. The famous eye specialists he consulted tried everything they knew, scratched their heads, and threw up their hands. Nothing worked; the infection would have its way. Young Okada—Meishusama—would have to face the future with the vision of his right eye greatly impaired. It was a crushing blow. In the context of the times, no one in the fine arts field could conceive of an artist with such a handicap. This meant he would no longer be accepted at the university. With heavy heart, Meishusama abandoned forever his dream of becoming an artist.

There was more to follow. First came stabbing pains in his side—the onset of pleurisy. "At the university hospital sanatorium," he wrote, "my lungs became a wellspring, yielding nearly seven ounces of water!" He suffered with this illness for six months, and in spite of every known medication, it made a nasty comeback a year later. The final prognosis was dire. He was just 18 when a famous medical expert confirmed that he now had advanced pulmonary tuberculosis. This was a death sentence, as the disease at that time was considered incurable.

Meishusama was despondent, but he refused to give up. After several years of searching for the right medication, he finally decided to try natural means, a strict natural diet. The result exceeded all expectations. "I had learned a certain tenacity," he later noted, "and this, combined with a change to a vegetarian diet, enabled me to throw off the TB."

Still fired up by the love of beautiful things, he took up the study of fine Japanese lacquer work and developed skill in the art of lacquer inlay. It was his hope to enter the antique and curio business in partnership with his father, but in May of 1905 fate intervened with the elder Okada's untimely death.

Business

Later that same year, Meishusama at age 22 overcame his deep sorrow and took an important step, and entered the world of business on his own. With his mother's guidance and a modest inheritance from his father, he acquired a small sundry-goods store in Tokyo, naming it "Korin-do" in honor of a great artist he admired.

Early in his business career he faced another test of fortitude—a permanent injury to his right index finger, the one he needed in order to apply fine gold-dust veneers to his artistic inlays. From that time on, he was forced to rely on others for this necessary handwork to bring his lacquer ware designs into being.

Nonetheless, his success was such that by 1907 he was inspired to enter the wholesale field. To gain more space for the venture, he remodeled the house in which his family was then living, located just behind Tokyo Station. In February of that year, his new Okada Enterprises store, specializing in traditional artistic handicrafts for women, threw open its doors to the wholesale trade. Here Meishusama's feeling for beauty and his background in painting and lacquer inlay began to pay rich dividends. His original designs won many prizes in exhibitions, and word of his talents began to get around. In June of the same year, he took a wife named Taka. Their glow of happiness may have helped to promote business; at any rate, Okada Enterprises quickly became a leader in the world of fashion.

Meishusama's life now seemed complete, but in terms of health, he paid a high price. With all the work, he was seized by a chronic cerebral anemia so severe that even the noise of a passing streetcar made him faint and dizzy. At last he found relief in moxibustion treatments combined with exercise and long daily walks through the city streets.

Following his mother's death in 1912, Meishusama continued to push ahead in the wholesale field and soon reached the pinnacle of success. By this time he was hiring numerous employees, and he was known for treating them well, earning their loyalty and inspiring them to give excellent service.

More Sickness and Pain

Still sickness never ceased to dog him. Tonsillitis, digestive problems, rheumatism, chronic fatigue syndrome, irritable bowel syndrome, valvular heart disease, scabies . . . it seemed he was going through the entire medical encyclopedia. Once he came down with severe typhoid, spent three months in the hospital, and at one point actually made out his will. Throughout his career, he was hospitalized three times and twice heard the doctors say he would die. Yet somehow his natural optimism always pulled him through.

Compared to everything else, a toothache might seem hardly worth mention, but when Meishusama faced this problem beginning in 1914, it almost drove him mad. Four teeth at once were screaming in agony. He tried all kinds of medicines, but all through the next year and into 1916, the pain just got worse. At times he even thought of suicide. When an acquaintance suggested a religious healer, he desperately stopped all his medications and consulted the man, though without much faith in the outcome. In a few days he began to feel better and was struck by a realization: the medications he'd been taking for pain were the actual cause of much worse pain. This gave him his initial insight into the possible side effects of modern medicine.

Despite this painful affliction, during this same period he created the beautiful Asahi Daiya (Morning-Sun diamond)—the sparkling artificial gemstone that earned patents in many countries and became one of the most fashionable jewelry items of the day in Japan.

Personal Tragedies

All through his youth, Meishusama's passions had flared when he heard of wrongdoings by politicians and others in responsible positions. His soul still burned with the desire to rid society of evil. At length he decided to start his own newspaper and use the power of the press to rectify injustices. Emboldened by his business success, he founded a finance company to raise the funds he would need. It was terrible timing. In the spring of 1919, following World War I, a floundering economy and the failure of his main bank left him deeply in debt, at the mercy of creditors. He tried desperately to save his wholesale business by incorporating it, but his efforts crumbled in the great market panic of March, 1920. About nine months earlier, he had also met with extreme personal tragedy. Taka, his wife of nearly twelve years, died of typhoid fever contracted during pregnancy. Their prematurely born baby could not be saved, either.

Spiritual Quest

At one time religion had appealed to Meishusama. "When I was young," he wrote, "I was so afire with love for the human race that I just wanted to become a man of religion and help the world." But as he got older, though his love for humanity never changed, he had come to consider religion pretty much a waste of time, and even thought of himself as an atheist. Now, however, at age 37, he was suddenly no longer sure of anything. Racked by the pain of his losses, he reached out for the only help that remained. There was nothing to captivate him in the established religions, but he was curious about Oomoto, a Shinto-related faith that was then growing in popularity. Often in those days he would stop by the Oomoto Tokyo center, taking time for meditation and learning to pray. Gradually he found solace and the courage to continue.

Early in this time of seeking, Meishusama also found consolation in a new marriage. For the next few years, buoyed by his natural optimism, he managed to keep his store afloat, eking out a daily existence for himself and his new bride. Then came a stunning shock—the giant Kanto earthquake of 1923, the most massive quake in Japanese history in which approximately 100,000 people died, and much of the city was destroyed. To the small Okada store behind Tokyo Station, it was a near fatal blow.

By this time, distracted by all the pressures of business, Meishusama had entirely lost touch with Oomoto. But now he could no longer ignore what Life was telling him. As he noted later, "There was nothing left to do but return to God."

Setting his misfortunes behind him, he rejoined Oomoto and began devoting long hours each day to an ancient form of meditation, seeking to refine his soul, explore the spiritual world, and to obtain oneness with a great force that he began to sense all around him. His dream of reforming things by starting a newspaper had been a delusion, and he realized that the only way to build a more perfect society was through universal spiritual awakening.

Over the next three years, Meishusama's personal warmth and dedication to helping others won him many friends, and he rose rapidly in esteem at Oomoto. With joy, he realized that just through the power of prayer he could be a genuine help to those suffering from illness. Then came an event that was to put his entire life in a new perspective.

Words from Above

It happened one night when he was at home. As he later wrote, "It was about midnight on a night in December of 1926 that I cannot forget. The strangest feeling I have ever experienced rose in my heart. It was a most peaceful feeling, yet it urged me to speak something out loud. I couldn't stop the words from coming. I was taken over by an irresistible force. The first words out of my mouth were, 'Get some paper and brushes ready.' I asked my wife for her help. From then on there came unbelievable words." Yoshi, his wife, hurried to get writing implements and began taking down his expositions, which continued page after page, and then day after day, week after week.

For three months the flood of words went on, laying bare the history of Japan and the entire world, and foretelling a great transition from the Age of Darkness to the Age of Light. The purpose of all Creation and humankind's divine mission were clearly set forth. God and man were to work as a team in building Paradise on Earth, creating a world of truth, goodness and beauty. But first would come worldwide catastrophe unless humanity could reform its ways, disperse negative clouds, and clear the way for higher spiritual vibrations in every field of endeavor.

Kannon[1]

Meishusama had grown up respecting but not really accepting the traditional Japanese concept of Kannon, the Buddhist deity of compassion who could manifest in human form. Lately, though, in his meditations he had begun to sense Kannon becoming one with him; and now, as he spoke his prophecies, he could actually feel this deity directing what he said. However, the words transmitted were not those of Kannon. The Buddhist deity was only serving as a messenger familiar to Meishusama. The words were clearly those of one single, universal God—the God of All.

At the time, the concept of such a single, universal God—the One Supreme Source and Creator of All, omnipotent and everywhere present—was still not entirely real to Meishusama. This idea played no great role in either of the two main religions he'd known from childhood, Shinto and Buddhism, and even in Oomoto there were several other prominent gods said to be aspects of the whole.

Now, however, staggering as it was, he could not deny the truth of what he had experienced. Later he would write, "That was the beginning of many spontaneous revelations that were beyond my normal perception. It seemed that whatever I wanted to know would be revealed to me. Yes, for sure God exists. He is very close. No, He must be within me. This was extraordinary!"

Gradually over time he came to understand that God was indeed real and was present inside his very being. In one of his teachings, he affirmed that at age forty-five he had, for the first time, "seen the Truth." It was an Oomoto expression, carefully chosen to signify his arrival at complete self-realization, a true state of enlightenment. The force he had felt in operation was the God-force, and God had given him an overwhelming mission—to inform the entire world of the Truth, to help disperse all humanity's negative clouds, and to demonstrate God's love by healing the sick. On February 4, 1928, having resolved to devote himself entirely to spiritual work, he gave all that remained of his business into the hands of his loyal employees.

---

1. *Kannon* is the well-known Buddhist deity of compassion popular in the East. She is known by other names in other countries, such as Kwan Yin, Chenrezig, and Avalokitesvara. Sometimes she appears as female, and at other times as male. She maintains order and harmony in the world through her wonderful ability of uniquely responding to the needs of each person and circumstance. Kannon bestows upon people the ability to live in balance and harmony. Meishusama had his own conception of this deity, whom he felt preceded and transcended Buddhism. In this book, Kannon is described as female for simplicity's sake.

Healing

In Meishusama's heart, the joy of healing others was now strongly reinforced. He had been depending on prayer alone, but from this point on, he worked to develop and refine his own original method of healing. From his untiring spiritual research and his own history of suffering came the realization that what we call sickness is really purification, the body's way of eliminating toxins. The key to healing, he perceived, is not medicine, but Light—clear spiritual Light, brought in to cleanse the human spirit of negative clouds, helping the body rid itself of its toxins.

Increasingly, his family members, friends, acquaintances, and everyone who came to him for help began witnessing cures that could only be described as miraculous. Even people who were seriously ill got well, even those diagnosed as incurable. At the same time, he became aware of a mysterious Sphere of Light that had come to dwell inside him: a Sphere of Divine Light in his abdomen, able to control his very thoughts, words and actions.

Before long, the sheer effectiveness of his healings, together with his growing body of followers, made him an influential figure in Oomoto. Everyone agreed he was a wonderful person to be around, a man who had fun doing things, lived life to the fullest, and who always spread happiness even in trying times. His laugh was infectious, the kind that makes everything seem funnier to others. He was always fair, never judgmental—a man of action who could give firm reprimands when warranted, but always with the aim of helping, always with consideration of the other's feelings. In short, he was loved and respected by all. It is not surprising, therefore, that in 1929 Oomoto advanced him to executive status, making him a regular member of the standing committee at their Tokyo headquarters and putting him in charge of his own Tokyo center where he began conducting regular healing services.

However, in those days, Meishusama's personal life was still haunted by the past. His meals at home were meager, at best. He was also hounded by creditors and his possessions were constantly being impounded. Still, he faced the future with his usual optimistic good cheer. "Don't worry," he told one visitor, "my finances will be abundantly blessed."

After work, he especially enjoyed going to the movies and other entertainments. He was fond of Western-made films, and would often take time off from his busy schedule to see them. In those times, it was considered daring for husband and wife to go out together, but to Meishusama, it was simply the way things should be. He enjoyed music, drama, and the whole atmosphere of the theater with his wife by his side.

Meanwhile, Meishusama's spiritual studies were going well, and there were small but helpful donations from his healing work. Often he went out to give treatments to those who couldn't travel, and when the need was extreme, he would take people into his own home.

Divine Revelation

Then it was 1931, and momentous events were in the air. It was the year Japan began its campaign of aggression by invading Manchuria. On June 15, guided by some inner calling, Meishusama led about thirty of his followers to the top of Mt. Nokogiri, which was across the Bay from Tokyo, to conduct a sunrise prayer ceremony. As the morning mists parted, he was overwhelmed by a great vision in which the events previously foretold in his spoken revelation now appeared before his eyes. He witnessed the great transformation of the world as part of an ongoing universal cycle. It was shown to him that the conversion from Night to Day had already occurred in the spiritual world, and would inevitably follow in the physical. But first would come a time of earthly cataclysm and great tribulation.

Meishusama came down from the mountain that day with the realization that his divine mission had now become imperative. The time was coming when he must extend his Divine Light healings to the general public, inform the world of God's Plan, and bring spiritual cleansing to all humanity.

For the next several years, he engaged in intensive spiritual studies, seeking to enhance his method of healing and map out plans for the future. Finally he felt ready. On May 1, 1934, in Tokyo's Kojimachi Ward, he opened a small clinic named "Ojindo." This marked the first official public appearance of the Divine Light treatment later known as Jyorei. The large number of recipients who returned to express their gratitude testifies to the effectiveness of these healings.

Initially, to fend off suspicions by the wartime government, he presented the new treatment as "Okada-style Spiritual Acupressure Therapy," with Light being directed into toxified areas of the body through touch. He would later refine the method several times.

Time of Decision

The police in those days had thought-control as one of their official functions. Unfortunately, they also despised religion, and Oomoto's popularity made it their likely number-one target. But equally disturbing to Meishusama was an inflexible atmosphere growing within Oomoto itself, which was arising partly in reaction to the militaristic regime of the time. In this environment, the more independence

Meishusama showed in following his inner guidance, the more he faced extremist opposition from within the organization itself. By 1934, the chaotic yet rigid mood in Oomoto, the instability within the leadership, and the surrounding social turmoil had all reached a peak. Meishusama felt this was a sign for him to move on and therefore in the fall of that year he sent a letter resigning his executive membership and withdrawing completely from the organization. The following year, all those in Oomoto leadership positions were arrested for "violations of the Public Order Act" and "contempt of the Emperor," and it was ordered that the organization be dissolved. All the accused would later be found innocent, but until the impending Pacific War had almost run its course, most remained in prison, and some even faced torture, were executed, or died from debilitation.

Kannon Society

Meanwhile, treatments at the new Ojindo clinic attracted so many people that within eight months, Meishusama had to seek larger quarters. As a temporary measure, on the first day of January, 1935, he moved his practice to the now-unoccupied Oomoto center that he had headed a few months earlier. Here he founded a spiritual organization of his own, naming it the Kannon Society of Japan (*Dai-nihon Kannon Kai*) in which most of its original members had been followers of his at Oomoto. Within the first year, their numbers had grown to 600, and eleven branch offices were flourishing throughout Japan.

At first, Meishusama's public resignation from Oomoto was enough to satisfy Japanese officialdom. He was allowed to go on mixing spiritual healing and religion under the watchful eye of the police. Inevitably, though, as his new organization grew, it encountered increasing police harassment. All its publications were eventually banned, and there was pressure from opponents to have it dissolved.

The storm signals were ominous, but Meishusama held firm to his purpose: the construction of Paradise on Earth. The wheels of progress he set in motion at the Kannon Society were basically two: first were his own presentations which centered on the "Kannon Lectures" dealing with his many revelations.

Ohikari

His other wheel of progress at the Kannon Society was something entirely new—the ohikari (then called *omamori*), which is a small parchment bearing his calligraphy and worn about the neck. In his personal healings, dating back to 1929, Meishusama had been using a white fan or *mite-shiro* on which his calligraphy or hand prints were inscribed. Now, in his continuing revelations, it had come to him that this new invention, the ohikari, would enable others to heal by Divine Light, much as he did.

At first Meishusama gave ohikaris only to thirteen of his close disciples. Then, at the Spring Grand Sampai (religious service) in 1935, he made a far-reaching announcement: from that time on, anyone would be able to receive an ohikari and give Divine Light healings. He knew that, despite the efforts of other great religious teachers, the world was still in dire need of being saved. By teaching his followers the joy of spreading Divine Light to make others happy, he aimed to set in motion an exponential wave that would progressively rise to envelop and transform the entire world.

Meanwhile his organization continued to grow, making it essential to find a good permanent meeting place. With help from his followers, he was able to acquire a mansion with spacious grounds above the Tamagawa River on Tokyo's west side. The official opening at the Tamagawa Grounds was held on October 10, 1935. Near the mansion, which was later named Hozan-so, Meishusama built a dwelling place for himself and his family, which now included six children.

Farming

Often at his new location, Meishusama could be seen directing work in the spacious garden area, showing his young helpers how to plant tea bushes, fruit trees, vegetables, and flowers, or how to channel water to the rice paddy. He was seldom at rest, and he didn't mind getting himself all muddy wielding a shovel, wanting always to set a good example instead of just issuing orders.

The poor farm villagers of that era had been weighing heavily on his mind. These tenant farmers had been suffering terribly. The weather for several years had been abnormally cold, causing many crop failures. When he first realized this, he wasted no time in educating himself and beginning his own experiments. Chemical methods were then new, and at first they looked like the answer, but experience taught him that chemicals only ruined the soil, and pesticides just bred stronger insects. He tried to point this out in his publications, but most of the public just jeered, few would listen.

After many trials and many failures, Meishusama found that he got the best results by using natural methods exclusively. No chemicals whatsoever, no pesticides, no fertilizers of any kind—nothing except natural compost to keep the soil loose and warm and moist. The soil itself was the key; along with nature's supply of nitrogen, it was the only fertilizer needed. There had to be love and respect for its spiritual nature, and understanding of its biochemical balance. Fresh soil, if needed, could be mixed in to restore the vitality.

One evening when his produce appeared on the family dinner table, Meishusama announced with pride, "I grew this with Natural Agriculture. What do you think? It's tasty, no?" He must have been pleased with the results of his labor. Crops grown using his Natural Agriculture method were tastier and of better quality, with more reliable harvests under varying weather conditions. And, additionally, the soil itself did not get depleted. Today Meishusama's Natural Agriculture techniques have silenced early critics and are winning increased recognition as the wave of the future.

Persecution

Nineteen Thirty-six, the year after Meishusama's move to Tamagawa, saw the beginning of a long persecution. In August of that year, he underwent a police "questioning" that involved threats and torture. Shortly thereafter he was jailed for eleven days and his practice was banned. At length, thanks to various public petitions, he was given a choice: he could operate either a religion or a treatment center, but not both. In 1937, just before his 55th birthday, Meishusama made his decision known that from then on, he would confine himself solely to giving treatments.

Despite his acquiescence, three years later he was charged with a minor violation of medical law and again thrown into jail. Enough was enough. Worn out, anyway, from treating scores of people every day, Meishusama announced his retirement. He returned to Hozan-so, where he limited himself to training "therapists" who were actually spiritual leaders and disciples. "I am stepping up," he told his followers, "From now on, the healing work is up to you."

But the very next year, fate played a hand. A number of prominent cabinet ministers, generals, admirals, and businessmen who had heard of his healings began visiting Meishusama, asking for his help. The police were stymied; they had no choice but to relax their restrictions. Meishusama was again free to give healings.

Although he had won a limited victory, the climate of oppression in Japan still remained. Until the war ended in 1945, his organization had little chance to grow. So in the meantime, Meishusama led a quiet life at Hozan-so, painting, doing calligraphy, writing, and conducting a poetry club with his followers. He still took daily walks, never complaining, and always talking cheerfully about his projects and plans for the future.

War and Peace

From the start of the Pacific War in 1941, Meishusama had known that Japan was morally wrong and had no chance of winning. Looking ahead, he saw that after the war he would need a larger home for his organization, a place where it could grow and fulfill its promise. Meanwhile, the threat of bombing raids on Tokyo meant that Hozan-so was no longer a safe place for his family and his followers. He conducted a search and managed in 1944 to acquire two attractive properties. One was at Hakone, a mountain resort about sixty miles west of Tokyo. The other was a scenic villa at Atami, a small bayside city seventy miles southwest. He visualized these properties transformed into miniature paradises, one for summer residency, the other for winter. In May of that year he took his family to safety at Hakone and commenced his project to create twin models for Paradise on Earth.

Following his move, Meishusama took on the monumental task of supervising the entire construction process at both new locations. Each day he made an extensive tour of the site where he was staying. To the workmen, both volunteer and professional, he gave instructions that took in every building site, every garden, every tree, plant, and rock on the grounds. He also designed a number of the buildings himself, including the new Hakone Hall of Worship, as well as Sunshine Hall at Atami, and the beautiful Crystal House.

In the wake of Japan's surrender in 1945, Meishusama faced a climate of fear in which he sought to be a stabilizing influence. He saw himself and everyone as citizens of the world, and viewed Japan's defeat as a rightful result of its treatment of other countries. True victory for anyone, he believed, could only come about with the realization of an ideal world for everyone, and toward that end he worked with renewed vigor. Along with all his other postwar responsibilities, he found time to write voluminously. Today his works fill over thirty volumes embracing every major field—religion, civilization, natural agriculture, healing, and the arts—including several thousand of his own hymns and poetry. He also wrote hundreds upon hundreds of articles for newsletters and other periodicals.

In 1947, Japan finally ratified a new national constitution that guaranteed freedom of religion and speech. Able at last to expand, within a few years Meishusama's organization grew to become one of Japan's most important cultural and spiritual organizations.

Art

Shortly before his move to Hakone in 1944, stirred by an old love, Meishusama began a serious endeavor to collect objects of art. The times were particularly favorable since the market was blessed with a profusion of lofty art treasures at down-to-earth prices. Over time, his purchases would become the foundation of a collection such as the Japanese art world had never seen.

At first Meishusama bought fine art objects just for his own enjoyment. But, whenever he found a wonderful art object, he could not fully enjoy it all by himself. Instead, he wanted to share the pleasure with as many people as possible so they could be happy, too. This trait had always been true about him. As he once wrote, "I am constantly thinking of how others can be made happy and more fortunate . . . . This way of thinking constitutes one underlying reason that I am a man of happiness and good fortune. And it is because of this that I say, 'If you do not make others happy, you can never be happy yourself.' "

In addition to this, Meishusama was now convinced that the love of beautiful things was a necessary touchstone for changing the human heart. Education, religion, and morals were all fine, but not in themselves sufficient. What was needed to create a beautiful society was more love of beauty in the lives of everyone.

To expand his already prolific studies in fine arts, Meishusama kept busy from dawn to the wee hours of the morning scanning textbooks and design manuals, going to exhibitions, and quizzing the leading experts. Year by year, he absorbed fields of art that would normally require decades to master. In an amazingly short time, he had become a recognized authority, with a true sixth sense for telling genuine masterpieces from secondary works and forgeries.

In those days, besides Art, Jyorei, and Natural Agriculture, Meishusama was also promoting efforts to "turn society into a paradise through flowers." Since his youth, he had always enjoyed cultivating and arranging flowers, and planting them wherever he could. Now he grew and distributed them widely, encouraging their display in homes and public places, in stores, offices, and plazas. His aim was to uplift and refresh all classes of people, creating a society based on beauty.

Oneness

In May of 1950, recurring troubles with the authorities brought Meishusama to an incredible spiritual climax. The police in Atami, suspicious of his growing success, first ransacked his home and then, though they found nothing, decided to throw him into prison anyway. At age 67, he found himself subjected to torturous daily questionings that left him exhausted and debilitated. After sixteen days of this, he developed a severe pain in his stomach that would not go away. The next morning he woke from a wonderful dream in which he found himself entering a beautiful palatial building high atop Mt. Fuji. Knowing that dreams of Fuji are traditionally good omens, he felt a sense of joyful anticipation. That pain in his stomach – could it not be a purification to advance God's work?

The following day was June 15, the anniversary of his revelation on Mt. Nokogiri. He recognized then that his stomach pain was in fact related to the divine Sphere of Light in his abdomen. The purification he was undergoing was nothing less than the final stage of his unification with God.

Some time later, after Meishusama's innocence was established by the courts, he wrote that, ever since his dream of Mt. Fuji, he no longer had to ask God for answers when people sought him out for help; he simply knew the answers even before he was asked. He was entirely One with the Sphere of Divine Light that was within him.

Museum

As that memorable year of 1950 drew to a close, Meishusama was taken by a new idea springing from his passion for beauty. Why not enhance society by making great works of art more accessible to the public? A corner site at the Hakone miniature paradise project was about to be vacated. He wanted to build something special there, to cap the project in an ideal way. Why not a museum?

It was the perfect solution—a place where everyone, of whatever social class, could come to experience beauty and find spiritual refreshment. The cost of the project seemed prohibitive, however, after discussing the matter with a loyal fund-raiser, Meishusama moved ahead, trusting in God. Work on his dream museum began in October of 1951. The necessary funds flowed in precisely as they were needed, and the work proceeded with record speed. On June 15, 1952—barely eight and a half months after construction began—members gathered for the dedication of the new Hakone Art Museum and also the rest of the Hakone miniature paradise.

Meishusama had designed the museum himself, playing the role of architect and supervising every part of the project: from the unique modern building with its stately Oriental roof, the innovative interior, all the facilities, even the placement of the art objects as well as every rock, tree, and flower outside in the beautiful Japanese garden. It was the first museum in Japan to be open to the general public at all times. "I keenly believe," Meishusama wrote, "that wonderful art works should not be secluded, but should instead be shown to as many people as possible . . . . In this way, fine arts contribute greatly to the development of culture, and this is the true purpose of art."

Although now past 70, Meishusama continued to oversee the daily efforts of his organization. Often he directed work in the garden at Atami or showed guests through the Hakone Museum. His habits had not changed with the years. Even when tired, he kept up a full schedule, seldom wasting a moment and often getting two things done at once. When out walking, he was apt to be followed by an attendant with a portable radio so he could keep up with world affairs. In the evening, he had the daily news read to him while he studied art books, wrote letters, or did calligraphy.

In those days he also made some seven tours of western Japan, inspecting construction of yet another of his earthly paradises, the villa Heian-kyo in Kyoto, while also visiting certain other religious sites, giving a few public speeches, and steadfastly searching out fine arts for the Hakone collection. To the end of his life, he remained devoted to gathering masterworks for public enjoyment and the betterment of society. Shortly before his passing, he acquired the Wisteria Vase, one of Japan's national treasures, even at the cost of giving up Hozan-so, his beloved home and former headquarters in Tokyo.

Taking Leave

In mid-April of 1954, on his final tour, Meishusama made an unpublicized personal visit to a group of his followers headed by Kaishusama (*please see page 266*) at their new sanctuary in Kyoto. This was a rare event; such personal visits were not at all his custom. In earlier times, he had given the group its name Shumei, and had instructed them as to the method of directing Jyorei light to two key locations on the recipient's head: the forehead and the crown.

A short time after Meishusama's visit to the Kyoto sanctuary, he fell ill. However, he remained in charge of things, directing activities from his bed and rising for important occasions. Therefore, few among his followers thought to be concerned.

June 15 was the day of the Revelation Ceremony, commemorating Meishusama's ascent of Mt. Nokogiri. This marked the beginning of a mysterious change in Meishusama. To everyone's surprise, he appeared at the ceremony in formal attire, his kimono, robe, and cloak all in white. This was totally unlike him, as he disliked formality and usually dressed in a casual mode. Another surprise was that he gave no speech, but instead presided quietly as the gathering joined in a prayer composed especially for the occasion, and then a chant. Again, this special prayer was the kind of "fuss" he normally liked to avoid.

Some time later, Meishusama revealed the reason he had not spoken at the ceremony that day. Something unexpected had overcome him—a strange sensation that deprived him of speech. It was as though he had been newly born, he said—not just "reborn" in some symbolic way, but actually newly born, like a child unable to speak.

Those who saw him at the ceremony noted that his skin now looked smooth like a child's, and his hair, which had been all gray, was showing strands of black. Also, on the palm of his left hand five deeply etched creases had appeared, extending to the tip of each finger. This was so mysterious that Meishusama's helpers consulted an expert in palmistry. The creases, they learned, were called "lines of a Master"; they gave evidence of God's Light in its purest form, in a divine being of the highest order.

Meishusama was able to speak at a dedication ceremony for Crystal Hall, the last building he ever designed, on December 11; whether or not he was dressed formally for this occasion was not noted. However, at his birthday celebration in December, and at the 1955 New Year's service, he appeared dressed formally, all in white. And just ahead lay more surprises.

As a rule, the spring celebration on February 4 was attended only by Senseis, however, in 1955, invitations went out to everyone. The members assembled not knowing what to expect. They were amazed to see Meishusama garbed all in golden yellow. It was the divine color of the spiritual realm—the color traditionally reserved for royalty. Normally, no one else in Japan would ever dream of wearing this color. In his brief speech that day, Meishusama gave no explanation, nothing to link his attire with what was to come. All he said was that everyone should be prepared for something unusual.

A few days later—at 3:33 in the afternoon of February 10, 1955 at Atami—Meishusama, at the age of age 72, departed from this physical world.

Firm and compassionate as always, he had given his mission over to the keeping of his followers.

In his reminiscences of Meishusama, Shuten Oishi, director of an interfaith organization to help new religions, wrote: "Of all the religious founders that I met . . . he is the one who had a truly special way with people... You never felt that he was trying to show his sensitivity and be considerate, but his considerateness nonetheless extended to the smallest particulars... When I think about him now, I feel that his personality was a true manifestation of universal love."

Summary of Meishusama's Spiritual Transformations

Most of us go through many transitions at various times in our lives. Some of the more significant ones include birth, puberty, marriage, and death. Other important transitions are graduations from high school and college, getting one's first full time job, and the loss of loved ones. Throughout our lives we continue to grow and mature. Major crises often force us to grow quickly and rise to the occasion so that we can handle them.

For someone on a spiritual path, the transitions can be even more profound, as they often provoke radical change in one's identity and ways of perceiving reality. Even though Meishusama experienced many worldly calamities, his spiritual transitions appear to have been initiated more by inner conditions than by outer events. These transitions finally led to an indescribable state of consciousness beyond duality and conflict. The following is an attempt to explain the more significant of Meishusama's various spiritual awakenings.

In retrospect, it appears that when the spirit of Kannon entered into Meishusama in 1926, placing a glowing sphere of Light in his abdomen, it deepened his connection with the Divine. He now experienced God's presence internally, as well as externally. After this, whenever he sought higher guidance, Kannon would internally give him the answers. She also continued to infuse Meishusama with spiritual Light, which transformed him into a humble servant of God, dedicated to the welfare of all beings.

The second phase of Meishusama's spiritual transformation process occurred in 1950 when the purification he experienced in prison appeared to throw him into a permanent union and identification with God. Here, his personal self gave way to the divine Self. The core sense of separation between himself and others vanished, and he now felt one with all things. From this time forward, his words and behavior were guided by an inner knowing. He no longer needed to ask Kannon for guidance because he no longer felt separate from Her in any way. Instead he would spontaneously speak out the replies to questions put to him by others, even when he had no previous knowledge of the subjects. When Meishusama spoke, it was Kannon speaking, and when Kannon spoke, it was him speaking. They were one but two, two but one.

When Meishusama emerged at the June 15, 1954 Revelation Ceremony[2], his divine condition seemed to extend deeper into the physical plane, transmuting

---

2. This was the first formal appearance of Meishusama in front of his students after the severe physical purification he went through in the spring of 1954. After the purification, Meishusama's body showed remarkable signs of rejuvenation (as described on page 18 of the biography section). These phenomena helped Meishusama to reassess his unique historical role as an agent of global transformation.

his body into a more perfect vehicle for serving the world. With this final development, there was little, if any, trace of separation between God and man, or between knowing and doing. The world was now seen as an outer extension of the Divine. There was only Oneness on all levels. This was considered unity of the highest order.

Meishusama was a living symbol of the ability to learn and grow through adversity. Despite grievous personal losses, debilitating illnesses, and financial ruin, he never lost his burning desire to help the world. These events only served to push him to discover deeper reservoirs of inner strength and to recognize God's profound guidance in his life. Through direct experience, Meishusama discovered the dangers of pharmaceutical medications, the power of Spirit to heal, the need to honor nature, the ability of beauty to uplift and inspire, and the importance of serving others.

If one focuses only on the difficult parts of Meishusama's prediction of the upcoming Great Transformation, the future might appear bleak. However, Meishusama was himself optimistic about our destiny. Although the times would be extremely challenging, he had strong faith in humanity's ability to rise up to the occasion. He never doubted the vision revealed to him that human civilization would continue to thrive at a higher level. Once Meishusama awoke to his divine mission, he dedicated himself tirelessly to improving the health and happiness of everyone, as well as to supporting their spiritual development. These all furthered the realization of an ideal world *here on earth*. And although Meishusama departed this world in 1955, many believe that his spirit still continues to work toward this goal from a higher plane of existence.

Three Prescribed Activities

Most significant of Meishusama's many contributions were the three main practices he advocated. Foremost is the practice of Jyorei, a form of spiritual healing that promotes inner purification and spiritual growth. Through his empowerments and blessings, great numbers of people were helped to improve their lives and to find a deeper sense of happiness.

Secondly, he developed Natural Agriculture, a spiritually based form of farming that does not use any chemicals or fertilizer. For people to stay healthy, he stressed, it is important to eat healthy food that is brimming with life force and that is free of toxic chemicals. He also felt that a return to a sacred relationship with the land and the natural world had a rejuvenating effect on the spirit.

Lastly, he promoted appreciation of the arts and encouraged people to incorporate beauty into their daily lives. According to Meishusama, beauty is a doorway into Spirit. Beauty inspires happiness and helps to balance and refine one's character. He saw beauty not as a self-indulgent luxury, but as a natural expression of spirituality.

Key Principles

Fundamental Spiritual Laws

All of Meishusama's teachings on sickness, healing, spiritual growth, transforming the world, and the attainment of overall happiness, rest on the foundation of two spiritual laws.

The Law of Spiritual Precedence – The first principle is that the spiritual always precedes the physical in both form and events. Events originate both directly from Divine Intent and from the conditions we have created in the spiritual world by our thoughts, words, and deeds.

The Law of Purification – The second principle is the idea that all suffering is a form of purification, the by-product of a cleansing process instigated for the purpose of eliminating unhealthy mental tendencies as well as physical toxins accumulated in the body.

Essential Inner Qualities

We can also point to various inner qualities and attitudes promoted consistently in Meishusama's teachings, all of which reflect the vantage point of a larger, more impersonal consciousness. The cultivation of any of these personal traits supports spiritual growth and is the outcome of spiritual awareness.

Gratitude – By our responding to life's experiences, both pleasant and unpleasant, with gratitude, our life is transformed for the better.

Loving Others – Love is an expression of Spirit, and when we recognize this Spirit within ourselves and within others, it is expressed as affection and compassion.

Makoto – Acting with sincerity, honesty, and integrity always generates the best results, even when outer appearances may seem to indicate the contrary.

Basic Perspectives for Living

In addition to the above spiritual laws and inner qualities, one can also discern a number of general perspectives from Meishusama's teachings. The following is a brief listing of some of the more important ones:

Respect for Nature – Recognizing nature as a gift from God and responding with reverence and respect promotes unity and harmony with all of life.

Aesthetic Appreciation – Creating beauty in our environment and harmony in our hearts uplifts our spirit, promotes social refinement, and deepens our appreciation of life.

Global View – Cultivating a broadminded point of view that appreciates variety, values each country's unique contribution, and realizes that humanity is one large family, promotes peace and harmony. This includes an awareness and concern for the global effects of our actions.

Long–term View – Anticipating the long-term effects of our actions, rather than blindly rushing toward immediate, short-term gratification, prevents unexpected problems from arising in the future.

Holistic Perspective – Recognizing that nothing exists independently, and that everything is interconnected and part of a larger pattern, helps us to value the whole as much as the individual parts.

Pragmatic Approach – Using common sense to determine whether our preconceived ideas need changing for the sake of helping others in practical and tangible ways.

Kannon's Way – Adapting to circumstances in a flexible, moderate, and balanced way that includes patience and tolerance, brings harmony to one's life.

These inner qualities and approaches to life (covered in greater detail in later chapters) are sprinkled throughout Meishusama's work, sometimes overtly, and at other times implied as a general background attitude. Understanding them is important for gaining a comprehensive grasp of his teachings. They are not abstract principles within a speculative philosophy, but are spiritual qualities that can be cultivated and embodied by sincere individuals. These qualities and approaches were critical for Meishusama to realize his vision of creating Paradise on Earth, an ideal world free from poverty, sickness, and conflict.

Creating Paradise on Earth was not just an imaginary vision, but also an urgent mission for him to fulfill. Being a pragmatic realist who had undergone a number of severe hardships, he did not naively believe that earthly paradise would be brought into existence by the mere passing of time. Instead, he encouraged and led people to walk a path toward achieving heavenly conditions in a practical manner. He cared about action, not words. Meishusama was a man of tireless industry who expressed his basic teachings in a variety of ways so that they could be easily understood by all different kinds of people. This is evident in all of his published works.

Philosophy only has value when it is expressed as action.
—*Religious Pragmatism. ET*

Style of Communication

Although Meishusama wrote prolifically, his writings and lectures were seldom intellectual or scholastic. The qualities of adaptability, flexibility, and simplicity of Meishusama's writings and speeches can be viewed as outer expressions of his spiritual insight. Nonetheless, because of his casual and spontaneous style of communication, and the way that it varied depending on the audience or context, it can be difficult for many readers to gain a comprehensive overview of the key principles of his teachings.

Another factor influencing the understanding of Meishusama is the recognition that, in Japan, communication is usually indirect, symbolic, and suggestive, and not necessarily requiring order and structure, in contrast to the more direct, overt, and logically consistent style familiar to Westerners.

It is helpful to be aware of two important factors. First, Meishusama varied his teachings depending on his audience. He could talk philosophically to an intellectual, simply and plainly to a child, in a very down-to-earth and practical manner to an ordinary worker, or softly and gently to an elderly woman. His primary concern was how well the person in front of him understood and could benefit from his discourse. He was pragmatic by nature, and was not overly interested in devoting his time to systemizing his teachings. Truth was expressed in living, not in words. Secondly, it is important to remember that he comes out of the unfamiliar context (to Westerners) of Japanese cultural references and historical influences.

Based on the mindset and character of the reader, there seems to be two basic approaches to the writings of Meishusama. One approach analyzes the teachings and looks for methodically presented explanations and well-defined terminology, oftentimes becoming confused by apparent inconsistencies and ambiguities. The other approaches the teachings sympathetically, looking for what is useful or inspiring, and tends not to be overly concerned with logical understanding.

Japanese Cultural Background

Meishusama spoke and wrote in Japan during the first half of the twentieth century, a time of enormous social, cultural, and economic turmoil. Japan went through rapid industrialization and social dislocation, suffered great economic depression, endured a militarist government, and experienced the ravages of World War II, along with the aftermath of total defeat.

Japan itself is also quite different from Western societies, with their Judeo-Christian heritage, rational empiricism, and individuality. Japan's cultural background is strongly influenced by the religions of Shinto and Buddhism. Shinto is an ancient folk religion without any known founder, no commonly accepted holy book, and no systematically formulated doctrines. Shinto idealizes a return to simplicity and harmony with the natural world—a world imbued with spiritual presence and mystical beauty. This return to simplicity is accomplished through purification of body and spirit by participation in ritual, cleansing with water, and immersion in the silence and beauty of nature. Shinto's ideal is the principle of mutually cooperative, peaceful coexistence.

Two different forms of Buddhism have also exerted a strong influence on Japanese culture. The first depends on "self-power," whereas the second relies on "other-power." Zen Buddhism seeks deliverance from Samsara, the world of suffering, through the pursuit of silent meditation, and by utilizing the power of one's own efforts. Pure Land Buddhism and Nichiren Buddhism, on the other hand, both seek salvation through faith and divine grace, or "other-power." Pure Land differs from Nichiren in that it seeks salvation in the Pure Land to the West through devotion and prayers to Amitabha Buddha, whereas Nichiren puts its faith in the saving grace of the Lotus Sutra and also requires its followers to undergo strict moral discipline.

Shinto is concerned with achieving harmony with community, nature, and the universe, whereas Buddhism tends to be more otherworldly. Neither puts a strong emphasis on the significance of the individual, and both are concerned with achieving an immediate, direct experience for their followers that will help them in a tangible way. Eastern traditions conceive of the ultimate reality in more abstract terms than the traditional Western concept of God, which tends to be more personalized. Curiously, Meishusama would alternate between both concepts of divinity, sometimes referring to a human-like God, while at other times using more impersonal terminology such as the "spiritual world." Overall, he could easily embrace a divinity that is both the One and the many, both personal and impersonal, and that can be found equally within and without all of creation. Meishusama made great efforts to live as a "Citizen of the World," incorporating ideas and values from both the East and the West.

The emphasis on purity, healing, and nature in Meishusama's teachings can clearly be found in the Shinto tradition, while his stress on the importance of spiritual growth and salvation parallels the teachings of Buddhism. Likewise, this dream of a "Paradise on Earth" can also be found in one form or another in the Western ideals of utopian civilizations. This is not to say that Meishusama superficially borrowed from all these various traditions. Rather, the union of these principles arose naturally from the universality of his revelation.

His synthesis and expression of these and other ideals were unique and very practical. The eclectic nature of his writings was natural for a thinker born in a country with a long history of incorporating foreign elements into its culture and society.

To be effective, a teacher must speak the language of the people he is attempting to reach. What is common sense in one culture might be considered superstition in another. Our environment affects all of us, and this was true of Meishusama as well. Wanting to appeal to the people in his immediate environment, he would incorporate their familiar customs and ideas in his communication. Yet, despite the many Japanese cultural and religious influences apparent in his teachings, beneath all of these can be found universal and timeless truths.

Meishusama was a divinely inspired teacher with a mission to help suffering humanity. Although he did not hesitate to borrow certain ideas from other sources, his teachings primarily originated from his own unique mystical insights. Not only could he directly perceive the spiritual influences operating behind external events, but also where others saw division, he saw unity.

The Achievements of Meishusama

- Founder of a new kind of spiritual movement, an "umbrella" organization open to all faiths.

- Master of positive thinking, triumphant over personal illness, poverty, and persecution.

- Effective spiritual teacher and guide to many.

- Originator of Jyorei healing Light treatments; successful healer of countless recipients.

- Leader in promoting gratitude, the happiness of others, and the Oneness of all humanity.

- Innovative thinker in the field of health: identified sickness as purification, and advocated natural healing instead of drugs.

- Successful business entrepreneur; inventor of the Asahi Daiya artificial gemstone.

- Pioneer of Natural Agriculture.

- Promoter of natural beauty and art as ways to create a beautiful society.

- A foremost art expert and prominent collector.

- Architect and builder of a major art museum.

- Author of extensive volumes of spiritual teachings, and an excellent poet.

- A man of constant high character, integrity, and wisdom—ideal candidate for Divine Revelation.

- Designer/builder of miniature earthly paradises.

- Inspired prophet of Global Transformation and Paradise on Earth.

CHAPTER 2

FUNDAMENTAL PRINCIPLES

My writings and speeches are all attempts to explain the Truth to all humankind in the most easily understandable manner. If you read them earnestly, with an open and appreciative mind, a perception of Truth will come unbidden into your heart.
—The Embodiment of Truth. ET

Is there an ultimate purpose of life, or are we just passing time until we eventually die? Too often the answers to this question sound like children's fables. In his teachings, Meishusama gives us a simple answer to this question. He says that the ultimate purpose of life is the spiritual growth and perfection of all creation. Although there is divine assistance, each of us remains responsible for our own spiritual growth and development, and all of us are encouraged to assist in perfecting the world around us. Meishusama also offers practical guidelines for realizing this objective.

First Meishusama's key ideas and principles will be explained so that you have a sufficient background to fully appreciate his more practical recommendations. What may appear linear and categorical at first will eventually emerge as part of an organic whole when later the topics of Jyorei, Natural Agriculture, and Art are covered.

Of course, as stated earlier, Meishusama was not normally inclined to write in this structured manner. Rather, he preferred to discuss current problems affecting humanity, and in the process, interject his various suggestions, values, and ideas. In his teachings, Meishusama was always looking to encourage the best in people, and to promote spiritual awareness, which are the foundations of real happiness.

Spiritual Principles

Universal Flux

Everything in the universe is constantly and ceaselessly moving. This year is different from last year in all respects. . . . Everything is in flux; nothing is at rest for even an instant. —Henri Bergson. ET

Everything is constantly changing and evolving from one state or condition to another. Night changes to day, and day changes to night. Flowers germinate, grow, blossom, wilt, and then decay back into soil. The seasons change from winter to spring, summer, and fall. Even giant mountains change their shape, although at an imperceptibly slow rate. We can also see this principle of change operating in our own lives by looking at how our lives have changed over the years or by witnessing the constantly changing thoughts in our mind at this very moment.

What were our lives like ten years ago? What were our relationships like then, and how are they different now? Because everything changes, the things that bring us comfort today may cause us suffering tomorrow. Family, job, home, and health—all are subject to disruption or loss. And the more we value and cling to them, the more likely we are to suffer at their loss. We do not know what will happen even one year from now, let alone in ten years ahead. Only one thing is for certain, and that is that everything will change.

If we pause to observe our mind, we will notice how our thoughts are constantly moving and changing from one image or idea to another. Throughout the day, our moods may vary from contentment to anxiety, anger, grief, boredom, joy, or humor depending upon the people and circumstances that we encounter. Sometimes we may receive praise from others, and at other times condemnation. Each person we encounter may have a different opinion about us and therefore treat us differently. The roles we play with people can range from parent to employee, sibling, spouse, enemy, or friend. Everyone depends on their relationship to everyone and everything else for their definition and identity. Also, over the course of time, nothing is solid, fixed, or enduring.

All things, whether mental, emotional, or physical, are subject to change. The only thing that does not change is the process of change itself. When we come to accept this fact and learn to embrace change, then we begin to flow in harmony with life.

Interconnectivity

There is absolutely nothing that spiritual cords are not connected with, be it the fundamental principles of relativity, the radiations that move through space, human society, or the individual. —The Spiritual Cords. ET

Nothing exists separately from everything else in the universe. A windstorm in the Sahara Desert can dump tons of sand on Mexico, thousands of miles away, and an ice shelf dropping off the continent of Antarctica can cause a hurricane to hit Japan on the other side of the world. Crop failure in the United States can cause famine in Africa, and a rise in the price of oil can make some rich while making others poor. From the largest galaxies to the smallest atoms, everything is linked in numerous invisible ways. At the level of Quantum Mechanics, according to Bell's Theorem, pairs of photons or electrons (two of the tiniest known particles in existence), demonstrate immediate awareness of each other despite their separation by vast distances of space. The natural sciences recognize the mutual interdependency of plants, insects, birds, and animals within a larger ecosystem. The food we eat links us to the farmers who grow the crops, with the plant kingdom from which they come, and to the earth that supports us.

Each part of our body communicates with all the other parts, from bones and organs down to nerves and cells. No part is independent of the rest, as all parts depend on each other for proper functioning. Thus, anything that affects one part affects all the rest. If one of our legs is wounded, our whole body is affected. Similarly, when we have the flu, the fever is not located in only one organ or limb, but in our whole body, because each part is intimately connected with every other part.

We are all interconnected like pieces of an elaborate, three-dimensional jigsaw puzzle. The convex curve of one piece is the concave curve of another piece, each shape complementing the other. On a spiritual level, we are all connected to God, people, places, and things by invisible spiritual cords. These cords bind us through thoughts, feelings, and sensation, and therefore, every thought and intention we hold affects others in some manner, either subtly or strongly. If we hold positive or loving thoughts, the people around us become cheerful, whereas if we become angry or judgmental, they feel badly. Each situation and environment has innumerable influences affecting it. Nothing occurs independently of the larger context within which it exists. Concurrently, everything we do is also reflected in the greater whole. These patterns of connectivity reflect a deeper underlying Oneness that unites all of existence.

Reincarnation

People are born and die and are reborn many, many times, just as the Buddhist expression, "the wheel of life turns and lives change," suggests.

—*Life and Death. ET*

We do not end with death. After we die, our soul returns to the spiritual world where it undergoes purification until it is ready to incarnate once again into the physical world. Meishusama wrote,

> Once the soul has returned to the spiritual world, the process of purifying it begins. The amount of spiritual clouds determines the position of the soul in the spiritual world and also the length of time it must stay there to be purified. At the shortest, the period would be a matter of years or decades, and it sometimes extends to centuries. After being purified to some extent, a spirit is again incarnated into the material world, according to Divine Direction, and charged with a Task from God. —*Life and Death. ET*

The soul continues to be reborn again and again, each time accumulating more experience, knowledge, and wisdom along the way. We also carry our limited conditioning, tendencies, and habits into each new lifetime, creating new circumstances based on old patterns of action. Each lifetime builds upon the previous one. Often, the reason a person behaves in a strange or compulsive way is because a past life experience left a strong mark on his or her soul. Physical deformities and health problems can also have their origins in past lives. Emotional bonds between people can be carried over from previous lives, often drawing these same people together again in successive incarnations.

According to the Greek philosopher Socrates, "Man has since ancient times thought it quite possible that the soul, after having left the world, descends to the underworld where it departs by degrees and returns to life. In this way the soul wanders from death to birth, from life to new life . . . .Time and time again the soul is called back to earth."

Each time a soul is born into a physical body, it tends to forget everything it experienced in its previous life, as well as what it experienced while inhabiting the spiritual world. Such memories might cause a person to dwell on the past rather than move on and seek new experience, which is the very reason for being reborn in this world, since new experiences provide the soul with lessons that further its spiritual growth. Amnesia, therefore, allows the soul to start over again fresh without being burdened by memories of the past.

Some people are born intelligent, some less so. This represents the differences between old and new souls. Older souls, who have been reincarnated many times, have richer and fuller experience of life than new ones, who have only recently been created. The latter, therefore, have little experience of material life, and cannot help but be unwise. Reproduction takes place in the spiritual world and new souls are constantly being born in the spiritual world.

Almost everyone will have had the experience of meeting or seeing someone they do not know, but who gives them a feeling of closeness and familiarity, as if they were a parent, brother or sister, or someone even more intimate. This person is the reincarnation of someone who has been a near relation or intimate associate in a previous life. This is what we call "karma."

Yet another example is that of a man and woman who fall blindly in love and carry on their affair with little heed of anyone else. This is the result of a previous life in which they loved each other deeply but never had the opportunity to culminate their relationship. If they are reborn and have this opportunity, their love affair is intense and passionate. —*Life and Death. ET*

Life always provides us with opportunities to learn and grow. Often, we are treated the very same way in this life that we treated another in a previous life. If in previous lives we helped others, were generous and kind, in this life we might receive assistance from others, inherit money, or attract kind friends. If we steal, slander, abuse, or betray, similar things will eventually happen to us. Often, we become that which we hate or wanted to hurt in a past life. The karmic pendulum always swings back the other way. Such reciprocity helps the soul understand what it feels like to be treated in hurtful ways, thereby encouraging empathy and compassion. These experiences help the soul grow and evolve.

To find happiness, the soul must let go of selfish attitudes and behavior, and develop wisdom and compassion. As the soul matures, it recognizes its essential Oneness with all beings and things, and discovers a shared spiritual identity. Once this occurs, there is no longer any need to return to this physical world.

Repeatedly reborn and repeatedly dying, man's spirit travels toward eternal happiness. —Life and Death. MK1

Spiritual Laws

The Law of Order

Materialism says, "Body first, spirit second," spiritualism says, "Spirit first, body second." —Methods and Results. ET

Underlying the diverse phenomena of the natural world are fundamental laws of order and structure that are fixed and immutable. These patterns and structures can be found in the studies of physics, biology, and mathematics, as well as in the cosmos, human society, and day-to-day life. Some examples are the ten fingers and toes of the human body, the hexagonal shapes within beehives, and the spiral patterns of galaxies. Other structures, such as those found in higher mathematics and logic, are invisible to the human eye and only recognizable to the mind.

> Order is present everywhere in nature. The seasons—spring, summer, autumn, winter—follow a fixed order. Day and night follow a fixed and unvarying order. Trees and plants, without exception, grow following the same natural order. For example, cherries never blossom before plums. *—Order. ET*

Because of natural order, objects fall down rather than up; water freezes when cold rather than when hot; round objects roll better than square ones; trees bend with the wind instead of against it; and we tend to rest when tired rather than when energized. Each of these common sense examples points to underlying laws of nature that rule our day-to-day lives.

As well as the above physical laws, there are also subtler laws governing human nature and society at large, although the specific application of these laws will vary from culture to culture. For instance, all societies require some sort of leadership, whether well-defined or vague, to give them structure and direction. Different countries uphold different role models for the individuals living within them. All cultures are defined by their collective customs, protocols, etiquettes, and values. And underlying these various social structures are the universal human needs for respect, affection, and social bonding. These basic needs also promote structure. Although customs and behavior may vary from place to place, most people can recognize genuine courtesy and politeness when they encounter it. Even social rebels who refuse to conform to a culture's particular norms actually cling to their own sets of values and principles. Order exits everywhere, even though we may not perceive it or understand it.

There is a correct time and place for everything. Sometimes these are obvious and sometimes not. As it says in the Ecclesiastes chapter of the Bible: "To every thing there is a season, and a time to every purpose under Heaven." Recognizing what these are, and then aligning oneself with them, is the key to success in the world. Such understanding also helps bring us into better harmony with the people and circumstances in our lives.

To put it precisely, the fundamental cause of failure is a lack of understanding of proper timing. Timing is critical for determining whether things will go well or not. For instance, flowers, fruit trees, and crops have their own natural sequence to follow. If the timing is not right, even if given favorable support, they will never grow well. The bulbs buried in soil in autumn come to bloom in spring, and likewise, the seeds sown in spring grow to beautiful flowers in summer and fall. The same can be said of fruit, which we cannot eat if it is not yet ripe. By picking it at the right time, we enjoy its best flavor. As for agricultural plants, there is a proper timing for sowing and transplanting seedlings, which of course needs to accord with weather and climate. —*Wait for the Right Moment. KW*

God arranges everything with perfect timing, and we cannot do anything about this divine arrangement but just go along with it.[3] —Meishusama

Only an unwise person will disregard the law of gravity, and only a foolish person will ignore the fundamental principles of social order or propriety. It takes a very high level of intelligence to successfully discover new laws of physics or to invent new technologies for harnessing these laws. So, too, does it require a greater than average intelligence and emotional maturity to successfully alter social norms. Only if the change to society fosters greater freedom, harmony, and respect for those affected can it be considered valuable—otherwise it is not. Although to some, such limitations may feel constrictive because, for most of us, freedom lies in creatively adapting to the natural order rather than in trying to fight it or ignore it. However, it is also better to help improve the world rather than escape from it.

If things do not go smoothly, the underlying cause can be found in the fact that the proper order has been disturbed. This is especially true of human affairs.

—*Order. ET*

---

3. Meishusama, "Lecture from a Trip to the Kansai Region," *Japanese Shumei Newspaper, no. 185* (August 1985).

Life entails a hierarchy of values, and that which deserves the highest value is Spirit. In a descending sequence, Spirit usually comes first, then mind, and then body. In our daily lives, if we follow this simple but essential order, things will go well because we will be in alignment with the underlying structure and forces of the cosmos. That which has spiritual value is usually placed first instead of last, up high rather than down low, or to the left instead of to the right. This is because first is more honored than last, high is more exalted than low, and left is more esteemed than right.

In most rooms, the further a location is from the entrance, the higher is its spiritual potency. Likewise, the left side has a more powerful spiritual vibrancy than the right. You can freely and practically apply this principle to almost any situation, knowing that no matter what you do, the most fundamental thing is to take into consideration the proper [sequential, spatial, or hierarchical] order.

—Learn From Nature's Order. KW

The Law of Order also applies to the act of giving Jyorei, wherein Divine Light is first directed to the forehead, followed by the top of the head of the receiver. Another type of order is helpful when sharing Jyorei with a group of people. About this, Meishusama advices: "When you give Jyorei to a group of people, one after the other, you should do this according to some kind of order. One way is to go from the most sick to those who are less ill. Alternatively, you can give Jyorei on a first–come–first–served basis. Sharing Jyorei sequentially according to age is another possibility. In addition, if there is no clear difference in the physical condition or age, a man should receive Jyorei before a woman. By doing so, both will obtain a better healing effect." (*God is Order. KW*)

It is best to give spiritual matters your top priority. In Shumei, one of the groups based on Meishusama's teachings, many of its members begin each day with spiritual practices such as prayer, contemplation, chanting, and Jyorei, as this will elevate their consciousness to a higher level for the rest of the day. They also begin most meetings with chanting and Jyorei before attending to the business at hand. Also, they place sacred objects such as spiritual books, significant photos, or items that have been blessed, in elevated places of honor because this helps them value the inner reality these things outwardly represent. When we honor that which is sacred, we reinforce the divinity within us.

The Law of Spiritual Precedence

The basic and underlying principle of the universe is that everything that exists in the material world has the origin of its existence and activity in the spiritual world.
—Natural Power. ET

The spiritual world, like the world of the mind, is a realm invisible to the senses. It is all around us, yet we cannot touch, taste, smell, see, or hear it. The spiritual world is where subtle energies coalesce into powerful forces that directly impact our lives. And although it lacks material substance, it is no less real than wood, stone, or flesh. Everything originates within the spiritual world.

Meishusama explains further: "As to the nature of the spiritual world, I would sum it up in the following way: it is the world of the fusion of thought and intention. That is, freedom in that world is wonderfully unhampered by the limitations of the physical body." *(Are There Ghosts? ET)*

Spirit itself is eternal and unchanging, whereas the physical is temporary and subject to change. The closer something is to pure Spirit, the greater its power to affect the physical and to create long-lasting effects in the world.

We can gauge the general proximity of something to Spirit by its corresponding distance from the physical. In other words, the more formless and insubstantial something is, the closer its association with Spirit. Therefore, conscious attention, which cannot be seen, touched, tasted, smelled, or heard, is intimately related to Spirit. This is followed by thought, which has form but lacks physical substance. Next come emotions, which, although invisible, strongly affect the body. Following this comes biological life, which stimulates the breath and animates the body. Finally, most distant from Spirit is physical matter, which has both form and substance. Although the physical world is the aspect of our experience that is most distant from the realm of Spirit, nonetheless, along with everything else in creation, it is contained within Spirit's all-pervading presence. Thus, the physical world is capable of being infused with Divine Light.

When power takes on a particular form, the more concrete and visible it becomes, the weaker that power becomes. Conversely, the less visible it is to the human eye, the stronger the power. This is a fundamental truth. The former kind of power can be measured in horsepower or kilograms, but the latter kind is immeasurable and infinite. *—Power. HT*

All things originate in the spiritual world. Physical objects do not cause things to appear but only affect what occurs in the outer world. The things of this world merely provide the necessary conditions for something to objectively manifest. Circumstances and conditions in the physical world are like the soil in which a plant grows; they provide the environment for growth but are not the source of life itself; that source is Spirit. Spirit provides the invisible spark of life that germinates the seed and causes it to grow into a fully matured plant.

What is conventionally viewed as cause and effect is, from a higher perspective, understood to be only a series of outer effects. The wind does not cause the tree to bend, nor does a bending tree cause the wind to blow. Rather, that which causes the wind to blow is also what causes the tree to bend. The wind is just as much a secondary effect of this prime mover, as is the bending tree. Both phenomena arise simultaneously just as mountains go with valleys, beaches go with oceans, and chickens go with eggs. Although we cannot see it, the spiritual world is the source and cause of all things, including chickens and eggs.

For example, one must first have the inspiration and intention to build a house before asking a draftsman to create a blueprint. After this, if everyone is satisfied with the blueprint and drawings, the craftsmen will put physical effort into building the house, which eventually gets completed as an actual material structure within the realm of time and space. The objective world is therefore a delayed outcome of the earlier conditions that existed in the spiritual world. First comes inspiration (which we receive from Spirit); then intention; then a mental plan; then an evaluation; then action; and finally the physical result. Similarly, if a child throws a rock through a window, did the window break because of the rock or the intention to throw it? What was the real cause of the event? What physical, mental, emotional, psychic and spiritual impulses lead to outer events? According to Meishusama, the primary cause lies in the spiritual dimension, and everything else is, at best, a secondary cause. In summary, all things are born within and then find their way to the outer world. Or, as the American transcendentalist Ralph Waldo Emerson stated, "The universe is the externalization of the soul."

Character is said to create destiny because it predisposes us to certain actions. Our character is made up of our thoughts, feelings, and desires, which spontaneously arise in our consciousness, largely beyond our personal control. How we interpret the conditions around us is especially significant because it determines how we respond. When we judge a situation as bad, we usually want to change it, or if we judge it as good, then we usually want to sustain it. Most of our attitudes and actions depend on subjective interpretations of fairness, rights, and obligations, as well as on personal evaluations of other people's motives and intentions.

It is surprising how many of us go through life mechanically, almost completely unaware of our true intentions. Dr. Sigmund Freud, the originator of Psychoanalysis, was correct when he stated that most of us are dominated and controlled by subconscious impulses. But these impulses reach much further back in time than he realized. We are molded by our childhood conditioning as well as by tendencies carried over from previous lifetimes in the distant past, and this conditioning is then stimulated by circumstances in our daily lives. We may like to think that we are the captains of our own ships, but in actuality we are controlled by numerous hidden influences. What we hold in our hearts determines our fate, and a heart corrupted by hurts, resentments, anxieties, and compulsions creates a world of conflict and suffering, whereas a pure heart creates a world of peace and joy. The place from where our tendencies and thoughts emerge, is the spiritual world. Although invisible to the senses, it is more fundamental than the world we experience.

> If a person thinks good thoughts and performs good deeds, he feels good inside because his conscience is satisfied and the pleasant thoughts originating from these actions become radiant Light. This Light increases and strengthens the radiance emitted from the spiritual body. This Light is also increased from the outside, for when someone performs a good deed, the gratitude and appreciation of the person he has helped become radiant Light that is transmitted to him through the spiritual cords, thus brightening his aura. —*Spiritual Radiation and the Aura. ET*

According to Meishusama, all living things are surrounded by an aura, an invisible body of Light unique to each individual. Only through special cameras using Kirlian Photography or through exceptional psychic awareness can this aura be detected. Meishusama writes, "It is a basic and true rule of the universe that auras cannot be seen by the eyes of ordinary people, but there are some who have the ability to see them. However, if an ordinary person stills his mind and gazes intently at another person, he can, to a limited extent, perceive that person's aura." (*Spiritual Radiation and the Aura. ET)* The aura is an outward expression of our soul, and its brightness and size are important factors determining our level of personal happiness.

Our thoughts, words, and deeds also leave imprints in the spiritual world. They either generate spiritual Light or produce spiritual clouds that darken our aura and cover our spirit. Negative thoughts such as anger, jealousy, and greed are the chief causes of disease and suffering. Thoughts of love, appreciation, and goodwill, on the other hand, bring Light to the aura, dispel spiritual clouds and create good fortune and happiness. When we understand this, the conditions in the spiritual world take on greater importance.

> Conditions in the spiritual world directly affect the spiritual body and are in turn reflected in the physical body. Thus, the fate of people is fundamentally decided by their conditions in the spiritual world. —*Jyorei and Happiness. ET*

On a practical level, this means that our spiritual life is more important than the physical things in life. Although cars, schools, jobs, and houses are important for comfort and survival, even more important is our relationship to these things, since it is what most determines our happiness. The same is true about our relationship to the people in our lives. Compared to the life of the spirit, these outer things are secondary.

What good is a promotion at work if it is obtained by manipulation, aggression, or deceit? Hurting the feelings of our friends or family members comes back to haunt us later, especially through the effects such behavior has in the invisible realms. When we take advantage of the people around us, we may benefit in the physical world, but lose out in the spiritual world. Lying, cheating, stealing, abusing, and other such unkind behavior immediately create disturbances in the spiritual world and directly impact the spiritual body. This is significant because our outer environment mirrors our inner environment; the one is not separate from the other.

> Watch your thoughts; they become words. Watch your words; they become actions. Watch your actions; they become habit. Watch your habits; they become character. Watch your character; it becomes your destiny. —*Lao Tzu (Ancient Taoist Sage)*

Our thoughts and intentions originate in the spiritual world and eventually manifest in the physical world. Healthy, positive thoughts create healthy, positive lives, whereas unhealthy, negative thoughts create unhealthy, negative lives. The more power we give to particular thoughts, the more they manifest outwardly. To have a good life, we need to take responsibility for our consciousness.

The first thing people need to understand is that every phenomenon in the material world reflects conditions in the spiritual world, and that every phenomenon in the spiritual world also reflects conditions in the material world.
—Do Not Deviate From Order. KW

The Law of Purification

It is a universal law of nature that if pollution gathers in any spot, then it will be cleared away and that spot will be purified.

—*A Third World War Can Be Avoided. ET*

In the beginning, our souls were created pure, but journeying through many lifetimes, their original purity becomes obscured by spiritual toxins. These toxins come from psychic pollution, physical poison, and most significantly, bad behavior. What we do and experience leaves residues in our souls, either positive or negative. This clouding of the spirit dulls our awareness and contributes to ill health and emotional suffering.

For example, if the toxins in our body make us feel irritable, and because of this we take it out on our family members over a period of many years by being mean to them, the resulting spiritual clouds generated by this behavior will lower our consciousness considerably. This negative effect on our consciousness will tend to then continue over into the next lifetime. Also, the less sensitive and aware we are, the more we make bad decisions and behave inappropriately, which results in negative consequences.

If we have the misfortune of being poisoned by fumes from a chemical factory or radiation from a power plant, these poisons leave a negative imprint that affects our spirit. After death, the physical poisons remain with the body, but the damage to the spiritual body may continue. The soul undergoes a purification process in the spiritual world and eventually returns to earth in a new incarnation. If the soul is not sufficiently purified, the effect of the poisons is carried into the new life, resulting in more suffering.

Although toxins have a harmful effect on the body, the underlying reason for the poisoning is spiritual. Why were we exposed to chemicals or radiation? Were we "accidentally" passing by the wrong place at the wrong time—or was it fated? The true reason for our behavior comes from unseen influences in the spiritual world. Nothing is an accident. The unseen laws governing all things determine when and where something will happen. Our soul may have needed to experience poisoning to further its spiritual growth.

Meishusama teaches that all suffering is purification. Nature initiates a cleansing process within the body through sickness and pain, and in the outer world, through natural catastrophes such as violent storms, floods, and earthquakes, as well as social calamities such as epidemics, wars and financial crisis. The body uses sickness to discharge internal toxins through fevers, sweating, diarrhea, vomiting, skin rashes, and other symptoms. These are all forms of purification. Interpersonal conflicts, financial difficulties, and other traumas are examples of external suffering that purify our souls.

> The thing that we term, all too simply, "sickness" is in fact a process of physical purification caused ultimately by the need to dispel the clouds accumulated on the human soul. Not only sickness, but all kinds of human suffering, stem from the same underlying cause. Thus, poverty and strife are also signs that a process of purification is taking place, and so it is obvious that there is no essential difference between sickness, poverty, and strife. —*Jyorei and Happiness. ET*

This does not suggest that suffering in itself is justified or good. Only the cleansing and educational effects of purification have value. Suffering is the inevitable result of erroneous behavior, individually or collectively. Great tragedies such as the Jewish, Armenian, Cambodian, and Rwandan genocides in the twentieth century are to be mourned. The need for humanity to grow up, and for individuals to learn to treat each other with kindness and respect has never been greater. If we learn from the ongoing lessons of life and finally create a world of health, prosperity, and peace, there will be no more mass purifications. Until then, we can expect more wars, poverty, injustice, crime, and disease. These events are outlets for the purification of collectively accumulated negativity. To grow, we need to take responsibility, individually and collectively, for these tragedies rather than blame others.

Words can be painfully inadequate following the death of a loved one or in the aftermath of wars, plagues, and earthquakes. At such times, the best one can do is give emotional and spiritual solace to the sufferers and provide physical assistance. Most people will begin searching for the reason behind these events because it is human nature to seek meaning. This is the time when wise counsel is valuable.

Purification's value is usually revealed in the future. To appreciate that suffering is purification requires one to suspend doubt, be open to the possibility of an intelligent pattern underlying life's events, and to know that this pattern is not only intelligent, but benevolent and compassionate.

When purification occurs, it is better to learn from it than actively resist it. We benefit greatly by asking ourselves, "How have I contributed to causing this purification? Have I eaten junk food? Have I smoked or drunk too much? Have I accumulated excessive debts? Have I been unkind?"

Those with the most spiritual clouds are not always those who suffer most, nor do those with the least amount of spiritual clouds suffer least. Gangsters who live extravagant lifestyles by manipulation, deceit, and violence might accumulate many dark clouds, but might not experience their negative effects until later in life. On the other hand, even saints, prophets, and humanitarians might have unresolved spiritual clouds from former lives that necessitate purification. Thus, even in the midst of lives dedicated to good works, they suffer hardship and disease.

With our limited understanding, we cannot know why innocent people suffer. There are hidden spiritual reasons for the death of a child, the illness of a generous person, or the financial problems of a great artist. Fortunately, from the long-term perspective of the soul, a lifetime's pain and suffering might seem like a momentary disturbance of one lifetime out of many.

That which is dying, as well as that which is birthing: each has its own reasons for following its fate. There are no accidents here, and everything is determined with exact certainty. —The Daijo Way. KW

Although no one wants to suffer, we can appreciate the general benefits of a detoxified body and purified spirit. As the clouding of our soul dissipates, health and happiness increase and our influence on others becomes positive.

Present suffering can lead to greater happiness in the future, especially when we learn from past mistakes. But there is no need to seek suffering, for the goal of life is happiness, not sorrow. Life is positive, and so purification can also be viewed as positive. Appreciating the positive value of purification can cause profound changes in our approach to life. We may find resistance to life's problems replaced by acceptance and even gratitude, which leads to an affirmation of life and greater peace of mind.

Fortunately, suffering is not the only way to spiritual purification and awareness. There are other ways, such as cultivating virtue and appreciating beauty. One cultivates virtue by doing good deeds for others. By helping others we also help ourselves. This is often a gentler and more effective way to purify our soul than through suffering.

Among the ways to help others, Jyorei is one of the easiest and most powerful. Jyorei is the art of focusing Divine Light for the sake of healing and spiritual growth, which results in increased health, awareness, and happiness. Jyorei clears negativity and toxicity on deep levels. There is no limit to Divine Light's benefits because it is not limited to the world of time and space.

Another way to purify without suffering is by experiencing beauty. Whether natural or man-made, beauty is of a high spiritual value that benefits all who approach it with an appreciative heart. It purifies us and raises our spiritual level.

Every one of us, despite age, gender, race, creed, or status, seeks happiness. This drive is at the core of human nature. Through purification of body, mind, and spirit, the obstructions blocking happiness dissolve. Eventually, we discover that happiness is not something to be earned, but our innate condition. When this is realized, we radiate happiness toward others rather than seek it solely for ourselves. This is the nature of true happiness.

The Law of Karma

Invisible to the human eye, there exists a spiritual world where laws are made by God, and people are judged according to these laws. —A Sense of Justice. ET

Actions have consequences. What we do to others returns back to us. When we treat others with kindness, our relationships improve and our well-being increases. On the other hand, behavior that harms others—lying, cheating, stealing, and physical assault—clouds our spirits and attracts misfortune. The universe is like a mirror reflecting our actions back to us. In this sense, we create our own reality through the energy we send out to the world. This principle is referred to as "karma." It can be restated by the well-known phrases, "As you sow, so shall you reap," and, "What goes around comes around."

Everything that you face and deal with in this world, such as people you interact with and the area where you live, is related to your own personal karma.
—Do Not Tighten Your Abdomen. KW

Most of our actions are neither overly good nor bad. They are usually a mixture of both. A parent yells at his or her children to stop them from fighting, to teach them proper behavior, and to protect them from harm. Although the motives may be good, the anger the parent expresses is bad. Yelling can hurt the children's feelings and set a bad example for them. Most actions like this generate mixed or mild karma because the good and bad tend to balance out. However, actions of intense passion generate stronger karma. The type of karma depends on the intention behind the action and the end results. If out of revenge a person harms someone through slander, theft, or violence, the bad karma and spiritual clouds generated will be immense. Whereas, if out of love a person sacrifices his or her own needs to help someone in greater need, the amount of good karma and spiritual Light produced will be large. The scales of karma always move toward balance and equilibrium.

Thus, a person's fate, his good luck and bad luck, depends on his thoughts and atti-tudes, and to understand this truth is necessary for an accurate perception of reality.
—A Sense of Justice. ET

The quality of our lives is more often determined by our state of consciousness than by outer events. All of our past thoughts, emotions, and sensory impressions accumulate within us and gradually drive our actions. Many of these tendencies are carried over from previous lives. The darker and more suppressed these tendencies are, the more they disrupt our lives. Aggressive actions tend not to improve situations, but often make things worse by provoking equally aggressive counteractions by others. Similarly, the tendency to judge others prompts them to judge us.

Openly accepting your karma helps you to handle things more easily.
—Do Not Tighten Your Abdomen. KW

Fortunately, when our spiritual condition rises to a higher level, everything else improves as well. This is because the way we interpret our lives, and the feelings that result from these interpretations, are dependent on the clarity of our perceptions. When the mirror of our soul is cleansed of dark, suppressed thoughts, emotions and impressions, everything becomes brighter and more positive. Our ability to perceive reality also improves and thus we are able to act intelligently and effectively. The darkness needs to be wiped from the mirror either by releasing it from our being or by embracing it with love. It is important not to act out these tendencies through negative behavior, but instead to allow them to dissipate naturally. This will result in a much better life.

A foolish person sows seeds of destruction, not realizing they will be his to reap.
—Good and Evil. MK1

Chapter 3

ESSENTIAL INNER QUALITIES

Spiritual growth affects all areas of our lives, including our thoughts, emotions, and desires. The cultivation of the following three inner qualities helps transform our behavior into that which supports greater happiness and fulfillment.

Gratitude

The source of human nobility is deep and abiding gratitude for all of God's gifts.
—Gratitude. MK1

Usually, we only pay attention to our body when we are in pain. When our comfort is disturbed, we take notice. Our immediate impulse is to resist the pain by tightening up the body, but this usually makes things worse. As pain lingers, we may sink into self-pity and resentment. Then, when the pain passes, we go back to ignoring our body.

Nobody likes to suffer, and the tendency is to become angry or depressed when in pain. This might become a lasting attitude if the pain continues for a long period. When the pain finally does go away, there may be some initial gratitude, but soon that fades too. One might expect this gratitude to endure, however, this is usually not the case, and most of us go back to taking our comfort for granted instead of appreciating it.

The mind is always looking for problems to solve. So, it focuses on what is wrong rather than what is right. Therefore, it does not notice when things are going well. About this, Meishusama says, "Humans have a tendency to focus more on the negative side of things rather than on the positive, and they like to complain." (*Maintaining Moderation. KW*) This tendency for problems to grab our attention appears to be a biologically inherited survival response. The mind guides us through the world and keeps us alive. It is always alert for danger. Yet this fixation on problems leads us to anger and self-pity when things go wrong.

We have a tendency to complain about what we do not have instead of being grateful for what we have. We might have a perfectly good house, car, job, or life partner, yet still envy those who appear to have something better. Instead of being grateful, we succumb to envy, resentment, or self-pity. Our cravings are never satisfied, even if we get the things we want, since there will always be others with better things than we have; thus, creating more envy on our part. No matter how rich a person becomes, there never seems to be enough money to satisfy greed. When holding greed and envy in our hearts, we produce misery rather than joy.

All that we are is the result of our thoughts. —Gautama Buddha

If we focus on the shortcomings of the people around us, our relationships with them will get worse. Conversely, when appreciating people's good qualities, our relationships with them improve and their behavior improves as well. This reciprocal principle is summarized in the Biblical saying, "As you sow, so shall you reap." Everyone appreciates compliments and expressions of gratitude, and it is wonderful to see how often appreciation brings out the best in people. Learn to thank people for the little things they do and see how quickly they respond to your kind words.

As well as its practical advantages, gratitude is in itself a satisfying reward. Gratitude does not ask for anything in the future, but gives thanks for what exists here and now. It arises when we look for things to appreciate in our present circumstances. We can view a glass of water as being either half empty or half full; the choice is up to us. It is possible to feel grateful in even horrible conditions because at least things are not worse. If for nothing else, we can be thankful for the simple fact of being alive. When we feel gratitude, life often reciprocates by improving. Meishusama adds, "[S]uppose that the value of life is the number ten. If one's gratitude for life also is ten, then one has achieved a kind of balance, and if it is above this, it is a plus that God will reward many times over with His blessings." (*The Rationality of Faith and Re-purification. ET*)

We create our own destiny by our actions in this and in previous lives. These actions either pollute our souls or draw greater spiritual light into them. The aftereffects in the spiritual world are what determine our destiny. As Meishusama puts it: "[T]he amount of suffering that affects a person corresponds to the degree of clouding of the soul." *(A Bad Person is Spiritually Sick. ET)* Instead of complaining about our misfortune, it is better to take responsibility for having earlier created this need for purification. Even under the worst of circumstances, the more grateful we are for our purification, the higher our consciousness rises, and as a result, the higher the quality of our lives. The way we do something is often more important than what we do, and it is the intention behind our actions that have the greatest impact on our spiritual body.

Meishusama recommends cultivating gratitude for not only the things we like, but also for those things we do not. Although his recommendation might seem strange, on closer look, we find profound wisdom. When Meishusama suggests that we feel grateful for our hardships, he does not mean that we should deliberately pursue suffering. It is not the pain itself, but rather the process of eliminating spiritual impurities that has value. This process is what we appreciate. The suffering caused by these bad experiences is a temporary hardship that we must endure while moving toward greater health and happiness. Purification opens the possibility for spiritual growth. Along with appreciating the present, it is also good to consider the future because it often arrives sooner than we expect.

Meishusama writes, "Gratitude breeds gratitude; discontent spawns discontent. This is the truth. For a grateful heart rises straight to God, while a discontented heart finds the evil spirits of Hell." *(You Are What You Think. ET)* This passage does not mean that if we grumble and complain a wrathful God will send us to hell. Rather, it points out that we create our own heaven and hell by our thoughts and attitudes. Gratitude gives rise to happiness, calms the mind, and dissolves feelings of want and need. About the significance of gratitude, the fourteenth century German Christian mystic, Meister Eckhart, stated, "If the only prayer you say in your whole life is 'thank you,' it will suffice."

Gratitude is a warm, appreciative feeling in response to the kindness or the benefits we have received. It is an affirmation of life and all its blessings. Anger, jealousy, and resentment melt when appreciation is held in our hearts. Fear and defensiveness shrink away, and are replaced by peace and love. Within gratitude are the seeds of joy. It can transform us beyond the reach of human effort. We may rush to self-improvement seminars and "instant therapy" workshops, but if our hearts are closed, they will be of no benefit.

A grateful heart draws spiritual Light to itself, and this Light then reflects outward to the world. Gratitude, at its core, is a divine quality. It is a doorway allowing God's presence to enter into our hearts. When we take one step toward God, God takes ten steps toward us.

So much has been given to me, I have not time to ponder over that which has been denied. —Helen Keller

The universe is not our creation, nor is our body. Everything was given to us. Even our first breath did not depend upon us. Our bodies spontaneously drew in the air. Our parents nurtured, providing food, clothing, and shelter. These and many more things are provided to us by society. Without bicycles, cars, buses, trains, and subways, we would not be able to travel daily to work, school, church, or stores. It is easy to take all these things for granted because we use them so often. However, in developing countries, these things are scarce and people walk long distances. The more we contemplate this, the more things we find for which to be grateful.

If you haven't got all the things you want, be grateful for the things you don't have that you don't want. —Anonymous

Start focusing on what you have, rather than what you lack. Even if you can find only one thing to be grateful for, by focusing on it your perception expands, as does your capacity for feeling more gratitude. Be grateful for whatever has nourished, blessed, or benefited your life, be it a person, place, or thing. The more gratitude we feel, the more that is given to us for which to be grateful.

A simple, good exercise is to say "thank you" throughout the day. Actively look for opportunities to express sincere gratitude to people. By doing so, we bring forth the beauty of others. Looking for reasons to be grateful increases our appreciation of life and helps us enjoy each moment more fully. As the American writer, Arthur Ward, puts it: "Feeling gratitude and not expressing it is like wrapping a present and not giving it."

Happiness comes mostly from our perception—from how we interpret things and the value we place on them. By changing our attitude toward what comes our way in life, we learn to want what we get rather than try to get what we want. In this way, we can feel grateful irrespective of what comes our way.

Trust in the divine order of things. Know that God does everything perfectly, giving each of us exactly what we need to further our spiritual growth. Expressing gratitude to God for all that arises, both the pleasant and the unpleasant, sanctifies everything and brings deep peace and joy to our hearts.

Our general attitude contributes more to our overall happiness than the specific circumstances in our lives. Thankfulness can improve the worst circumstances, revealing hidden gems that are immensely rewarding. Gratitude gives us wings to soar above our daily problems and guides our arms to embrace the many gifts that come our way.

At times I feel there is no one as fortunate and happy as I, and I am always full of heartfelt gratitude to God for this. —About Myself. ET

Loving Others

When you love the world and help people, God protects you wherever you go.
—Loving Others. MK2

Everyone wants love. Unfortunately, the human need for love is a source of much pain and confusion. Children who do not receive enough love and approval from their parents often become angry, bitter adults. And when forming close relationships, they often struggle to dominate the other person rather than express mutual affection. Society reflects this sad condition by creating institutions such as workplaces, schools, government agencies, and hospitals that are also based on control rather than love. These impersonal environments are mostly devoid of warmth and caring.

> In this society, no matter where you go and what social status you have, it is important to care about your duty as a human being: to love and respect your inner self, your parents, and others. Whatever you do, if your actions do not originate from a core of love and respect, they are almost devoid of value. It is like a body missing a backbone. *—Izunome: The Movement of the Universe. KW*

People whose hearts are closed feel cut off from others, including their spouses, children, parents, and friends. They also feel estranged from society and nature. Often they lead solitary lives of silent desperation, enduring painful feelings of alienation and loneliness even when surrounded by people they have known for years. And, most of their efforts to improve their relationships fail because they do not know how to express warmth or affection.

One of life's major challenges is cultivating and maintaining loving relationships. Success in this area depends as much on avoiding conflict as on being friendly and likable. And although making such positive efforts is essential, one's outer behavior, no matter how pleasant, cannot guarantee a return of genuine love. Such love must be inspired in others, and we can only inspire love if we have love within our own hearts.

> In essence, what determines the kind of impression people make is the condition of their souls, which we can feel spiritually. In the same manner, I think that people who give us a warm feeling have more love in their hearts, compared to those who give us a cold feeling. —*Warm Hearts Attract People. KW*

The essentials of life are difficult to define. Words tend to describe the outer surface of things rather than their inner reality. Love is also like that. It is essential to who we are, but is hard for the mind to grasp. In personal relationships, we experience love as caring and affection for each other. At a deeper level, love is a response to our perception of the spiritual presence within others. Love reveals to us their uniqueness and inner beauty. The greater the purity of an individual's soul, the more capable that person is of perceiving the spiritual essence within others. Love reveals our common humanity beneath our superficial differences, thereby fostering unity instead of separation, and bringing us closer together. It extends our sense of self to include the other. The French theologian-biologist-paleontologist Pierre Teilhard de Chardin wrote, "Love alone is capable of uniting living beings in such a way as to complete and fulfill them, for it alone takes them and joins them by what is deepest in themselves."

To love is to not judge. The more we connect with another's spiritual essence, the more we are able to love the many facets of their character, such as their attitudes, personality, and mannerisms. Love inclines us to accept the whole person, not just their admirable qualities, but even their less than perfect aspects. People know when they are truly loved because they feel acknowledged and accepted. They feel safe in revealing more of themselves to the person who does not judge, but accepts them just as they are.

Your task is not to seek for love, but merely to seek and find all the barriers within yourself that you have built against it. —Rumi

When the light of love illuminates our own inner darkness, we become beautiful. The same happens when we shine love on others—they become beautiful as well. All of us yearn for this unconditional love. To love is to not judge.

Love is one of the most healing forces in life. As psychologist Karl Menninger said, "Love cures people—both the ones who give it and the ones who receive it."

In the Harvard University Mastery of Stress Study, which began in the 1950s with 126 healthy male undergraduate students, the most accurate predictor of future health was the perception that these men had of their parents' love and caring. This factor far superseded other factors such as family and genetic history of disease or lifestyle conditions. Further, it turns out that those men who rated their parents high in love and caring not only proved to be more open to receiving love, but also more capable of communicating love to others.

The closer one moves toward God, the more one's heart fills with love. Although it might be easy to perceive love as an abstraction when in solitude, the true test of love is found in the way we treat others in our day-to-day lives, especially those we do not like or who cause us problems. It is possible to communicate effectively to those who mistreat us without expressing anger or hostility. Love is demonstrated by acts of gentleness and kindness. It always thinks of others and seeks to serve. When we love someone, we give that person our energy and attention, which makes him or her feel recognized, valued, and cared for. Most adults are easily impressed by outer appearances and social status, confusing this with inner worth. Children, however, care very little about these things. Children respond naturally to love and are not fooled by outer appearances or falseness.

A life lived only for oneself is a life of isolation. At the end of our lives, everything unessential will fall away and each of us will be left with the question: "What was my life all about?" The only satisfying answer is found in how much good we leave behind us. As Meishusama says:

If you want to be happy, you have to make others happy. What is absolutely essential here is love. —The Izunome Principle and Love. KW

Our life has greater meaning and value when we are able to help others. The extent that we are able to contribute to humanity, and especially to the people we encounter daily, is the extent to which we can feel good about ourselves. Helping others is a natural expression of the love we feel. As Mother Teresa said, "We can do no great things; only small things with great love." It is love that counts.

The ability to see ourselves in others is the basis of love. It is as simple as seeing through another's eyes and knowing that deep down we are fundamentally the same. This is the recognition of Spirit within form. God radiates love, and this love is at the foundation of all existence. The closer we move toward God, the more we, too, radiate love. And when God resides securely in our heart, our love partakes of divinity. This love is both impersonal and all-encompassing. Like the sun, it radiates outwardly on both the good and the bad, while attracting to itself all that its rays illuminate. God's love is unconditional, whereas human love is usually limited by personal needs and affinities. About this, Meishusama writes, "When looking into the vast sky, the expanse of God's love enters my heart." (*Divine Compassion. MK2*) We all have the essence of God within us, and thus partake of God's goodness. To love others is to touch God.

Love is an expression of the Oneness of all life. It removes all divisions and allows us to feel our essential unity with people, nature, and God. "Faces may vary in shape and color, but in God's eyes all are of the same land," writes Meishusama. (*Peace on Earth. MK1*) At the level of Spirit, we are one and the same.

When we truly love others, there is no room for judgment or suspicion. These ways of thinking separate us from love by projecting negative motives onto others. When we judge others, we are focusing mostly on their outward behavior, whereas when we empathize with them, we are identifying with their feelings and needs. Empathy prompts us to sympathize with people's pain and to celebrate their joy. About himself, Meishusama writes, "It is my essential nature to care for people and to work to make them happy. In addition to this, since my heart clearly mirrors other people's thoughts and feelings, when I listen to them expressing their pains and worries, it feels as though their troubles were mine." (*Helping Others. KW*)

Possessiveness—trying to control people—pushes them away. We cannot force people to love us; it must come naturally. Love is genuine when spontaneous, not coerced. So, we need to allow people the freedom to be themselves. When we exhibit selfishness, by making our needs more important than those of others, we create division, which in turn blocks the flow of love. A selfish heart tends to use others for personal gain, thereby fostering resentment rather than appreciation. Love flowers best in an atmosphere of selflessness, kindness, and generosity.

However, loving others does not require us to accept their negative attitudes or behavior. We need to discern right from wrong, as well as positive from negative. People can be selfish, destructive, or cruel, and this must be dealt with appropriately, but always with kindness. There is a difference between a person's behavior and their essence. Behavior can be good, neutral, or bad, but our essence is always good, as it partakes of God's Spirit. And it is through people's essence that we learn to recognize and love them, regardless of their actions or beliefs. This unconditional love is what will heal the world and bring peace and harmony to all.

The psychoanalyst and social psychologist Erich Fromm, in his book The Art of Loving, describes love as being not so much a relationship to one person as a general attitude and orientation of character. It is a forgiving, nurturing, and supportive way of relating to people. This loving orientation determines how we relate to the whole world and not just toward an individual. If this love is directed exclusively toward one person, rather than universally toward everyone, then it is really a dependent attachment, and the person one loves is likely an extension of one's own ego. As Fromm put it, "If a person loves only one other person and is indifferent to all others, his love is not love but a symbiotic attachment, or an enlarged egotism."

"To be loved, be lovable," wrote the ancient Roman poet Ovid. If we desire love, we should be gentle, kind, and forgiving toward all beings, including ourselves. We should put aside selfish desires, personal agendas, and self-serving justifications that interfere with love. Especially, we must not be judgmental. We must learn to be compassionate both toward others and toward ourselves. By itself, being compassionate and non-judgmental does not cause love to appear, but it does create a space within us where love can spontaneously arise.

The quality of our love is the measure of its authenticity. In its highest expression, love is unconditional and impartial, and is not dependent on people's actions. It is a universal attitude that is not restricted or constrained by anything that happens in the outer world. Such love excludes nothing and applies to all things. Unconditional love is like the sun that shines on both the good and the bad, without discrimination or favoritism. Its warm glow nurtures all. The more we are like the sun, the more we shine from within, happy to glow brightly.

Love is its own reward, and is an end in itself. Its blessings flow like waves through water, soothing and nourishing all that it encounters. Love lightens the soul and creates happiness for no particular reason. Love is a force that sustains the universe. Love is the motivation for aiding others. It is both a means to an end and an end in itself, as love begets love. The more we love, the more love increases throughout the world.

The true goal of love is to draw us into its larger sphere, which is the all-embracing unity of divine love.

Go with God's love and extend this unconditional love to others, and then you can be a person whom everybody feels comfortable to talk to and to be around.

—Being Daijo. KW

Makoto

A person who has Makoto will keep his promises whatever happens.
—How to Find Makoto. ET

The way we live is a reflection of the quality of our soul. While it is easy enough to think idealistically or feel fine sentiments, it is through our deeds that we truly reveal our character. Most of us would be upset if our car malfunctioned because our mechanic neglected to attach a wheel or a fan belt properly, despite promises to do a good job. If he did a bad job, we would end up suffering the consequences of his carelessness. Like the mechanic, what we do matters because there are consequences to it that affect others.

One who does not neglect small things can achieve great things.
—Spiritual Cultivation. MK2

All the little things we do throughout the day add up to a larger picture that reflects our general character. If we leave the faucet dripping in the kitchen, our bills unpaid, the oil unchanged in our car, and our shoes untied, then there is a good chance that we are just as negligent with our thoughts. It is easy to rationalize and justify our laziness or procrastination, but it is not so easy to deal with the consequences. This is especially true when we neglect the people around us, and our relationships deteriorate. How can we focus our mind on accomplishing anything important when our life is in chaos? The best we can do is dream and talk about big things rather than take decisive action.

Always do right. This will gratify some people and astonish the rest. —Mark Twain

When what we think matches what we say, and what we say matches what we do, then Meishusama would say that we display "makoto," a Japanese word for sincerity, honesty and integrity. It denotes a fundamental unity in a person's thoughts, words, and deeds. A person with great makoto tends to live according to a high code of ethics and never wavers from it.

Act the way you'd like to be and soon you'll be the way you act. —Leonard Cohen

How often have we said or done something wrong that later we deeply regretted? This often happens because of unconscious divisions between our thoughts and feelings, and between our selfish tendencies and our altruistic intentions. Most people have mixed motives for what they do. They may halfheartedly attempt to serve others while pursuing self-gain. Consequently, sometimes their actions are helpful and sometimes not. If a person volunteers to do charity work, but then starts bragging about his good deeds, he is operating under false pretenses. Eventually people will notice that he has been putting more time and energy into promoting his social image than into helping others. Questions will arise about his sincerity. Such behavior reflects a desire for admiration and respect rather than a desire to help others. If he continues like this for too long, he might attract scorn and contempt.

People who do not attempt to impress others seem modest and courteous, and are viewed with heartfelt respect. —The Spirit of Izunome. KW

Makoto's foundation is purity and wholeness. It is only possible to become inwardly whole to the extent that our desires are sufficiently purified and brought into alignment with our conscious intentions. The more we dedicate our actions to a higher purpose or ideal, the more these actions will begin to demonstrate inner wholeness. To be whole is to be free from the distraction of conflicting desires and purposes. This wholeness allows us to put our hearts more fully into our actions, which not only improves the quality of our work, but lets us draw greater satisfaction from it as well.

Sincerity is also an expression of makoto because it depends on consistency. We cannot be truly sincere if our left hand acts contrary to our right one, or if our words do not match our actions. It is false to declare our love for animals if an hour later we kick our dog because it damaged our furniture. Some would call this hypocrisy. Similarly, if we proudly proclaim our love for humanity and grandly promise to dedicate our lives to serving world peace, and then in our next breath start condemning the homeless and the poor, we will probably fail to convince anyone about the sincerity of our convictions. They will quickly dismiss the things we say. Such discrepancies between a person's actions and their words reveal a divided self that is full of inner contradictions and self-deception.

Be a genuine person: one who is always concerned for the truth, for the world, and for others. —Poems of Inspiration. MK1

Maturity is another expression of makoto. It requires maturity to keep one's commitments. Dr. Fritz Perls, the originator of Gestalt Therapy, defined maturity as "the transformation from environmental support to self-support." He says that mature people mobilize their own inner and outer resources rather than manipulate others to get what they want. They stand on their own two feet and take responsibility for their actions rather than blame others for their mistakes.

Living with makoto means that we have integrity and act in accordance with our convictions. We follow our conscience and are true to our word. If we promise to do something, we do it. People can rely on us because of the honesty of our character, which itself is an expression of our concern for others. If we have makoto, we truly care for others and are considerate. Being grounded in our own experience, we do not find it threatening to view things from another person's perspective. We are not divided against ourselves, but speak with one voice. We are integrated and whole.

To develop makoto, we must continuously examine our attitudes and motives for any sign of falsehood or deceit. The lies we tell ourselves undermine our ability to attain makoto. Self-deception leads to self-destruction. Therefore, to practice honesty and sincerity is the best way to cultivate makoto and find peace and happiness. The importance of true sincerity is affirmed in an ancient Shinto saying: "Where you have sincerity, there is also virtue. Sincerity is a witness to truth. Sincerity is the mother of knowledge. Sincerity is a single virtue that binds divinity and man in one."

Only when free of self-deception are we capable of sincerity in all we do and say. Sincerity is a beautiful personal quality in which the inner and the outer self align in perfect harmony. A truly sincere person has the inner purity of a polished mirror that accurately reflects the outer world without obstruction or distortion. This purity derives from a state of selflessness and honesty. Such a person is trusted because people sense that he means what he says.

It can be said that love is an attribute of the heart, gratitude is an expression of both the heart and the mind in balance, and makoto is a product of the heart, mind, and will, all fused together in perfect harmony. The quality of our will is determined by our desires, motives, and intentions. Someone with impure motives suffers from continual conflict with others, whereas a person of inner purity finds harmony and happiness in society. As self-centered motives give way to altruism and concern for others, a person will increasingly tend to do what is best for everyone, not just for himself. When an individual's soul becomes pure, his desires and intentions are aligned with Divine Intent. Such a person chooses to serve God in whatever way he can.

Makoto is an outer expression of our character. Only when we keep promises, act in accordance with our values, and communicate with honesty and sincerity, do we truly embody makoto. To have makoto is to behave maturely and with uncompromising integrity.

Because everyone and everything is infinitely connected, our actions have widespread consequences. Knowing this, a person with makoto takes responsibility for everything he thinks, says, and does, and dedicates himself to the betterment of the world and its inhabitants.

Return to your heart of makoto, let God's Light brighten your soul.
                                                                    —*Restoring Integrity. MK2*

Chapter 4

MYSTERIES OF
THE SPIRITUAL WORLD

Miroku⁴ Omikami

If you acquire a deep knowledge of the spiritual world, then life is joyful and even death itself is pleasant. —Preface. ET

Miroku Omikami is a Japanese word for God that Meishusama uses when referring to God as an all-pervasive spiritual presence. "Miroku" can be interpreted as Ultimate. "Kami," in Japanese, refers to an individualized god, spirit entity, or conscious energy localized in a particular place, object, or phenomenon. Shinto, the indigenous religion of Japan, holds that trees, rocks, mountains, lakes, and rivers each have a conscious spiritual energy, or kami, residing within them. Such a world is experienced as alive and full of divine power. "Omikami" means Great God or Great Spirit. Therefore, Miroku Omikami means Ultimate Great God, the one universal, all-encompassing spiritual reality at the heart of all existence.

On a deeper level, Miroku Omikami exists undivided in each and every particle of existence. As humans, we tend to see the world around us as fragmented into discrete objects, and therefore do not perceive the infinite nature of God, which is always whole and complete. Although Miroku Omikami is present everywhere,

---

4. *Miroku* is most commonly recognized as a Buddhist term that refers to Maitreya, the future Buddha of all-encompassing love. According to Meishusama, there is not merely one, but actually three Mirokus. These are the well-known figures of Kannon, Amitabha, and the Buddha, who respectively symbolize the elements of fire, water, and earth, or sun, moon, and earth. The Miroku explained in this book indicates the One that unites and surpasses the power of these different Mirokus, in other words, three ultimate spiritual elements. Meishusama also identified the spiritual nature of Miroku Omikami with that of Maitreya in Buddhism.

it is much greater than manifest creation, and can exist complete unto itself even in the total absence of all phenomena.

God, or "Miroku Omikami," is formless and everywhere. It is infinite consciousness and eternal presence. It is not separate from the natural world, but exists within each one of us, as well as within all things. "The Divine Power of God is present in the world in many forms," says Meishusama. (*True Faith. HT*) This divine presence reveals itself in the patterns of nature, and can be found in the flowing movements of a mountain stream, in the blossoming of a flower, and in the flight of a bird in the sky. There is nowhere in nature that Miroku Omikami cannot be found.

Miroku Omikami is both nature and that which animates it. To view Miroku Omikami as completely formless is to limit it, for this would exclude the world of form. Miroku Omikami is both formless and form, infinite and finite, and Spirit and matter. It is an undivided totality.

God, or Miroku Omikami, knows everything because God is everything. But God does not know things objectively because nothing exists as an object outside of Him. Instead, God knows things subjectively, because everything exists within the vastness of His own infinite being. Everything that God sees is a manifest projection of Himself, like images in a mirror. Divinity sees Itself in all things because there is nowhere that It is not found. This unitary perception is the basis of unconditional love. It is God loving Himself (or Herself) through the agency of others.

God is not limited to any particular time or place. Everything that we see, taken together, is an aspect of God. The Light of God is in everything and beyond. It is porous, and fills all space. All of creation is surrounded by and pervaded by divinity, like the water in the sea that both flows around the fish and infuses every cell within their bodies. Each of us is like these fish, which never even for a moment lose contact with this life-giving water. But, just as fish are oblivious to the water that surrounds them, so too are we oblivious to God's eternal presence. Both are invisible and all-pervasive realities to those who live in them.

Although God is constantly guiding and influencing everything, we need to raise our consciousness to a higher level before we can perceive this. We can do this through internal purification and also through contributing to the happiness of others. How we treat others affects how we relate to God, because God dwells within each and every person, animal, plant, and thing. Everything we do affects our relationship with God one way or another.

To grow spiritually, we must first establish a loving relationship with God. To do this, it is helpful to feel that he is close, rather than distant, because intimacy depends upon close proximity. Not only is God's Spirit nearby, it is even closer than our nose, more intimate than our breath, and more constant than our heartbeat. God's divine presence accompanies us everywhere, whether we know it or not. So, in this sense, we do not need to create a relationship with God because it already exists. However, most of us may find that we have room to improve on the quality of this relationship. If we think of God as our close companion, as our spiritual guide, and as our helper and protector, then our relationship with the Divine will become closer and more personal. Over time, this relationship may become so intimate that we will find God's presence within us, as well as within all things. After this, we will never again feel alone, because we now feel continuously embraced by God's invisible loving hands.

The eyes of God see to the furthermost depths of the human heart.
—Good and Evil. HT

Each of the three primary ways of relating to Miroku Omikami produces different effects. Discovering God's presence as our indwelling spirit promotes inner serenity and joy; relating to God interpersonally as the Supreme Being in heaven encourages love and devotion; and perceiving God's Spirit in the world of nature fosters reverence and gratitude.

Miroku Omikami refers to the absolute unity of the Supreme Being, which encompasses all apparent contradictions and dualities within a larger, unifying whole. Not only does God contain everything, as water contains fish, but the essence of God also exists within all things, like the water within each fish. God is equally immanent (dwelling within the world of time and space) and transcendent (existing above and beyond that which we can perceive). We, and all of nature, are part of God's extended body, and are supported by God's divine presence. Although manifesting in diverse forms, Miroku Omikami never loses its wholeness.

Beyond the Mind

Neither wisdom nor intellect can penetrate God's design. —Meishusama IV. MK2

Meishusama teaches that although Divinity is immanent in the world of space and time, it is difficult to perceive this Divinity because of the spiritual clouds that block our perception. So, for most of us, God appears more transcendent (out there) than immanent (in here), or, in other words, more distant than near. Yet, fortunately there are ways to connect with Divine Presence. This Divine Presence can be sensed in the beauty of nature, through the healing effects of Jyorei, and in the loving kindness of others. We can also discover divinity in simplicity, because this quality allows space for something greater to appear. For most of us, though, God will seem distant and unknowable until we can free ourselves from excessive attachments to worldly things that distract us and cause emotional distress.

At first, faith is helpful in our journey toward God. But eventually, faith must be transformed into direct experience because then God's Presence will become immanent and obvious within our very own soul.

God is neither exclusively transcendent nor exclusively immanent. Either concept of God, by itself, is incomplete because it reduces God to a partiality. Each concept expresses only half of the larger truth and thereby limits that which is by nature unlimited. To single-mindedly embrace one point of view at the expense of the other would result in locating God either wholly inside or wholly outside of creation, but not both. Yet to conclude that both are true is logically contradictory, and therefore seemingly impossible. To resolve this apparent discrepancy, it must be realized that this contradiction exists only on the level of the rational mind, which thinks similarly to the binary logic of a computer chip that uses on and off switches to make calculations. In actuality, the essential nature of God is a profound mystery that is beyond words and cannot be understood with the limited capacities of our minds.

Paradoxical descriptions of God have been uttered since the dawn of time. An ancient axiom attributed to the legendary Hermes Trismegistus declares that, "God is a sphere whose center is everywhere and whose circumference is nowhere." Another way of saying this is that God is within everything and everything is within God. This double-sided description is an expression of Kannon's Way, which is an inclusive frame of mind that always sees both sides of an issue and, as a result, approaches life with flexibility and balance. (*See chapter 9.*)

Meishusama is flexible in matters of theology. He describes his teachings as both monotheistic and polytheistic in nature. Out of the One emerges the many, however the many never separate from the One. Meishusama claims that God can manifest in numerous forms, each an expression of a different spiritual quality, such as peace, love, truth, or harmony. This variety of forms might confuse people and lead them to think that there are many gods because they fail to perceive their underlying unity.

Even though you tie a hundred knots
The string remains one. —Rumi

God's presence can be found in the world, as well as within each of us, as the Light at the center of our souls. In a similar sense, goodness and beauty can also be found everywhere if our eyes are sufficiently open to seeing it. But first, the mind needs to become free of obscurations so it can unite with the beauty and Light that is everywhere.

See things from a spiritual perspective—a God-centered viewpoint.
—Seeing from a God-Centered Viewpoint. KW

The more we progress spiritually, the more we tend to lovingly embrace the world rather than reject it. This is because, when we have love in our hearts, we feel an affinity to the things around us. Spirituality does not remove us from life, although it does free us from binding attachment to it. By becoming detached and peaceful, we become increasingly "in the world but not of it."

Personal and Impersonal

In this body Kannon has taken up humble abode. —Meishusama I. MK1

In contrast to the impersonal concept of Miroku Omikami, Meishusama often personified God as one who frowns on those who do bad, and smiles on those who do good. This is a God who takes a personal interest in people and who actively cares about their welfare and spiritual evolution. On a grander scale, God also oversees the spiritual progression of the entire Cosmos. In this matter of how to view God, as with everything else, Meishusama was quite flexible, and his wording and description of God varied according to the subject matter and the person he was addressing.

Use the Light that is in you to recover your natural clearness of sight.
—Lao Tzu (Ancient Taoist Sage)

When looking inwardly, one can discover God as the eternal Spirit ever-present at the core of our being, whereas when looking outwardly, one can discover God as the ultimate power and intelligence that directs all things. Of course, these are both the same God because there are not two Supreme Beings—only one. Again, this division between inward and outward is created in our own minds, not in God's, for God is beyond the limitations of inner and outer, as well as subject and object. These opposites are like the two sides of the same coin. Stated simply, God, or Miroku Omikami, is both everywhere and beyond.

According to Meishusama, Miroku Omikami is continually personifying itself as the deity Kannon, the compassionate power of God. Meishusama claimed that this deity merged with his inner being and thereafter began to move and speak through him. Meishusama describes this condition: "[I]t was Kannon who approached me to use me as Her instrument. I am, one could say, a physical embodiment of Her. I am used completely as Kannon thinks fit and do not have the freedom of an ordinary person, but I do have a freedom that the ordinary person lacks. This spiritual state is very difficult to explain as it is beyond normal comprehension." (*My Testament. ET*) As a result of this, Meishusama became a living embodiment of God—a fusion of the human and the divine. Now that Meishusama is no longer physically alive, but instead dwells within the spiritual world, many believe that he continues to intercede on their behalf and so they extend their prayers and gratitude toward him.

Whether one views God in a personal or impersonal way, or both, is up to the individual. Both views can support one's faith and trust in divinity. In any case, God is not accessible through philosophical speculation, but only through direct spiritual perception. This is gained through inner transformation, not through ideas.

To be free, we should not create fixed images or frameworks. —Kannon Faith. ET

The Three Spiritual Elements

Miroku Omikami is infinite, eternal, ever present, and changeless, and also finite, temporal, elusive, and changing. Change is a creative process that occurs within the realm of manifestation, whereas the changeless is a non-occurrence within the unmanifest realm, the "World of the Ultimate Mystery." Miroku Omikami creates the world from the metaphorical elements of fire, water, and earth, the three fundamental components of existence. Meishusama writes: "Everything in the universe is composed of three great elements. There is not a single thing that does not owe its creation to the power of these three elements. They are related to the sun, the moon, and the earth. The sun is the source of the spirit of fire; the moon is the source of the spirit of water; the earth is the source of the spirit of earth. These three elements flow and mingle inextricably together." (*The Spirits of Fire, Water, and Earth. ET)*

In line with this, the essential qualities of the sun and the moon are respectively height and width. Looking at the planet earth through this concept, ... one sees that its air is filled with the spirits of water flowing laterally and fire moving vertically. The spiritual elements of the vertical spirit of fire and the horizontal spirit of water are intertwined in space like the warp and woof of a fabric. The density of their fusion cannot be perceived or measured. — *Vertical and Horizontal. KW*

The spirit of earth is the gross, material dimension; the spirit of water is a subtle, semi-material dimension; and the spirit of fire is a luminous, immaterial dimension. The distribution and balance of these three elements determine the nature and condition of our world. Within human beings, they represent body, mind, and spirit. The body is dense—like earth; the mind flows—like water; and spirit radiates—like fire. Earth, water, and fire can also be interpreted as symbols for qualities and processes in the natural world, such as solid, liquid, or gas.

The Three Spiritual Elements

Fire	Water	Earth
Sun	Moon	Earth
Sunshine	Rain	Soil
Divine World	Spiritual World	Physical World
Spirit	Mind	Matter
Perception	Feeling	Action
Oxygen	Hydrogen	Nitrogen
Subjective	Inter-subjective	Objective
Thoughts	Words	Deeds
Heart	Lungs	Stomach
Immaterial	Semi-material	Material
Gas	Liquid	Solid

Symbols are images that represent complex realities: a heart can symbolize love, a bird can symbolize Spirit, and a car can symbolize freedom. A symbol cannot be reduced to one single definition or a simple sign, but is open to multiple interpretations. Symbols are meant to evoke, not represent, and therefore, some symbols have many possible meanings.

Although the three spiritual elements are described symbolically, they are real things. They are the energetic qualities that underlie all of manifestation, similar to the way atoms and molecules underlie all forms of matter. How they manifest in the world depends on how they combine with each other, as well as the environment in which they appear.

The Inconceivability of God

The longer we think, the more the divine and spiritual wonders surpass our words of description. —Atheism. HT

The human mind is constantly accumulating knowledge. While this might be useful for dealing with the complexity of the world, in spiritual matters it often creates confusion. This is because God is not an object, not even in the subtlest sense, and so cannot be understood through symbolic representation. When relying solely on thought, we disengage from Spirit, because the mind is only capable of thinking "about" things, and cannot know them directly. Once God is perceived as an idea, additional concepts inevitably get attached until entire religious systems and philosophical traditions arise, further binding Spirit to the conceptual realm.

If a person's spiritual understanding is based on concepts rather than a direct, living experience, they might easily delude themselves with problematic ideas and beliefs. Or worse, they might use religious doctrines to justify their own poor behavior while condemning the behavior of others. Bound in the mind and lacking the living touch of God, they become susceptible to dogmatism, exclusivity, and self-righteousness, which, in turn, give rise to intolerance, religious persecution, and violence.

One gains authentic spiritual insight from direct inner experience, not from facts and opinions. What people need most are experiences that open their hearts and purify their souls. They need love, kindness, and beauty. These gentle qualities are what will bring peace on earth and goodwill toward all.

Use the Light that is in you to recover your natural clearness of sight. —Lao Tzu

The Spiritual World

The spiritual world, like the material world, is divided into a considerable number of levels. It divides roughly into three major ranks: upper, middle, and lower. Each of these major ranks is subdivided into sixty levels and these sixty are collected into groups of twenty. If the divine world, which transcends all these levels, were to be included as one of them, then there would be one hundred and eighty-one levels in total. Except for God, who resides in the divine world, all other deities or divine beings belong to one of these one hundred and eighty levels of the spiritual world.

—Jyorei and Happiness. ET

Everything originates in the spiritual world, a realm that encompasses and surpasses the world of our physical senses. The spiritual world is subdivided into three main levels roughly corresponding to heaven, purgatory, and hell. Beyond this is the divine world, which is the realm of pure Spirit, in contrast to the spiritual world, which contains images and forms. Spirit itself is formless. All forms arise out of the formless realm, like water out of steam. Spirit, the World of the Ultimate Mystery, can neither be thought about nor imagined, and thus remains a mystery to the mind.

The conditions in the spiritual world create events and circumstances in the physical world. What appears to be a chain of events, with a specific cause and effect, is actually a secondary effect resulting from its true cause, the conditions within the spiritual world. The spiritual world influences our ideas, which then form our values, which then determine our behavior on both an individual and collective scale. The civil rights activist Rev. Martin Luther King, Jr., put it this way: "Everything that we see is a shadow cast by that which we do not see."

One level of the spiritual world acts as a repository of the mind, and can be viewed as a reflection of the collective psyche of all humanity, which can be subdivided into specific cultures such as American, Arabic, Japanese, and so on. This collective psyche can think and dream, much like individuals do. A dream is both subjective (because it is an expression of the mind), and also objective (because it contains people, places, things, and events, not to mention abstractions, memories, and moods). Some gifted individuals such as psychics and visionaries are believed to actually see into the spiritual world and report back to others what they have seen.

The spiritual world is inhabited by many dis-incarnate beings, including our departed friends and ancestors, a variety of animal spirits, as well as other non-human beings. This is also the place where we ourselves go when we die. It is a transition place where our soul can heal and grow until we are ready to incarnate again in the physical world.

There is no death; only a change of worlds. —Chief Seattle

The Three Worlds

The three worlds can be summarized in the following manner:

The physical world is objective in nature. — It can be perceived by the five senses, and can be experienced and validated by more than one person. It is subject to the laws of time and space.

The divine world is subjective in nature. — It is silently aware of life's changing phenomena and is the impersonal backdrop of all experience. It is the causal source of all that arises and cannot be known objectively. Although unseen, it is the harmonizing, transformative agent within all that can be seen. It is the source of Light. The divine world (which Meishusama sometimes refers to as "the World of the Ultimate Mystery" or as "the world of the third dimension of profundity") can also be defined as the highest aspect of the spiritual world, depending on how you divide it up.

The spiritual world is everything that lies in-between the subjective and objective poles of experience. — It is made up of thoughts, feelings, desires, and dreams, which can be simultaneously subjective and objective. They are subjective because they color our perceptions, and are objective because they are observable to the mind. The spiritual world is a dreamlike realm hovering between conscious awareness and deep sleep, between the manifest and the unmanifest realms of experience.

The three worlds operate simultaneously, and overlap in time and space. All three are components of day-to-day experience. The spiritual world and the physical world interact with each other in a dynamic, living process. Commenting on their relationship, Meishusama says, "The spiritual world is a continuation of the material world." (*Aspects of Death. ET*) The divine world, on the other hand, resides above the world of time and space, illuminating all things, like sunshine on a spring day.

Levels of Reality – The Three Worlds

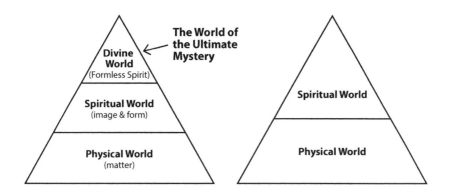

God is the creator, and material things are the creations made from denser vibrations of God's Spirit. Everything can be seen as a manifestation of divine energy, and the three elements are the three main levels of vibratory frequency. As Meishusama said, "To summarize: earth is material, water is semi-material, and fire is immaterial." (*The Spirits of Fire, Water, and Earth. ET*)

We can compare the relationship between the spiritual world and the physical world to the difference between phenomena that we can touch, taste, smell, hear, or see, and phenomena such as radio waves, ultraviolet rays, and X-rays which are invisible and inaudible. One is a world of tangible experience, and the other is intangible (except through the agency of secondary devices such as a radio or a camera). In this analogy, the divine world would be the space in which these phenomena occur.

Much like the subatomic world, the spiritual world is imperceptible to our senses, yet no less real. It affects us just as significantly as the physical world, and even more profoundly.

I refer to the world that lies within a person's immediate knowledge as "the material world" and the world unknown to most as "the spiritual world."

—Natural Power. ET

Chapter 5

SOUL AND SPIRIT

The Soul and its Spiritual Influences

According to Meishusama, the human soul is primarily affected by three invisible spirits: the divine spirit, the instinctive spirit, and the guardian spirit. The divine spirit infuses the soul with awareness and sensitivity, the instinctive spirit activates its desires and instinctual behavior, and the guardian spirit affects its conscience and good fortune. How the soul responds to their combined influences determines the degree to which it evolves spiritually.

Soul

Humans are not simply material bodies; they also have spiritual bodies that we cannot see. Humans are made up of both physical and spiritual elements, the spirit being the most important of these. As the spirit moves—in other words, as the will dictates—so the body moves. —Methods and Results. ET

The soul is individuated Spirit. It is a condensation and crystallization of the inherent Oneness of God's essential nature. The soul is related at one end to God and at the other end to the sensory world. The soul is subject to change, in contrast to the Spirit, which is unchanging. Located within the center of the soul is the divine spirit, which illuminates the soul's form with pure awareness. Just as the moon is but a dim reflection of the sun, so too, is the soul but a dim reflection of the inner spirit. Each borrows its light from another source: the moon borrows light from the sun, and the soul borrows Light from the divine spirit. The source of the former is outer whereas the source of the latter is inner.

We are not really separate from God, even though we may think so, due to the layers of impurities that cloud the soul's innate awareness. The more impurities we have, the more the Divine's positive influence is blocked from affecting us. A pure soul is gifted with natural wisdom and is inclined toward good, whereas an impure soul is restrained by ignorance and is dominated by selfish desires and reactive compulsions. The impure soul feels heavy and slow because it is impeded by negative impressions and binding attachments.

The soul acts like a container for accumulating memories, habits, emotions, and desires. One can imagine the soul as being similar to a soap bubble with swirling transparent colors floating around its surface. These swirling colors represent the various memories and tendencies accumulated by the soul throughout it's long journey through time. These swirling shapes tend to create an illusion of separation between the space inside and outside the bubble. However, despite appearances, it is always the same unbroken space on each side of the bubble's skin. The apparent division between inner and outer makes no difference to the space any more than cutting air with a knife makes a difference to the air. Similarly, the spiritual awareness within the core of the soul is at one with the greater field of spiritual awareness that surrounds it. There is only one Spirit—not two. The soul, by its transparency, occupies an intermediate position between form and the formless, time and the timeless, and the personal and the impersonal.

The soul is the animating principle, that which makes things come alive. It is the carrier of the life force, which is synonymous with movement and breath. Although God's Spirit takes residence within all things, it lies dormant until the soul activates it. When the soul enters into an organism, the organism inhales a breath and comes to life, and when the soul leaves it, the organism exhales and dies. Breath is the difference between a lifeless rock and a living being. Indeed, the quality of the breath reflects the mood and temperament of the soul. Not only do humans have souls, but so do animals, insects, and plants as well, although their souls are much less individuated than those of humans. Even soil, which is alive with billions of microorganisms, may have something resembling a group soul. Unlike the body, the soul is indestructible. It is the personal essence that survives beyond physical death, after which it moves on to other realms.

The soul is also the emotional or feeling aspect of our being. It is our inner character—that which makes us unique. We can sense this inner character in others by looking into their eyes, which are often referred to as "the windows of the soul."

After the soul has completely purified itself and surrendered all traces of egoic separativity, it becomes one with God. This is what Jesus Christ meant when he said, "I and the Father are One," and what Meishusama indicated when he stated, "As the saying goes, I have 'the Light of God in my heart.' This is the supreme God, and everything I do and say is guided by God. In other words, there is no distinction between God and man. I am God personified." (*God Personified. HT*)

Whereas the divine spirit is impersonal in nature, lacking individual characteristics, the soul, by contrast, is personal, containing many unique qualities and tendencies, all of which were slowly developed over the course of many lifetimes. At birth in the physical plane, these soul qualities and tendencies exist as dormant potentialities similar to the invisible plans for an oak tree that exist within an acorn. All that is required for the soul to grow and develop into a well-defined individual are the proper supportive conditions, such as a mother, father, food, shelter, education, and love. Similarly, the acorn needs air, water, sunlight, and soil to grow into a giant oak tree. As the soul grows toward adulthood, its past life tendencies, combined with genetics and the environment, determine what type of person it will become. The soul functions as an intelligent matrix for organizing and integrating its various internal qualities, memories, and tendencies. Just as the physical body dwells within the physical world, the soul, in turn, dwells within the spiritual world. However, when the soul incarnates within a human body, it does not leave the spiritual world. Instead, it continues to reside within the spiritual world, within a spiritual body, while only partially entering the physical world. This enduring connection with the spiritual world gives the soul continuity from one lifetime to another. During physical incarnation, the soul temporarily loses awareness of the spiritual world, only regaining this awareness after it leaves the body to continue to reside solely in the spiritual world. However, there are some exceptions. Some rare individuals retain the ability to remember the spiritual world or are able to develop the ability to perceive it later in life.

The soul is an invisible field of energy and awareness, although, unlike the spiritual body, it is without fixed dimensions. We cannot see the soul but we can feel it, or rather, feel its responses to things. The soul is a vehicle for embodied experience.

Each of us has a particular mission to accomplish in this life which will further the evolution of our soul in the spiritual world. To discover this mission we need to undergo extensive purification and spiritual renewal.

Divine Spirit

It is said that man is the child of God, and that God is enshrined in man. This means essentially that humans are charged with a mission by God and, when born into this world, are given a part of God's Spirit. This is their divine spirit.

—Guardian Spirits. ET

Our soul, as it travels through countless lifetimes, is subject to numerous influences and conditionings, both inner and outer. The highest and most important influence comes from our divine spirit. "The divine spirit is the best part of one's personality, the conscience," writes Meishusama. (*Guardian Spirits. ET*) It is our inner core, and is that part of us which partakes of divinity. The divine spirit is the formless presence behind, within, around, and between our thoughts. It is eternal and unchanging, and operates as the core awareness within our soul. It is the subtle spark which lights up a person's eyes, and the unmoving force that moves our breath. The divine spirit is our very essence.

God dwells within all things, from the natural world of animals, vegetables, and minerals to man-made inventions and creations. Life forms are capable of expressing this inner divinity through conscious action. The more evolved a biological organism is, the more consciously it can act. The paleontologist, theologian, and Jesuit priest Pierre Teilhard de Chardin writes, "Whatever we may think of, we can be sure that…a richer and better organized [physical] structure will correspond to the more developed consciousness."

Rocks do not contain sufficient organic complexity to sustain life, nor do they have any mechanism for consciously perceiving the outer environment. Living things are able to breathe, consume food, grow, respond to stimuli, and reproduce. And although animals are alive and conscious, in general, their souls are much less conscious and evolved than those of humans. As a species, humans have a much greater capacity for self-awareness, intelligence, and moral conscience than do the lower creatures of the animal kingdom. The human range of experience extends much further up into the mental realm than does that of the lower creatures. Humans read, compose music, design buildings, create machines, and communicate in sophisticated languages. They also reflect upon the past and plan for the future. And most uniquely, humans have a reflexive capacity that allows them not only to be self-conscious (as an object observed by others), but also to be conscious of their own consciousness (as an object to itself). In other words, they are aware that they are aware. Although God's Spirit can be found within each of us as our innermost essence, this spirit cannot fully express itself in the world until the soul has been thoroughly purified in the spiritual world. The purer the soul, the more it tends to exhibit various spiritual qualities in its thoughts, words, and deeds.

Unlike the soul, the divine spirit is essentially pure. Nothing can affect it because it is without form or substance. Nonetheless, it can become covered with spiritual clouds to the extent that its presence within us is obscured. Again, unlike the soul, the divine spirit does not evolve. Instead, it acts like an impartial observer of the soul's changing fortunes. It is unmoved by our personal joys and sorrows, and is forever peaceful and serene. The divine spirit functions much like the spotlight at a theatre, illuminating the various scenes of the play but remaining unaffected by any of it.

The divine spirit, despite its intimate association with the body and soul of an individual, remains forever one with God, just as a wave, despite its surface level movement, always maintains an inseparable unity with the ocean. Our divine spirit, as an aspect of divinity, exists beyond time and space, patiently waiting for us to rediscover its eternal presence deep within our soul.

Instinctive Spirit

At birth everyone receives an animal spirit that merges with him or her and functions as an instinctive spirit. This is unavoidable due to the very nature of human existence in a world where fleshly desires are to some extent necessary, and God permits this kind of animalistic tendency for that reason. A bad person, on the other hand, is possessed by yet another animal spirit, or finds that his or her instinctive spirit has degenerated into a purely bestial form. Both these conditions are brought about by the clouding of the person's soul. —A Bad Person is Spiritually Sick. ET

The spiritual world is inhabited by a variety of beings, both human and nonhuman. Among the nonhuman beings are those of animal spirits such as wolves, fish, hawks, bears, foxes, turtles, snakes, and so on. Similar beliefs about animal spirits can be found in the cultures of indigenous people throughout the world.

According to Meishusama, early in life each person is assigned an instinctive spirit (or secondary guardian spirit) that exerts a guiding influence over the physical body, activating its various physiological processes, instinctual drives, automatic reflexes, and sensory perceptions. Similarly, we do not consciously control our respiratory, digestive, circulatory, or nervous systems, but rather depend on the body's own innate intelligence to regulate these internal functions for us. Although the divine spirit, through the vehicle of the soul, breathes life into the physical body, it is the instinctive spirit that actually animates the body by stimulating its desires and passions. This influence is quite appropriate since, physiologically, humans are a type of animal with an anatomy and a DNA code quite similar to many simian species, most notably the chimpanzee.

Most animals are driven by their instincts in relation to food, sex, and territorial defense. They do not think about music, art, mathematics, or science. Animals have well-developed sensory perception, but only limited mental capacity. The same is true for the instinctive spirit.

The instinctive spirit tends to be selfish and unconscious and has little sense of ethics or morality. Psychologically, it often operates in a manner similar to the Freudian concept of the Id, which is driven by lust and aggression. The instinctive spirit's actions tend to be compulsive and automatic, rather than conscious and deliberate. It often gravitates toward the lower emotions of hate, anger, resentment, jealousy, depression, sorrow, and fear, and can also be consumed by the lower appetites of lust, ambition, and greed.

Despite its lower tendencies, the instinctive spirit performs a useful and needed function: the survival of the human body. The instinctive spirit's instinctual nature provides us with a sense of healthy boundaries, the aggressiveness necessary to defend ourselves from harm and to acquire what we need. Without these instincts, we would not have the motivation to eat, procreate, or succeed in the world.

The instinctive spirit is not an enemy to be attacked or conquered, nor is it an evil to be annihilated. Rather, it needs to be tempered by our conscience, which (in its pure form) is an expression of our divine spirit. Sometimes the instinctive spirit will respond best to compassionate understanding rather than judgmental repression, but at other times, if it is too wild and impulsive, then it must be kept on a tight leash. While it is important to appreciate our body and to take care of it, it is also important to understand that the body sees things from the perspective of separateness, and is most concerned with sensual pleasure and physical survival. In a purified state, the body is a useful vehicle for manifesting awareness, intelligence, and love, but is not really the source of these higher qualities. That source is our divine spirit.

Within the spiritual world there also exist other animal spirits that can temporarily inhabit and possess the bodies of human beings, thus overpowering the beneficial influence of the divine spirit. Meishusama elaborates, "These evil entities are, of course, of the bestial type, such as fox-spirits, badger-spirits, dragon-spirits, and so on, and their behavior when they take over a person is, accordingly, very much like that of a beast. They are capable of cruelties and callousness beyond the limits of what a human being can tolerate." (*A Bad Person is Spiritually Sick. ET*) Spiritual possessions like this can occur when a weak soul becomes too clouded with impurities that accumulate as a result of wrong actions in the past, or from excessive drug or alcohol usage that dulls our consciousness. Spiritual clouds block the higher influences emanating from our divine spirit, leaving us in spiritual darkness. To remedy this unfortunate condition, a person needs to increase the Light within their soul through purification, positive actions, and faith in a higher goodness. It is important to remember that darkness cannot exist where there is Light.

> There is no one who is totally without any spiritual deficiencies, and therefore everybody is to some extent controlled by possessing spirits, and to that extent is suffering from some mental disorder. —*Mental Disorders, God's Way to Health. HT*

Individual animal spirits can function as instinctive spirits or as externally possessing spirits. The first is constructive and useful, and the second is destructive and harmful. It is not necessary to know what type of animal is operating behind either of these functions because excessive interest in them tends to strengthen their negative influence over us—which can be problematic. Instinctive spirits have necessary functions to play in our lives, but our main interest and concern should be the soul's spiritual development, which is the only thing that guarantees true happiness.

Guardian Spirit

Souls that have been purified to some extent in the spiritual world are chosen as guardian spirits and extend protection to people in this world through the spiritual cords. —The Spiritual Cords. ET

The guardian spirit (also known as the ancestor spirit) is a discarnate being residing in the invisible spiritual world that is assigned to guide and protect a particular soul living in the physical world. In this regard, it is similar to the Western concept of a guardian angel. However, unlike guardian angels, which are selected from among the community of angels, the guardian spirit is usually selected from among an individual's ancestors in the spiritual world. It is their job to accompany and watch over the soul of a person until his or her physical death. On certain rare occasions this guardianship position has instead been assigned to a uniquely divine animal spirit. The guardian spirit has the responsibility of encouraging the soul to behave in a virtuous manner, and of pointing it in a higher direction. In this way it supports the soul's spiritual advancement. The guardian spirit often communicates to us through symbolic dreams, creative inspiration, and through the silent voice of our inner conscience.

> Guidance dreams are caused by guardian spirits wanting to tell human beings something. Dreams created by guardian spirits are often allegorical or metaphorical, and frequently require specialized interpretation. As I have said before, the material world reflects the changes of the spiritual world, and therefore the guardian spirits who live in the spiritual world know of things that will inevitably come about in the material world in the future. They use dreams as a means of informing humanity about these. When you have a presentiment that something is sure to happen, this is due to the influence of a guardian spirit. —*Dreams. ET*

Because of their higher vantage point, the guardian spirits can see more clearly what the future holds, and can benefit us by providing protection and advice. They can also contribute to our good fortune by various magical means. The instinctive spirit within us, which is selfishly motivated toward survival at the expense of others, is tempered by the beneficial guidance of our guardian spirit. The effectiveness of this guidance depends on our inner purity as well as our receptivity to the higher influence. To this, Meishusama adds: "It is one's own instinctive spirit that urges one toward vice, and it is one's guardian spirit that urges one toward virtue. Above all, however, is the divine spirit that firmly directs the soul toward absolute good. Therefore, what is necessary is to help increase the power of the divine spirit, which is the way to conquer the fundamental cause of vice. People should be very careful to develop this power as much as possible." (*Controlling Your Worldly Desires. ET*)

Physical Body

All of us have physical bodies through which we can see, hear, taste, smell, and feel. The body is made up of tissues, organs, muscles, bones, and nerves. Each body has an endocrine system, digestive system, skeletal system, respiratory system, nervous system, and circulatory system. On a smaller scale, the body is made up of trillions of cells, each with its own DNA code and special functions.

The body is part of our personal identity, as are our various social roles such as plumber, teacher, accountant, soldier, shopkeeper, student, housewife, parent, and so on. Just as our social roles are temporary, so, too, are our physical bodies— they usually last for only seven or eight decades, at best.

It is important to keep the body healthy. Toxins, malnutrition, and injuries can affect how we think, feel and behave; and these, in turn, determine how far we advance spiritually. Good actions help us evolve quickly and bad actions slow us down. Then, when we die, the body is left behind, whereas the soul continues to exist in the spiritual world.

The instinctive spirit has a powerful influence on the physical body, influencing the instincts and desires that motivate it. To be healthy, we need to love our bodies, but at the same time not be overly carried away by the body's appetites. We need to find a healthy balance between the needs of the body, the mind, the soul, and the spirit.

The body is the soul's vehicle for operating in the physical world. How we treat others indicates a lot about our character. It is how we outwardly reveal our inner condition. The more we truly embody our higher values and ideals, the more aligned we are with Spirit.

Lamp Analogy

Our divine spirit, which expresses itself through the agency of the soul, can be viewed as the essence or foundation of our personal identity, whereas the instinctive spirit and the guardian spirit can both be viewed as outer influences that support our life in this material world. Although we each also possess a physical body and a conscious mind, these too are not part of our fundamental self. Rather, they are temporary structures inhabited by us in this lifetime that are eventually discarded at death.

The divine spirit is the impassive witness of all phenomena. It is like clean lenses on a pair of eyeglasses, whose transparency allows us to see through them clearly, without distortion. Anything that can be perceived, including sensory phenomena and internal thoughts and feelings, is not the divine spirit, because these are objects whereas the divine spirit is not. The divine spirit is pure subjectivity, and a subject is unperceivable as an object. The divine spirit is the observer, not the observed, the perceiver, not the perceived. It transcends death and is eternal. Although the divine spirit may identify with the various bodies and minds that it temporarily inhabits during its journey from one lifetime to another, it is also capable, through grace, of dropping this limited identification and awakening to itself as pure Spirit. When this happens to someone, he or she becomes selfless.

One possible way to visualize the relationship of the soul to the three types of spirits is to use the analogy of a light bulb within a lamp. At the center of the light bulb is the bright light radiating from the metal filament. This light represents our divine spirit, which is pure awareness. Surrounding the brightly lit filament is the glass bulb, which is the soul. The soul is illumined by the spiritual Light radiating from deep within the center of its being. If the glass is clean and transparent, the light shines brightly, whereas if the glass is dirty or darkly tinted, then less light filters through. The amount of light that shines from the bulb indicates the purity of the individual soul. The physical body, which is under the control of the instinctive spirit, is the lamp itself, which stands on a table or floor. The lampshade represents the mind, which can also block the Light if it is too cluttered with rambling thoughts. The light bulb needs a lamp to hold it in place and to conduct electricity, just as the soul needs a physical body to function in the world. But the light is the most important factor to the user—not the lamp—just as Spirit is the most important factor to the soul—not the body. The electricity is God's Power, which brings life to that which is otherwise inanimate. The guardian spirit is the one who comes by regularly to dust off the light bulb and the lampshade, thereby allowing an increased amount of light to shine through.

Lamp Analogy – Spirit, Soul, Mind, and Body

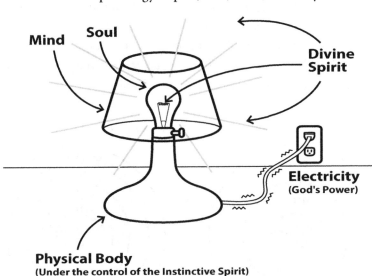

Mind Soul

Divine Spirit

Electricity
(God's Power)

Physical Body
(Under the control of the Instinctive Spirit)

Throughout a person's lifetime the guardian spirit and the instinctive spirit compete for influence over the soul. For some people, the instinctive spirit may be more dominant, thereby influencing them toward negative action. Other individuals may find that the guardian spirit is more persuasive, thereby helping them to be better people and also bringing them good fortune.

An example of this might be if a person came upon a child drowning in a rushing river: the animal spirit, being selfish, would be primarily concerned with its own personal safety, whereas the guardian spirit, being altruistic, would be inclined to save the child despite the risk. The stronger influence of the two would determine the resulting behavior of the person.

The Soul in Relation to the Spiritual World

One must first heal the spirit by Divine Light in order to bring a cure to the body. The soul of a human being belongs, of course, to the spiritual world and a human being's physical body belongs to the material world. —Natural Power. ET

Spirit within the Soul

Meishusama, demonstrating his typical flexibility, uses a variety of examples to explain certain concepts. An alternate way of viewing the inner structure of the soul and its relation to the spiritual world is to locate the divine spirit in the center of a circle that is surrounded by the mind, which, in turn, is surrounded by the soul at the outer circumference. This can be illustrated using a diagram consisting of a series of concentric circles with each succeeding circle more distant and removed from divinity, which is located in the middle.

The Soul in Relation to the Spiritual World

Meishusama's Diagram　　　**Expanded Diagram**

The reason for placing the divine spirit in the middle should be obvious, as it is the true center of our being. Spirit is the core essence from which all else emerges. However, some might question the reason for placing the mind ahead of the soul in its proximity to the divine spirit, as the soul is often regarded as being subtler than the thinking process. For example, most people can consciously experience their thoughts, but not their soul, and therefore have only a vague idea about the latter. To help clarify this confusion, a simple distinction can be made between the lower mind, which focuses on objects of the senses, and the higher mind, which is abstract and analytical.

Each soul is on a long journey through countless lifetimes during which it experiences a full range of possible conditions, including health and sickness, peace and conflict, and success and failure. Such a variety of conditions help the soul learn and grow spiritually. The essence of these experiences is accumulated and stored deep within the soul as unconscious memories and tendencies.

The universe is God's extended body, and thus a part of God evolves in conjunction with the evolution of that body. Just as our arms, legs, nose, and teeth are each a part of us, so too is each and every thing in all of creation a part of God. Humanity, as the highest life form on the planet, leads this evolution like the crest of a wave, and so carries a great spiritual responsibility. Each of us, individually, as we continue to learn and grow, has a valuable role to play in the Creator's cosmic drama.

Outside the soul is the lower mind, which tends to focus on biological needs, instincts, and sensory awareness. It thinks in concrete terms, and labels and classifies things in a simple manner. The lower mind is mostly concerned with pleasure and survival; it is closely associated with the physical body.

Located further within than the soul is the higher mind, which is logical, rational, and intuitive, and has a greater capacity for morals and altruistic behavior. The higher mind is not the source of awareness and perception; it merely analyzes experiences from the past and then imagines possible futures. The divine spirit, however, always functions in the here and now, and is the true perceiver. The divine spirit, with assistance from the five senses, feeds information to the lower mind in a manner similar to how the light from a film projector illuminates images on a movie screen. That light is pure awareness. In order to access the past, the higher mind must reach into the soul, which contains most of our memories. These memories and conditionings are unavailable to the higher mind except under unusual circumstances, such as through hypnosis or dream recollection. With this understanding, we could say that the mind is both inside and outside the soul, depending on whether one is referring to the higher or lower component. The mind is actually one unified entity, but is divided by function.

In addition to expanding Meishusama's model to include this distinction, with the higher mind contained within our soul, and the lower mind located outside its perimeter, we can also extend this model by depicting the relationship of the physical body to the mind. Our brain temporarily houses the mind, as well as most of its memories and emotions. In relation to our diagram, we can say that the outer ring of the lower mind is surrounded by and encased within the physical body. Both lower and higher mental functioning are stored in the physical body like software stored in a computer. Each outer ring of the circle is further removed from Spirit, manifesting a progressively denser and slower frequency and vibration. Physical matter is the furthermost removed from Spirit.

Meishusama also sub-divides the mind into three main components: reason, emotions, and will (or desire). He writes, "To analyze people's thoughts, we can say that they consist of reason and emotions, and a desire to put them into motion. The organs of the forebrain are connected to reason, and the rear parts of the brain are the sources of emotion. Whichever it may be, reason or emotion, it must be rendered into action, and when this happens—indeed, every time it happens, however trifling—will or volition is necessary. This will is strengthened by an invisible energy center located in the middle of the stomach. This is what we may call the source of action. A combination of these three components makes up the tripartite entity of human thought." (*Mental Disorders, God's Way to Health. HT*)

Arrangement of the Spiritual World

As explained above, the spiritual world can thus be arranged in a circular diagram. In the center is God, or Spirit, and at the outer circumference is physical matter. Although God's Spirit exists in everything, in both the center and the circumference, the further away from the center one gets, the less consciousness there is of this divine presence. Physical matter is solidified energy vibrating at a slower frequency than more subtle forms of phenomena such as sound or light. Matter is neither good nor bad in itself. Its purpose is to function as a container for Spirit. The human body is a necessary vehicle for our soul to journey through this world, and as such it supports our spiritual growth.

From another perspective, this diagram can be reversed, with the physical body situated on the inside, surrounded by a much larger spiritual body (the aura, or morphic field), which, in turn, is surrounded by Spirit, which is infinitely larger. This configuration can be illustrated by a series of concentric circles with

God, or Spirit, on the outside, the mind inside that outer ring, and the physical body located in the middle.

Another way of viewing the spiritual world is as a vertical hierarchy, with God, or Spirit, at the top, and the physical body at the bottom. Meishusama writes, "The above is the vertical arrangement of the different levels, each of which expands laterally. The condition of each level is different in some way from that of its neighbors. If, for example, your soul belongs to one of the lowest twenty levels in the lowest major rank, then the conditions of your experience are the worst and deepest hell, a world full of pain and suffering. This is inevitably reflected in your physical body, which is oppressed by the worst kind of afflictions. On the other hand, if one's soul is nearer the divine level, it has a much more pleasant time. Overall, the closer one's soul is, the better the conditions become. Each level's balance of pain and pleasure is different from those of its neighbors." (*Jyorei and Happiness. ET*)

One's soul is on a journey from the outer material rings toward the spiritual center. With each progressive step inward, one experiences greater peace and joy. Meishusama adds, "Thus we can see that as one's fate on earth is decided by his position in the hierarchy of the spiritual world, one should strive to rise as high as possible, for the higher one rises, the less hardships and suffering one must endure and the greater the happiness within one's grasp. Or, to put it another way, the higher one goes the less impurity one has and the less purification one needs to undergo." (*Jyorei and Happiness. ET*)

The spiritual world is less constricted by time and space than is the physical world. This non-dimensionality is also why there are so many possible ways to represent the spiritual world in a diagram. The higher up in the spiritual world, and the further away from the senses, the less everything can fit into any single form of symbolic representation. This is why spiritual experiences are so hard to describe. About this, Meishusama writes, "One problem is that spiritual phenomena are not approachable through the five senses, and so it follows that to gain a direct perception of their existence and reality is very difficult indeed. However, it is not a case of conjuring something out of nothing, but rather perceiving something that already exists, and this perception definitely lies within everybody's grasp." (*Preface. ET*)

Although Spirit is invisible, we can recognize its expression in others by how well they demonstrate love, truth, humility, patience, humor, generosity, purity, kindness, and wisdom. People will automatically tend to exhibit these traits after having sufficiently purified both their spiritual and physical bodies. At this point, there is less of an effort on their part to be virtuous because their innate goodness manifests naturally.

Spiritual Cords

The term "spiritual cords" has seldom been used until recent times. Their importance has been neglected for so long primarily because these cords are much finer and subtler than air, and therefore invisible. However, their influence on all human affairs is impossible to ignore. They are the causes of human happiness and misery, and in the widest sense they shape history. Therefore, the human race must learn to recognize the nature and importance of spiritual cords. —The Spiritual Cords. ET

Each of our lives is defined by relationships. These include relationships with parents, spouse, children, friends, co-workers, neighbors, as well as with possible rivals or enemies. Beyond this, we are each related to our community and our country and, beyond this, to the planet and the entire universe. We are also in relationship to the animals, plants, and inanimate things. All of these relationships affect our state of mind and behavior.

Beyond the outwardly visible forms of relationships, there are also invisible components to our relationships with people, places, and things. Meishusama labeled these components "spiritual cords."

Spiritual cords are invisible lines of energy that stretch between various people, places, and things. Like the aura, they are invisible to most people, yet exert powerful influences on everyone. There are literally thousands of spiritual cords attached to each person. The relative significance of a relationship can be measured by the thickness and strength of the spiritual cords connecting two people. The strongest cords are usually between husband and wife, then parent and child, next between brother and sister, and so on. There are also long-lasting spiritual cords connecting us with our deceased ancestors. Thoughts and feelings flow invisibly along these lines from one person to the other.

There are tens, hundreds, thousands, indeed, uncountable numbers of spiritual cords attached to you. Some are thick, some thin; some are long, some short; and some of them are good, while others are bad. They all, to a varying degree, influence and change your life. It is no exaggeration to say that human beings stay alive because of these spiritual cords. —*The Spiritual Cords. ET*

The Varieties of Spiritual Cords

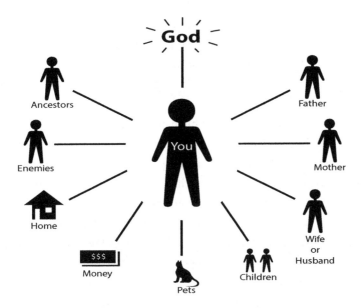

In reality, all of life is interconnected and interrelated in numerable ways beyond our imagination. Spiritual cords can affect us in both positive and negative ways, depending upon the type of thoughts that pass through them. Negative thoughts weaken us and positive strengthen us. If we associate with people of noble character, we tend to become good, but if we associate with people of poor character, we tend to become bad. This is why we often become like the friends we keep. The effect is largely derived from the influence of the spiritual cords we share with them.

Not only are we affected by the thoughts of others, but our thoughts affect them as well. Therefore, it is important to hold kind thoughts of the people in our lives. When our relationships are based on mutual love and respect, beneficial energies are exchanged through the spiritual cords.

The spiritual cords of God and divine beings are radiant Light.
—The Spiritual Cords. ET

Of all our relationships, the one we share with God is the most significant. As the spiritual cords connecting us to God become thicker and stronger, our soul begins to glow with peace and joy. These most significant of all cords extend deep into the heart of existence itself, into our innermost core where our divine spirit resides. It is here, in this silent inner core, that God's blessings can be found.

Evolution of the Soul

The greatest aim of the discipline undergone in the spiritual world is the removal of attachments, and the height to which a spirit can rise depends on the degree to which it has been able to rid itself of these attachments.

—Self-will and Attachment. ET

All of nature is subject to the cycles of birth and death. Only Spirit is unchanging and eternal. Death is not the end of existence, but only a transition from one realm to another. At death, the physical body is left behind, and the soul continues to accumulate experiences in the spiritual world. If a person is burdened with excessive attachment to the people or conditions in their earthly life, after death they risk becoming trapped in one of the lower realms. This can happen because they are obsessively looking backwards to their former life rather than letting go and moving forward toward something new.

The lower realms of the spiritual world are populated by many otherworldly beings, including ghosts, animals, and various other disincarnate spirits. Usually, depending on the individual's level of spiritual evolution and the amount of spiritual clouds he or she has managed to burn off, his or her soul will bypass this dimension and move on to the level of existence most appropriate to it. After it has been sufficiently purified, the soul will reincarnate again into another physical body.

In the spiritual world, human souls are purged to some degree of the many and various transgressions they have committed in the material world, and they are subsequently born again into this world. *—The Spiritual Cords. ET*

Our relatives and ancestors remain spiritually connected to us after they pass on to the other side. These connections are like invisible wires or cords through which psychic communication travels back and forth. Consequently, it is not just through our genetic heritage that our ancestors influence us, but also in subtler, nonphysical ways such as through their thoughts and feelings.

Many people in Asia pray for the happiness of their deceased ancestors. They believe that by honoring and appreciating their ancestors, it encourages the ancestors to provide valuable assistance from "the other side."

The view from the spiritual world is similar to the view from atop a tall mountain. It allows one to see the vast panorama down below. Living in this physical world, we may not see the traffic jam further down the road, but from the vantage point of the spiritual world, our ancestors can see it quite easily. They can also see what we need to do in order to avoid the traffic jam, and can also inspire us to take an alternate road to our destination. Or, they might draw outside help to the scene to quickly clear it up.

When the body reaches a state of complete powerlessness through old age, illness, injury, or loss of blood, the soul and the body part company. This is death. In other words, death is when the soul breaks away from the material world. The soul reverts completely to the spiritual world for a time and is subsequently born again into this world, while the previous body rots and returns to the earth. This is what people know about the process. One implication of this knowledge is that the soul is capable of unlimited life, while the body is limited and exists as a thing of secondary importance. —*Natural Power. ET*

After we die, we discard our physical body and lose most of our personal identity, along with its accumulated memories, possessions, and habits. What remains afterwards is our soul, which was only temporarily visiting this world of density and form. Upon being reborn into a physical body, an infant appears to be empty of all past memories and thoughts; but just as an acorn has the invisible blueprint for the giant oak tree hidden within it, so too does the infant contain latent tendencies and memories from past lives. Although these are not usually conscious to the infant, nonetheless they begin to influence the soul as it gains experience in life. During the soul's interactions with people and events, the old tendencies begin to reassert themselves. The physical body, under the influence of the instinctive spirit, also conditions the soul through genetic, neurological, hormonal and other biochemical processes.

The relationship between reborn human beings and the spiritual world is as follows: Each of us has a mission assigned to us by God. As one carries it out, one accumulates, knowingly or unknowingly, spiritual clouds within one's soul. At the same time, one's body becomes weak with illness or old age and one's mission becomes harder and harder to carry out. Eventually one casts off one's mortal body and returns to the spiritual world. In Japanese, a dead body is referred to as a "hollow shell." In other words the body is merely an empty container. —*Life and Death. ET*

The soul learns and evolves by experiencing the various consequences of its actions. Ignorant or harmful behavior generates suffering either immediately, in the afterlife, or in the following incarnation, whereas actions that are wise and helpful create happier experiences in the future. This process of cause and effect is an immutable law that governs all things; it is the Law of Karma.

> When a human being dies, in other words, when the spirit leaves its physical shell, it leaves mainly from three parts of the body. These are the forehead, the navel, and the tips of the toes. The reasons for these three distinct exit points are that the purest kind of spirit leaves by the forehead, the more defiled through the navel, and the most muddied and corrupted through the toes. A pure spirit is one that has been purified by good works and virtue while the person was alive; while the muddied and corrupt spirit is one that has been stained by a lifetime of debased behavior. There are also spirits that fall between these two extremes. All actions on earth affect spirits and all spirits are thus divided into these three. —*Life and Death. ET*

In this sense, nothing is really lost because we cannot escape the repercussions of our actions. Justice regulates the cosmos. Good deeds brighten our soul, and bad deeds diminish its luminosity. Sometimes we move forwards, and sometimes backwards, but always with the opportunity to learn from our actions. It is through the continual cycle of reincarnation that the soul grows and matures. Through the experiences of countless lifetimes, the soul eventually develops wisdom and spiritual maturity and thus rises higher up in the spiritual world.

Everything in the universe is constantly evolving toward conscious union with the "Object of Eternity," the divine presence that surrounds and permeates all things. Meishusama refers to this Presence as, "The World of the Ultimate Mystery, that is, the world of the third dimension of profundity." (*Repent, For the End of Night Is at Hand. ET*) This "World of the Ultimate Mystery" can be found within us. It is the spiritual home that we've all been endlessly searching for beyond the sufferings of this physical world. It is the realm of eternal peace and happiness.

CHAPTER 6

SPIRITUAL CLOUDS AND PURIFICATION

Physical and Mental Toxins

In each and every person is a certain amount of polluting toxin, some of which is inherent and some acquired after birth.
    —The Three Great Disasters and the Three Lesser Disasters. ET

Much of our sickness and suffering occurs as the result of toxins that have accumulated in our bodies throughout life. The food we eat is full of chemicals from pesticides, artificial flavorings, and preservatives. More and more of our food crops are genetically modified organisms (GMOs) that are engineered with gene splicing biotechnology to withstand heavy doses of pesticides or to produce their own internal pesticides. The animals we eat are usually fed GMO soy, corn, and alfalfa, which makes them toxic. Most of our meat and dairy products are loaded with synthetic hormones and chemical antibiotics. We are surrounded by air and water pollution, as well as harmful radiation. Fumes from cleaning fluids and chemical gasses released from new carpeting and furniture pollute indoor air. Personal hygiene products and cosmetics also contain poisonous chemicals that soak into our skin. Dental fillings contain mercury and other heavy metals that slowly seep into our body. In our modern world, it is hard to escape this constant onslaught of physical toxins.

Most of these physical toxins fall into one of three main categories: heavy metals, molds and yeasts, and man-made chemicals, although some can also come from radiation, plants, insects or parasites. In addition to these, some toxins can be genetically inherited from our parents and their ancestors.

As well as environmental pollution, we can also suffer from autotoxemia, the self-poisoning that occurs because of poor digestion caused by systemic yeast or parasites or the malfunctioning of the liver, kidneys, or digestive track. When toxins are not adequately filtered by the kidneys or broken down by the liver, they begin to accumulate in those organs, as well as in the blood, the lymph glands, the joints, around the nerves, and in other sensitive areas of the body.

Subtler than physical toxins are the mental toxins that cloud our judgment and cause stress and emotional suffering. We live in a sea of negative thoughts generated by all of humanity. Negative thoughts and feelings pollute the environment, disturbing our peace of mind. When anger and hostility are directed toward us, they can be just as damaging to our health as physical toxins. More significantly, we also generate our own internal toxins from the negative thoughts and feelings that we hold within us. Actions that hurt others, whether deliberate or through neglect, can generate some of the strongest and most enduring toxins by leaving negative impressions deep within our soul. All toxins leave their mark in the spiritual world, thus causing negative outcomes in the physical world.

Life consists in what a man is thinking of all day. —Ralph Waldo Emerson

Our physical body is a living canvas on which we paint our thoughts and emotions. Every thought is a chemical messenger that tells the body what to do, when to do it, and to what degree. Anxiety causes the heart to pump faster, the adrenal glands to work overtime, and brainwaves to speed up. Anger causes the lungs to constrict, the muscles to tighten, and the blood to flow to the surface of the skin. Sorrow depletes energy, slows down the metabolism, and makes the breath heavy. These types of thoughts and feelings also disrupt the hormonal balance within the brain and the internal organs, which exacerbate the misery.

Negative thoughts are self-perpetuating. They paint a dark picture of the world for us, and we respond by becoming even more negative. Each reinforces the other. That is why it is hard to change a bad mood once it takes hold.

If a person thinks bad thoughts and behaves badly, the clouding of his spiritual body increases accordingly. Resentment, hate, jealousy, and other such feelings cause cloudiness, and when these feelings are transmitted to another person they, in turn, cloud his spirit. —*Spiritual Radiations and the Aura. ET*

According to Meishusama, all suffering originates in the spiritual world. To a large extent, our lives are the result of thoughts and feelings generated in the past or present, by ourselves or others. Selfishness, animosity, judgment, envy, despair, lust, greed leave negative impressions in the spiritual world that eventually generate corresponding conditions in the physical world. Meishusama called these negative impressions "spiritual clouds." The collective thoughts and actions of whole societies and entire countries also generate spiritual clouds, which can result in such catastrophes as earthquakes, floods, economic crises, wars, and plagues.

The sufferings of society such as the havoc of storms, natural calamities, earthquakes, and riots are all methods of purification similar to individual sickness. The most considerable suffering is, of course, that brought about by war, and it must be obvious that the only way to prevent this kind of disaster is to clear away the clouds from the souls of humankind, which includes all the individuals who make up society. —A *Third World War Can Be Avoided.* ET

The more we can eliminate physical toxins from our bodies and mental and emotional toxins from our minds, the quicker we can regain health and happiness. The spiritual healing practice of Jyorei (*please see chapter 10*) is very helpful for this, as is kind and loving behavior, as well as a happy and positive disposition. Together, these actions and attitudes brighten the aura and also enhance the cellular activity within our physical body. In fact, there is always a biochemical response within our body from every thought and emotion we hold. Recent discoveries in microbiology and mind/body medicine are beginning to confirm these and other psychosomatic connections.

Most noteworthy are the recent discoveries by cellular biologist Dr. Bruce Lipton, demonstrating that the cellular membrane is intelligent and aware, and is the active agent responsible for programming the DNA. According to Dr. Lipton, our genetic conditioning is not fixed but is constantly responding and adapting to our thoughts as well as to conditions in the outer environment. For instance, he points out that stress causes blood to leave the internal organs of the body and to rush to the outer muscles in a "fight or flight syndrome." Peaceful and loving thoughts, on the other hand, induce the blood to nourish the inner organs, allowing the body to regulate and repair itself.

All living things emit invisible energy fields called "auras" that vibrate at various rates. Although most people do not see auras, we all can sense them to some extent, especially when in close proximity to others. These energy fields surround the body and reflect both a person's spiritual and physical condition. The auras of human beings vibrate much faster than do those of less evolved creatures, and even amongst humans the range of vibration can vary tremendously from one person to the next. Auras can vary in size, brightness, and color depending upon a person's condition. A small, cloudy aura reveals an unhappy or sick individual, whereas a large, bright aura reveals a happy or healthy individual. Someone who is spiritually advanced will have a large, bright aura. Meishusama writes, "An ordinary person's aura is one or two inches in thickness, a virtuous person's is two or three feet, and a great saint's is infinite in size. In contrast, the aura around a clouded soul is thin and feeble." (*An Examination of Miracles. ET*)

Spiritual Clouds

The clouding of the soul that we talk about is in fact a deficiency of power, of Light, on the part of the divine spirit. —A Bad Person is Spiritually Sick. ET

Our spiritual nature is like the sun in the sky. On sunny days, the sun shines brightly, but on cloudy days it is obscured. According to Meishusama, these clouds superimposed over our spirit, cause inner darkness, resulting in a dulling of awareness and a corresponding increase in suffering. The amount of spiritual clouding polluting the aura determines its overall size and brightness. Spiritual clouds are created by environmental toxins that have accumulated in our body, and also from impressions left in our aura as a result of our wrongful thoughts and actions

Although all human souls were created pure, over time, because of errors and misdeeds, we all became corrupted by negativity and spiritual pollution. Our thoughts and actions create immediate changes in our personal energy fields, which, by radiating outward, influence the world around us. The way that we view the people and circumstances in our lives determines our responses. Negative thoughts lead to negative actions, whereas positive thoughts lead to positive actions. Appreciation, empathy, gratitude, love, and humor magnify the aura and promote greater awareness and happiness. By contrast, resentment, worry, judgmentalism, jealousy, and hatred create spiritual clouds that weaken the aura and promote unhappiness.

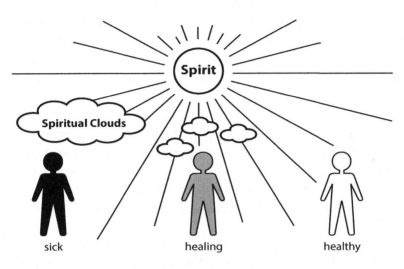

Three Stages of Purification

This same principle applies to our actions. Everything we do either brightens or darkens our soul. We are a product of our past actions, which is summarized in the common expression, "character is destiny." Helping others with kindness and consideration is a powerful way of improving our lives because of the effect it has upon our consciousness and character. By serving others, we serve the greater good.

As you embark on a spiritual path and turn to God, Divine Light flows into your soul through the spiritual cords, increasing its radiance and dispelling spiritual clouds. —A Bad Person is Spiritually Sick. ET

The spiritual clouds that we create continue to affect us until they are purified by either our actions or by painful external events. By covering and diminishing the radiance of our spirit, spiritual clouds can burden our thoughts and moods as well as attract unfortunate events into our lives. Based on this principle, we can say that the radiance of our soul is the primary determinant to the quality of our life.

People whose minds are heavily shrouded in spiritual clouds fail to see the essential unity of all things. Instead they see only division and separation. Coming from a place of want, they are compulsively driven by desires and bound by personal attachments. They imagine the world as a hostile place full of potential enemies and are quick to attack others or withdraw in fear. Some will overcompensate by striving to succeed in the world, hoping to demonstrate their superiority over those around them. Others try to escape their pain through alcohol and drugs, co-dependent relationships, burying themselves in obsessions or compulsive work. These people are subject to fear, anger, depression, insecurity, alienation, and low self-esteem.

When we see things in this light, the reason for humans becoming bad is to be found in the clouding of their souls, which makes them inwardly sick. Of course, the violence with which they are purified depends on how bad they have become, and a very bad person can suffer greatly, even to the extent of becoming seriously ill. —*A Bad Person is Spiritually Sick. ET*

This is not to equate being ill with being bad. After all, many "good" people become ill, including Meishusama. Instead, it makes the connection between being bad and becoming sick. "Bad" behavior generates spiritual clouds, and spiritual clouds produce suffering and illness. Spiritual clouds also tend to generate "bad" behavior in those so afflicted. Most of this behavior is reactionary, and fails to produce any real peace or happiness. Because of lack of awareness, these clouded people tend to project all sorts of false images, fantasies, and motives onto others. Additionally, they are prone to delusions and self-deception. This condition is a breeding ground for neuroses, emotional instability, and mental confusion. These are all symptoms of the negative influence that spiritual clouds can have on the mind of an individual.

Diseases of the soul are more dangerous and more numerous than those of the body.
—*Cicero (Roman Statesman and Scholar)*

Not only do thoughts and actions have this influence, but toxins from the outer environment can also create spiritual clouds by polluting our physical bodies and poisoning our blood. Also, because we are not separate from our society, spiritual clouds generated by the social order affect us as well. The more repressive or dysfunctional a culture or society, the greater is the damage it causes. Countries that oppress women, minorities, and other nationalities are good examples of this.

Finally, we are subject to spiritual clouds carried over from our past lives, inherited from our ancestors, and acquired from childhood conditioning. All of these factors influence our behavior to an enormous degree.

Toxins and spiritual clouds block the beneficial influences of our divine spirit and guardian spirit, allowing the instinctive spirit to drive us towards destructive behavior, resulting in increased personal suffering. According to Meishusama, criminals are spiritually sick people whose ability to distinguish right from wrong is severely clouded. Individuals who are mentally ill also suffer from oppressive spiritual clouds that confuse their minds, disturb their emotions, and generate irrational cravings, leaving them vulnerable to domination by malevolent animal spirits.

The most important point here is that the primary cause of all suffering is found in the spiritual world, not the physical. Nonetheless, physical toxins contribute to impurities in the spiritual body, since the physical and the spiritual are related. But if we examine the fundamental reason behind why we were originally exposed to toxins in the physical world, we find that it lies in the spiritual world. This is why it is always useful to look to the spiritual world to find the meaning and purpose behind events.

When impurities accumulate to a sufficient degree, a natural process of elimination occurs that can be unpleasant or painful. The essence of Meishusama's teachings is to remove these spiritual clouds gently and pleasantly, rather than through suffering. We can avoid suffering by doing things that create more Light in the spiritual body, and by not indulging in activities that generate spiritual clouds. The healing energy of Jyorei is an especially powerful way to eliminate clouds and to infuse Light within the spiritual body. The overall movement of the universe is toward greater consciousness, harmony, and unity, and from this perspective, all forms of purification can be seen as necessary occurrences brought on to further this ongoing evolution.

Refine your heart so as to cleanse the world of baseness.
—Refining Body and Soul. MK2

Purification and Health

To purify means to remove unnecessary elements that corrupt the integrity of a substance or object. For individuals, it means to eliminate those things that are not essential to our original nature. Whatever pollutes the body, mind, or spirit must eventually be removed through a process of purification.

Suffering and Purification

By its very nature, the spiritual body rises and falls according to the amount of its clouding. A pure spirit is light, and rises; a clouded spirit is heavy, and sinks.
—*The Strata in the Spiritual World. ET*

We inevitably experience the effects of negativity or pollution as sickness, emotional disturbance, and external problems. The more these harmful influences accumulate, the more powerful the resulting purification will be. Purification disperses the negativity or pollution so that we can return to health and harmony. All suffering can be seen as a process of purification. Meishusama gives an example of physical purification:

In each and every person is a certain amount of polluting toxins, some of which is inherent and some acquired after birth. These toxins gather at the places of greatest nervous activity, that is, the nerve centers of the part of the body from the neck up; for the brain, eyes, nose, mouth, and ears function the whole time a person is awake—unlike, for example, the limbs, which are sometimes at rest. It is therefore inevitable that the toxins should accumulate in this upper area, and this is why a great many people complain of stiff necks and shoulders, and so on. As time passes, these toxins gather and solidify into lumps, and when these lumps exceed a certain limit, the process abruptly reverses itself. In other words, the lumps are dissolved and expelled from the body. This is what we call the process of purification. Also, this process is always accompanied by a fever, which is necessary to change the solidified lumps into a form easily expelled by the body. In other words, the lumps are melted down from the fever's heat into a liquid. This natural purification is what is called a cold, and the signs of its activity are phlegm, nasal mucous, perspiration, and other excretions. This kind of cold varies from quite serious to a semi-permanent type of purification that most people undergo all the time. This condition is so mild that it is unnoticeable to the person, who considers him or herself to be healthy. —*The Three Great Disasters and the Three Lesser Disasters. ET*

However, although all suffering can be viewed as purification, it is important not to use this insight as an excuse to avoid acting responsibly. Sometimes we are presented with purification as a way of drawing our attention to a circumstance that needs correcting. The best way to learn and grow is to recognize our mistakes and to take responsibility for our actions. Doing so promotes wisdom and maturity.

When confronted by the suffering of others, the best response is empathy and compassion, not apathy or dismissal. Empathy is communicated when the recipients feel that we share in their misfortune and can identify with how they feel. And compassion, which is motivated by the desire to alleviate the suffering of others, is expressed by offering a helping hand. Sometimes just listening with an open heart is the most effective way to help.

Understanding and accepting the theory of purification promotes detachment from pain, which can help us endure our own suffering more easily. However, this detachment, if directed towards others, can appear as cold indifference. There is no need to label others' suffering as "purification" or to lecture them on spiritual philosophy. That only alienates them. Lecturing others makes them feel dismissed rather than cared for. When people are suffering, they want empathy, not philosophy. Therefore, when confronted with the suffering of others, try to remember what it feels like when you yourself suffer. This allows you to sympathize with them and offer genuine emotional support.

Extreme purification is always painful. And when those who are exceedingly negative and harmful to others finally do undergo purification, it can be quite terrible. About this, Meishusama says:

> Thus the underlying cause of this spiritual corruption is the clouding of the soul, and as this clouding directly results in impurities of the blood, there is sure to be a time when the bad person is purged and purified in a violent and dreadful way. At that time, the amount of suffering that affects a person corresponds to the degree of clouding of the soul. —*A Bad Person is Spiritually Sick.* ET

Although the clouding of our spirit leads to suffering, the resultant process of purification eventually brings us to increased health and happiness. But there is no need to deliberately seek out suffering in order to quicken this purification. That would be like "putting the cart before the horse." Suffering occurs when it is needed, and only the higher intelligence of the Creator knows when and how it should occur. For those individuals who want to speed up their quest for greater health and happiness, Meishusama recommends being of service to others, engaging in Jyorei healing energy, improving one's character, appreciating beauty, and adopting a healthy, natural diet. These are the most effective ways for us to actively promote positive purification and healing. The rest is up to God.

Physical Health

Health is the state wherein all cells are functioning optimally.
　　　　　　　　　　　—Raymond Francis (Naturopathic Physician)

To be healthy is to have abundant inner strength and power. It is to feel vital and alive, and be full of energy and enthusiasm. Good health is a condition in which all the various systems within the body, such as the respiratory system, nervous system, immune system, cardiovascular system, skeletal system, and digestive system, function optimally, and work in harmony with each other. On a psychological level, this means a state of mental peace and emotional balance. We exist on many levels: structural, chemical, electrical, emotional, mental, and spiritual. Health is a condition of the whole person, not just one level, part or system of the body.

To keep the body in good health is a duty . . . Otherwise we shall not be able to keep our mind strong and clear. —Gautama Buddha

According to Meishusama, health is the result of a physical body that is free of toxicity and injury, and a spiritual body that is free of spiritual clouds and is full of spiritual Light.

Raymond Francis, a chemist and naturopathic physician, explains the practical effects of health on the cellular level:

When your cells are functioning as they should, you have ample adaptive capacity to thrive in our constantly changing environment without ill effects. With properly functioning cells, you have strong resilience to various kinds of stress—physical, chemical, biological, and emotional. You have the ability to make daily repairs to your cells, the ability to build healthy new ones, and the ability to efficiently remove pathogenic microorganisms and toxins from your body. You become an optimally balanced organism, with integrated mental and physical equilibrium. Perhaps most important is that achieving good cellular health gives our society the ability to produce healthy offspring. (*Never Be Sick Again*)

When we live in harmony with nature, including both the internal terrain of our bodies and the external terrain of the world, we enjoy abundant health and happiness. Unfortunately, the societies we live in are out of touch with nature, and hence create unbalanced lifestyles and toxic environments. Even the remedies that society promotes for its problems are unbalanced and toxic, which leads to still more problems. All of this poses great challenges for those of us who seek to avoid sickness and misery.

If we examine the way in which people enter the abnormal state called sickness, what do we find? The reason for their illness, above all, is that they go against nature. True medical treatment consists of perceiving this anti-natural condition, correcting it and restoring the person to his or her normal and natural state. —*The Truth about Health. ET*

Despite the industrial world's many advances in safety, sanitation, food productivity and health care, statistics reveal that most of the population suffers from a variety of health problems. Obesity, diabetes, cancer, heart disease, arthritis, mental disorders, and many other health problems continue on the rise to epidemic proportions.

In fact, many primitive societies—those that have managed to avoid excess exposure to modern civilization—tend to enjoy far greater health and vitality than those living in technologically advanced countries. Their lives tend to be simple and free of inordinate stress. They live close to nature, and maintain strong ties with their fellow family members and local communities. Their food is fresh, organic, and locally grown, and their air, water, and land are clean and free of pollution. Most get plenty of exercise and sunlight. As we get further removed from nature, our health and vitality tend to decline.

The truth is that humans are born to be sound and healthy.
                                                    —*Humans Are Born to Be Healthy. ET*

Sickness and Modern Medicine

So-called "medicines" are all poisons, and it is precisely because they are poisonous that they have an effect. To be exact, the poisons we call medicines act in a toxic way to reduce the symptoms of disease, and thus give the superficial appearance of a cure. However, no real cure takes place. —What is Illness?. ET

When people get sick, they usually want to eliminate their physical discomfort as soon as possible. Often they run either to their local pharmacy for a somewhat toxic over-the-counter drug or to their doctor for a prescription to a stronger, more potentially dangerous drug. Unfortunately, most pharmaceutical drugs do not cure disease, but only suppress its unpleasant symptoms. They do this by disrupting normal cellular functions. According to Doctor Raymond Francis, abnormal cell function is the very definition of disease, and because drugs tend to cause our cells to malfunction, they actually promote disease rather than eliminate it. In the long run, they do more harm than good.

In his book, *"Never Be Sick Again,"* he describes the effects of poor cellular health as follows: "For a more meaningful understanding of disease (cellular malfunction), we must consider the health of our cells. Remember that noticeable health problems begin when a large number of cells malfunction. As this happens, important cellular chemicals are not produced, cell-to-cell communications become garbled and the body ceases to regulate itself properly. Our tissues suffer and noticeable symptoms appear, e.g., allergies, fatigue, aches and pains, colds, flu, depression, anxiety, cancer, or any of thousands of other complaints." (*Never Be Sick Again*)

Modern medicine is usually quite toxic to the body, and despite the temporary benefits it may bring, one has to wonder what the long-term effects of these toxins might be. Drugs can be severely damaging to the liver, kidneys, or other vital organs in the body because poisons are designed to kill, not cure. And vaccines, which bypass much of the immune system by being injected straight into the bloodstream, pollute the body with not only harmful bacteria and viruses, but also toxic chemicals and heavy metals. About this, Mahatma Gandhi stated, "Vaccination is a barbarous practice and one of the most fatal of all of the delusions current in our time. Conscientious objectors to vaccination should stand alone, if need be, against the whole world, in defense of their conviction." We need to question why anyone would want to ingest more toxins into a body already suffering from toxic overload. Might not modern medicine, because of its toxicity, actually be contributing more to the problem than to the solution?

Not only do drugs harm the cells of the body, but so also do many other therapies offered by Western medicine such as chemotherapy and radiation therapy. The former poisons the cells, and the latter burns them. Both destroy health rather than improving it. Meishusama was equally critical of radiation therapy:

Another example is cancer, which is often attacked and destroyed using radiation. This would be fine if it were only the cancer that is destroyed, but in fact the tissues surrounding it suffer, and the negative effects of the treatment far outweigh the positive ones. —*What is Illness?. ET*

The article, *Doctors Are the Third Leading Cause of U.S. Deaths,*[5] presents some startling statistics:

Medical errors constitute the third leading cause of death, after deaths from heart disease and cancer, according to a study by Barbara Starfield, M.D., M.P.H., from the Johns Hopkins School of Hygiene and Public Health, in Baltimore, Md. Published in the July 26, 2000, Journal of the American Medical Association, the article lists 225,000 deaths per year in hospitals alone, broken down as follows:

- 12,000 deaths/year from unnecessary surgery

- 7,000 deaths/year from medication errors in hospitals

- 20,000 deaths/year from other errors in hospitals

- 80,000 deaths/year from infections in hospitals

- 106,000 deaths/year from non-error (adverse effects of medications)

The figures were even higher in the 1999 Institute of Medicine (IOM) report, *To Err is Human.* (Please note that these figures include, for the most part, deaths caused by doctors in hospitals, so deaths from medical errors outside hospitals would be another subject.)

Too often, assembly line medical care fails to sufficiently educate patients in the proper use of medicines. Sadly, many deaths occur shortly after discharge from hospitals due to a patient inadvertently adding another medication to their current one without considering how the two might interact. Sometimes something as innocuous or as common as Tylenol or Benedryl can cause severe sickness or death when combined with a prescription drug.

Poisoning from prescription drugs has risen to become the second-largest cause of unintentional deaths in the United States, according to the federal Centers for Disease Control and Prevention. In its Morbidity and Mortality Weekly Report, researchers found that deaths from prescription drugs rose from 4.4 per 100,000 people in 1999 to 7.1 per 100,000 in 2004. This increase represents

5. *The Whole Life Times Magazine* (September 2000).

a jump from 11,000 people to almost 20,000 in the span of five years. Among the 20,000 that died, more than 8,500—double the number from 1999—were from "other and unspecified drugs." Psychotherapeutic drugs, like antidepressants and sedatives, nearly doubled from 671 deaths to 1,300.[6]

Most medicines are composed of toxic ingredients derived from petroleum or other synthetic chemicals. Although some drugs may be derived from various plants or herbs, these also tend to be toxic because they are made from isolated chemicals instead of whole plants. The human body was designed to consume either plants or animal products as food, not synthetic or isolated chemicals. Whereas food is composed of many nutrients (such as protein, fats, carbohydrates, vitamins, minerals, and various natural phytonutrients, all bound together at the molecular level), chemicals, on the other hand, are relatively simple substances. When one ingests these chemical formulas, they tend to create stress and imbalance within the organs, glands, and tissues of the body, rather than nourishing them. How do they do that? In general, drugs operate by blocking or restricting the natural functions of the body, whereas by contrast, good nutrition operates by boosting the body's natural functions. Some drugs, such as various forms used in chemotherapy, indiscriminately destroy cells throughout the body, ruining one's health in the process.

Taking a survey of the damage can be alarming. It is becoming increasingly obvious to many that antidepressant drugs can make you psychotic; cholesterol/lipid-lowering drugs can destroy your liver, hormones, and entire nervous system; diabetes drugs can destroy your liver and pancreas; chemotherapy can ruin your immune system; and anti-inflammatory drugs can cause gastric ulcers, GERD (gastric esophageal reflux disease), and liver and kidney disease. Meishusama adds: "Drugs and treatment by medical devices bring temporary good effects, but as time passes the effects reverse themselves and become harmful. Despite this, people are dazzled by the initial good results and pursue the same method of treatment, come what may. The result is that harmful effects grow greater and greater." *(It is Not True that "Honesty does not Pay". ET)*

I no longer believe in modern medicine. I believe that the greatest danger to your health is the doctor who practices modern medicine. Don't trust your doctor. Assume that if he prescribed a drug, it's dangerous. There is no safe drug. —*Robert Mendelsohn, MD (Confessions of a Medical Heretic)*

6. Adams, Mike. "Unintentional Poisoning Deaths – United States, 1999–2004" (February 9, 2007). Centers for Disease Control and Prevention [Online], Available at: http://www.cdc.gov/mmwr/preview/mmwrhtml/mm5605a1.htm

Marica Angell, a physician and author, along with being the first woman to serve as editor-in-chief of The New England Journal of Medicine (regarded as one of the most prestigious peer-reviewed medical journals in the world), wrote, "It is simply no longer possible to believe much of the clinical research that is published, or to rely on the judgment of trusted physicians or authoritative medical guidelines. I take no pleasure in this conclusion, which I reached slowly and reluctantly over my two decades as an editor of The New England Journal of Medicine."

Toxic residue from pharmaceutical drugs affects everyone, even those who do not personally consume them. "Apart from the vast number of drugs taken directly, people are also, unknowingly, consuming large amounts of drugs and other chemical substances indirectly from the food they eat. Most food industries rely on chemical substances from soil to supermarket, and the animal products industries are by far the most excessive users of these substances. The avalanche of drug and chemical usage by these industries occurred with the shift in production methods from free-range farming to factory and feedlot farming in the last 20 to 30 years." (The Pharmaceutical Drug Racket Part-1[7])

Modern medicine is based on the presumptions of Newtonian physics, which maintains that both the universe and the human body are like machines—entirely composed of collections of individual parts—and that by isolating the parts and studying them separately, we can understand the whole. Health writer Mike Adams writes, "M.D.s practicing today literally believe the body is divided into isolated compartments that have no effect on each other; hence the dividing up of doctor duties into roles like foot doctor, ear doctor, eye doctor, brain doctor, and heart doctor. What happened to the WHOLE patient?"[8]

This mechanistic model stands in great contrast to more holistic models, which explain how the whole can only be understood through the synergistic functioning of all of its parts. The mechanical model promotes a fragmentary approach to health that treats only one or two malfunctioning organs in the body at a time rather than working to heal the entire body.

This leads practitioners of modern medicine to view the human body as a battleground on which wars are waged against malevolent invaders and tumors. Their main weapons in this war are synthetic chemicals, surgery, and radiation. What doctors and pharmacists fail to realize is that diseases are not separate from

---

7. John Leso, "The Pharmaceutical Drug Racket Part-1," Nexus New Times Magazine, vol. 2, no. 13 (April/May 1993).

8. Natural News. "Medical Quackery" (2007, February 14) Retrieved from http://www.naturalnews.com/CounterThink/Medical-Quackery.html

the person. In fact every disease can be more accurately called an expression of the patient's lifestyle, beliefs, and subtle energies, which in turn are strongly influenced by the culture and civilization that they live in. (Thus, a toxic society breeds toxic individuals.)

By attempting to attack and destroy disease, modern medicine invariably ends up damaging the greater person in the process. Such injuries to the overall health and functioning of the body are viewed as unavoidable casualties of war— the war against disease. If the patient ends up losing his or her kidneys, heart or liver, it is considered the lesser of two evils because at least they did not die (hopefully).

The person who takes medicine must recover twice, once from the disease and once from the medicine. — William Osler, M.D.

This is a shallow approach to healing that only attempts to treat the symptoms of an illness rather than its underlying cause. It is like dealing with a fire by taking the batteries out of the fire alarm! Yes, the alarm has become quiet, but the flames are still smoldering, causing even more damage, and by the time you see the flames, it is too late, everything is already being destroyed.

Similarly, a tumor or malignant growth is only the symptom, seen or felt, of deeper, systemic disorders within the body, such as toxicity, malnutrition, or metabolic malfunction. Therefore, removing the tumor through surgery is not usually sufficient to overcome illness because it does not address these vital health issues. In addition, on a deeper level, the underlying negative energy connected to the tumor will continue to remain in the spiritual body and continue to cause damage. Usually, the best that surgery can do is to buy some extra time for the patient, although the price is high: the injury and disfigurement of the body. And how can the body function well if an essential part of it has been removed? Surely there must be another way—one that respects health rather than destroying it.

To overcome illness and attain true health, first the spiritual body must be purified of its clouds, and then the physical body must be cleansed of its internal toxins. Good nutrition is also important. Junk food should be avoided, including sugar filled desserts such as cookies, pastries, donuts, ice cream, and candy; and processed foods such as hotdogs, instant coffee creamer, corn and potato chips, margarine, artificial sweeteners, sugary breakfast cereals, sports drinks and soft drinks. A diet consisting of a wide variety of fresh, chemical-free fruits, vegetables, whole grains, beans, and nuts will help the body to recover and regain strength.

Ideally, choose locally grown food, in season. In addition, fresh air, sunshine, pure water, moderate exercise, and a positive attitude should also be included in one's overall lifestyle.

As I have previously explained, curing an illness is a process of dispelling or breaking up an accumulation of toxins in part of the body. When this process takes place in the soul, the accumulated toxins take the form of clouds that dull the spiritual body, and the "dissolution" is the dispelling of these clouds. Medical treatment until now has been directed only toward dealing with physical symptoms, and this misdirection has not resulted in true cures. — *Natural Power. ET*

Current medical technology has been quite successful in treating victims of car accidents, patients suffering from life-threatening infections, and those in danger of imminent organ failure. It offers much needed help during trauma and emergencies, but is not very useful for chronic, long-term health problems. This is because it assumes an adversarial approach to illness, rather than a supportive approach to wellness. Such practices will never cure anything, but only postpone recovery. The medical establishment needs to understand that health is not the absence of disease; it is a condition of optimum vitality. And in order to promote true health, they need to focus more on what is good for the body and less on what is bad for it.

These same problems of suppression and toxicity also hold true for psychiatric medications, as well: they do not cure mental illness, but only make people emotionally numb. Although the emotional pain may lessen by taking these psychiatric drugs, the underlying problems of guilt, depression, anxiety, confusion, and rage do not go away, but only get buried for a while. The patient soon becomes dependent on these drugs to maintain a tight lid on their troubles, because if they dare to stop taking them, their old problems resurface with increased energy. It is like using a pressure cooker with a clogged steam release valve; the pressure soon builds up to a dangerous level. Thus, the longer they suppress their problems, the worse they get. There are many stories of people, both young and old, exploding into violent behavior after having been on psychiatric medications for long periods of time. According to recent studies and stories, these drugs also increase the chances of suicide by those who use them. Plus, the toxicity of these drugs presents serious dangers to the patient's physical health, including potential damage to his or her brain, nerves, liver, and other vital organs. Although the use of psychiatric medications may sometimes be required to control extreme behavior, it is important to understand their limitations. True healing must go beyond chemical suppression. It must work to purify the underlying problem and to nurture the whole person, spiritually, mentally, emotionally and physically.

Body and spirit are one and indivisible. —Awaken to God's Intention. ET

Viruses and Bacteria

Modern medicine considers viruses and bacteria to be the enemy, and sets out to destroy these harmful invaders. Meishusama viewed the occurrence of a cold or flu as the body's attempt to rid itself of accumulated toxins. Viruses and bacteria are instrumental in initiating a healing process by actually feeding on toxins in the body. A runny nose, sweat, diarrhea, vomiting, etc. are often healthy symptoms of the body purifying itself of toxicity. A similar condition occurs in nature, where toxic or decaying substances are quickly broken down and assimilated by various bacteria, worms, and insects. This is nature's way of maintaining balance and harmony.

Understanding this, Meishusama advocates that we appreciate the benefits of purification, despite how unpleasant it might feel at the moment. If we keep in view the possible benefits of a clean and purified body, we would not try to suppress the purification process, but would actually support it. The physical body must throw off its toxins, whether inherited, ingested, acquired, or generated in some particular manner, if it is to remain healthy and functional. Better to eliminate them now, while the body has sufficient strength to handle the effects, than to wait until a serious illness occurs. When the body is weak, the purification process is more difficult. Receiving and giving the healing energy of Jyorei will strengthen the body, ease the pain of purification, and bring illness to a speedier conclusion.

Dr. Antoine Bechamp—a medical doctor, pharmacist, chemist, microbiologist, and university professor who lived in the nineteenth and early twentieth century France—postulated that disease is usually the result of an unhealthy "terrain" within the body. He found that when the internal condition of the body was weakened from poor nutrition or environmental toxicity (such as smoking, over-consumption of alcohol, ingesting drugs, or exposure to harmful chemicals, heavy metals, or radiation) then the natural, healthy bacteria inside the system would change and evolve into harmful microorganisms. He called this phenomenon pleomorphism (having many forms). According to Dr. Bechamp, the most important approach to healing is to reverse this condition by cleansing the body and strengthening it with healthy food, fresh air, sunshine, and exercise.

Natural Forces within us are the true healers of disease. —Hippocrates

One of his students, Louis Pasteur, advocated the opposite theory that disease was the result of hostile, invading germs and viruses. He claimed that bacteria do not change or evolve, and promoted the use of aggressive applications of synthetic medicine to kill them. This was a theoretical model resembling the violent tactics of open warfare, rather than the gentle art of promoting health and healing. Yet, despite his dismissal of the importance of strengthening the physical body—what many would consider to be common sense—his approach became more popular than Bechamp's because it was more in sync with the prevailing paradigms of the time, and also because it supported the financial interests of the medical establishment who wanted to promote profitable chemical drugs. Preventative medicine was not profitable.

Of course, Pasteur was correct in his declaration that illness can occur from outside sources. Some viruses and bacteria can indeed be deadly, such as Anthrax or Ebola, and an open wound can easily be susceptible to infection. Pasteur also deserves credit for championing the once-controversial practice of doctors washing their hands before performing surgery. This single procedure alone has probably saved millions of lives since it was accepted within the medical community a century ago. But Bechamp's point is that a healthy body, full of vitality, is much less susceptible to contracting a virus or bacteria, because its immune system is strong and its internal organs are functioning well. And Pasteur—despite his lifelong advocacy of the germ theory—on his deathbed seemed to have a change of heart, and was reported to have exclaimed, "The germ theory is nothing; the terrain (internal environment) is everything." Antoine Bechamp's theories are currently being rediscovered, and the fundamentals of these theories might well have been embraced by Meishusama had they been better known in Japan during his time.

Although the life expectancy of men and women in industrialized countries has risen during the past 100 years as infectious illnesses have been controlled, according to German nutritionist, M.O. Bruker, M.D., the primary reason is improved hygienic conditions, not better medicine or the use of antibiotics. "People live statistically longer, but they are not necessarily healthier," he explained. "Today we have sewage systems, water faucets, and better sanitary conditions that have helped eliminate mass epidemics, such as typhus, cholera and tuberculosis. But more people are becoming sick from heart disease, cancer, and intestinal illness than ever before. The idea that antibiotics and modern medicine deserve most of the credit for improving both the length and quality of people's lives is a fraud."

Accidents and Spiritual Clouds

Humans are purged of their spiritual clouding through suffering.
—A Bad Person is Spiritually Sick. ET

Sickness can also be caused by injuries or from exposure to harmful chemicals in our environment. These externally caused illnesses are also forms of purification. Our spiritual clouds may have drawn these experiences to us in order to help facilitate a particular purification. Thus, from Meishusama's perspective, events are not interpreted as resulting from chance or coincidence, but rather, are understood to have their origins in the spiritual world. Outer events are the secondary effects of pre-existing inner conditions that were generated in the past.

To be cheated and suffer a loss, to suffer damage by fire, to be injured or robbed, to encounter family bereavement, to suffer business setbacks or failure, to lack money or fall deeply in debt, to argue with your wife or husband, to be alienated from your parents or children, to be on bad terms with relatives or friends—these are all without exception examples of this process of purification. As there is no way other than suffering to remove clouding from the soul, suffering cannot be avoided as long as such clouding exists. *—You Are Free to Make Your Own Destiny. ET*

Mental Purification

A small amount of mental disorder seems to be the common lot of mankind. The so-called "man in the street" is slightly mentally ill.
—Mental Disorders, God's Way to Health. HT

There are many types of purification, including physical, mental, relational, financial, environmental, familial, and societal. Mental purification can involve depression, anxiety, insecurity, jealousy, guilt, resentment, and anger. The main cause of these emotions is usually our pre-existing attitudes and tendencies, not the outer circumstances in which we find ourselves. Financial problems, accidents, or encounters with rude and aggressive people merely act as triggers for unresolved mental and emotional patterns that already exist within us. This is why some people can explode in rage over an innocent remark made to them by a friend, family member, or stranger. When we hold unresolved emotions within us, they tend to distort our perceptions and judgments, causing us to misinterpret other people's feelings and motives. Our emotional reactions based upon these misinterpretations only tend to provoke negative responses from others, resulting in further interpersonal conflict. Each person will, of course, mentally justify his or her actions, no matter how negative or irrational, while simultaneously criticizing the other person's actions. These dysfunctional cycles are at the root of most relationship problems, and are a chief cause of much personal unhappiness.

All clouds caused by misdeeds are purified according to the law of cause and effect.
—Awaken to God's Intention. ET

Our emotional disposition tends to color everything we experience and can sometimes blind us as to what is actually going on around us. Most interpersonal conflicts are the result of mutual misinterpretations and unconscious projections. We usually tend to take things too personally, frequently expect too much from others, and often fail to consider the needs of others. Until we purify our minds of the spiritual clouds that dull our awareness, interpersonal conflicts of one sort or another will continue to plague our lives, promoting misery for all concerned. One of the fundamental truths in life is that *the inner world of our thoughts and feelings actually determines what we experience in the outer world.*

The truth is that all suffering comes from a lack of wisdom.
—Divine Writings. MK2

An especially significant cause of mental purification is the suppressed feelings we accumulate from the past. Feelings of inadequacy, low self-worth, neediness, anger, resentment, loneliness, anxiety and compulsiveness remain within us because we refuse to acknowledge and release them. Instead, we blame others. When we judge feelings such as anger, fear, or sorrow as bad, we inevitably try to avoid them, both in ourselves and in others. This causes us to repress our feelings, and the more we repress them, the more deeply entrenched they become, thereby locking us into limiting behavior patterns that are exceedingly difficult to change.

But, like a pressure cooker, whatever gets suppressed has to eventually burst out because it is the nature of energy to move—not stand still. Often, when we judge and blame others, we are actually reacting to qualities in them that remind us of those same qualities within ourselves—although we refuse to admit this to ourselves. One of the main ways we tend to grow psychologically is by experiencing ourselves mirrored objectively in the outer environment. Consequently, we often attract people and circumstances to ourselves who can reflect disowned or projected parts of ourselves back to us. By triggering our repressed feelings, they provide us with opportunities to learn more about ourselves and to expand our consciousness. Furthermore, this is why we draw the same types of people and circumstances to ourselves, again and again. Until we learn and grow from our problems, we are destined to repeat them.

However much we refuse to see and acknowledge negative feelings within ourselves, to the same degree will we have difficulty dealing with those same negative feelings in others. This type of avoidance prevents meaningful communication, because healthy relationships depend on openness and honesty, not secrecy and deception. How can people resolve interpersonal conflicts if they chronically avoid dealing with each other's feelings? Plus, people tend to get frustrated and angry when they feel they are being ignored or avoided, which then makes relationships deteriorate even more. The emotional suffering caused by these continual rounds of avoidance and reaction are good examples of mental purification.

Each time an emotional reaction occurs within us, it is a chance to learn and grow by acknowledging and releasing it. Through mental purification, life is giving us the chance to free ourselves from the old conditioning that has kept us bound and unhappy for so long. So this type of mental purification, although painful, is actually something to feel grateful for. It is a gift from the Creator for the sake of our own long-term benefit.

What joy that the dark side of my heart has cleared and shines with the brightness of noon. —My Salvation. MK1

One might notice that good things often happen to bad people and that bad things often happen to good people. But it would be a mistake to conclude that life is therefore unjust or cruel. In actuality, life is not so much concerned with our limited views of fairness as it is with giving us whatever experiences will most help us to grow spiritually. Meishusama himself suffered enormously in his life, but this did not imply that he deserved to suffer or that he had a great deal of negativity he needed to burn off. On reviewing Meishusama's life, we discover that the tremendous suffering and adversity he experienced throughout his life actually furthered his purification and thus supported his dramatic spiritual growth. Because of this, he tended to look back on his suffering not with regret but with gratitude for all the blessings that he received from it.

Terrible tragedies in our lives that we cannot understand are often the result of accumulated spiritual clouds either in ourselves or in those around us. When a sufficient amount of negativity or darkness accumulates in the spiritual world, purification inevitably follows. Not only can this take the form of sickness, strife, financial problems, natural disasters, or wars, but it can also present itself as moodiness, neurosis, or in extreme cases, schizophrenia or psychosis. Cultivating purity of mind and body is the best prevention against these terrible conditions.

The only good way of improving your fortune is to lessen your spiritual clouding. In other words, if clouding is reduced, then there will be less need for purification and what would have been bad fortune will be transformed into good fortune. —*You Are Free to Make Your Own Destiny. ET*

Viewing hardship and suffering as forms of purification can encourage feelings of acceptance and trust rather than bitterness and resistance. This view also promotes a positive attitude toward life and greater hope for the future. When we understand that the true source of happiness is our internal spiritual condition, then our priorities begin to change. Instead of the transitory rewards of this world, we begin to value that which promotes spiritual growth, including purification and the challenges that accompany it. Gradually, purification draws us closer to eternal peace and happiness.

Luck comes not to one who waits, but to one who is purified.
—*You are Free to Make Your Own Destiny. ET*

CHAPTER 7

TOWARD A WORLD OF LIGHT

Paradise on Earth

If I were to express as simply as possible what is meant by the words 'Paradise on Earth' I would say it is the world of beauty. That is to say, people have beauty in their hearts, a beauty of the spirit. Words and deeds should embody this beauty. This is beauty at the individual level. And when beauty spreads, social beauty comes into being.[9] —*Meishusama*

The story of humanity in many ways is a tragic tale full of wars, poverty, disease, social oppression, and injustice. Past attempts to correct these problems seem to have made little meaningful difference in the overall picture. If things got better in one place, they inevitably got worse somewhere else. After much disillusionment and despair about the condition of humanity, Meishusama received a revelation—a vision of a rapidly approaching New Age, which he labeled "Paradise on Earth." This paradise would be a world of truth, goodness, and beauty: a world free of the three perennial afflictions of sickness, poverty, and strife.

> We must ask ourselves for what purpose God, the Creator of all things, made humans. His purpose, according to my understanding, is that we are meant to create an ideal world of absolute truth, goodness, and beauty.
>
> Perhaps some will find this too large a concept to take in. Of course, how long it will take to create such an ideal world—how many hundreds or thousands of years—is beyond human conception. However, the world

---

9. Meishusama, "An Inquiry on Heaven on Earth," *Japanese Shumei Newspaper*, no. 262 (January 1992).

is certainly moving in that direction. Little-by-little, step-by-step, it is progressing and improving. No one who looks around will be able to deny this obvious fact. For the truth is that God as Spirit and humans as body are involved together in an upward progress that is seemingly boundless and endless. This means that the human race is the agent charged with physically carrying out this cosmic task.

Thus, we can see that humankind is of great importance and has equally great responsibility. —*The Truth about Health. ET*

Although things will improve dramatically after the arrival of this New Age, we do not need to wait until then to find individual freedom and happiness. We can establish our own personal "Paradise on Earth" right here and now, during this very lifetime, to the extent that we can purify our souls and also begin to live a life dedicated to the happiness of others. This world of ours was created to be a place of genuine happiness—not misery. But humanity, through the long-term effects of its ignorant and selfish behavior, has gradually corrupted and ruined it. Indeed, the world has been darkened to such an extent, that for universal happiness to finally arise, the human heart must first go through a dramatic transformation. This will require no less than a deep and thorough purification of the spirit. Mahatma Gandhi expressed a similar awareness when he said, "You must be the change you wish to see in the world."

Meishusama's vision of Paradise on Earth incorporates not only the higher ideals of spiritual growth, but also the lower ideals of ordinary worldly happiness as well. He was not a religious extremist like those who denigrate or dismiss the world. He was neither ascetic nor otherworldly. Instead, he valued this world for all the love, beauty, and joy it provides. Meishusama understood that for most people, their outer circumstances were at least as important to their happiness as was their inner state of consciousness. They need family, friends, jobs, homes, and food. No one is an island unto himself, despite how detached or inwardly free they might be. For example: how can one's body stay healthy and pure if the food and the surrounding environment are full of harmful chemicals and other poisons? How can one feel comfortable if one (or anyone of us) is living on the streets without food, clothing or shelter? And how can one maintain a peaceful and loving heart if one is in the midst of violent hostility and conflict?

I am urging the human race toward a great awakening through the flowering of a spiritual culture. —Preface. ET

Not only is happiness important in its own right, but for many it is also the foundation for the cultivation of spiritual growth. The humanistic psychologist, Dr. Abraham Maslow, argued that people usually must have their basic needs met before they will begin to focus on higher matters. The following is a brief summary of Maslow's famous "Hierarchy of Needs":

1. Physiological: the need for food, water, and physical comfort.

2. Safety: the need for structure, order, security, and predictability.

3. Belongingness and love: The need for social acceptance and intimacy.

4. Esteem: The need for social recognition and status through personal achievement.

These first four are the most basic needs that must be satisfied before higher interests and drives can emerge within the individual. After this, people tend to demonstrate "higher needs" or interests as their chief motivating factors:

5. Cognitive: the need to know, understand and explore new things.

6. Aesthetic: the need to appreciate and express beauty, order and symmetry.

7. Self-actualization: the need to find self-fulfillment and realize one's potential.

8. Self-transcendence: the need to connect to something beyond the ego or to help others find self-fulfillment and realize their potential.

The more that each of these latter needs is fulfilled, the more the individual starts to exhibit a greater degree of wisdom, altruism, and awareness in his or her life. Meishusama and Maslow both agree that people's basic needs for safety, comfort, and good health must be satisfied before they can realistically hope to obtain greater happiness and authentic spiritual development. To these basic things, Maslow would add the needs for love, social acceptance and personal achievement. Meishusama writes, "There are the desires for wisdom, the sense of superiority, the competitive urge, and the desire for progress on one hand, while on the other there are the physical cravings for love and pleasure. They all find a place within the human mind." *(Atheism. HT)* Although everything has value, from the most basic physical needs to the most abstract, real happiness depends upon attaining a higher level of consciousness. And it is a basic truth in life that what we value we become, in accordance with our actual priorities.

Meishusama dreamed of a world of warm-hearted people who were naturally inclined toward treating each other with kindness and generosity. His primary objective was to create a world where everyone was free of sickness, had good food to eat, attractive clothes to wear, and beautiful homes to live in. He envisioned a society that would nurture the sick and feed the poor, not abandon or shun them. It would be a world free of war, conflict, and crime.

According to the contemporary American philosopher, Ken Wilber, life's activities can be divided into four general categories or quadrants:

1. Interior-Individual: Our subjective state, such as thoughts, feelings, and intentions.

2. Exterior-Individual: Observable behavior such as bodily actions or physiological activities.

3. Interior-Collective: The beliefs, attitudes, and values of each culture.

4. Exterior-Collective: The outward structures and collective behavior of entire societies.

Here is an example of these four categories in action. The statement, "I love the taste of fresh fruits and vegetables," expresses Interior-Individual (1). The statement, "Not only myself, but many other people seem to love fresh fruits and vegetables," expresses Interior-Collective (3). The statement, "I can often be seen shopping at the local farmer's market for fresh fruits and vegetables," expresses Exterior-Individual (2). And finally, the statement, "More and more people are shopping for fruits and vegetables at farmers markets and also growing them in their home gardens," expresses Exterior-Collective (4).

The comprehensiveness of Meishusama's teachings is evident in the fact that he addressed each of these four aspects of experience in one way or another. To create a world free of disease, poverty, and strife, all facets of life need to be healed and spiritually transformed. Jyorei, Natural Agriculture, and beautiful art promote a healthy mind (1), body (2), society (3), and external environment (4). Each of these four facets is inseparably linked because if any one of them is unbalanced or toxic it will inevitably affect the others. The inner (1 & 3) affects the outer (2 & 4), and the outer affects the inner. Similarly, the individual (1 & 2) affects the collective (3 & 4), and the collective affects the individual. This is why a total revolution in human affairs is necessary if we are to create a significantly better world. Again, the basis for this revolution is a deep spiritual purification and transformation in all areas of our lives.

The great American civil rights crusader, Martin Luther King Jr., expressed similar sentiments when he stated, "On the one hand, I must attempt to change the soul of individuals so that their societies may be changed. On the other [hand] I must attempt to change the societies so that the individual souls will have a chance."

Regarding this upcoming transformation of the world, Meishusama writes, "Material culture has already advanced to a level high enough so it can contribute to the creation of perpetual and universal peace. Yet, unfortunately, humanity's spiritual progress still lags far behind its material success. It seems that God is now busily working to assist us in closing the gap between material and spiritual progress." *(Progressing Upwards. KW)*

Spiritual Development

I, myself am striving with all my heart for progress and elevation from last year to this one, and from this month to the next. —A New Person. ET

In our busy lives, it is easy to become over-preoccupied with such worldly concerns as earning a living, recreational activities, and interpersonal relationships. We worry about such things as job security, our finances, and our health. We spend our time shopping for the latest fashions in clothes, the newest electronic gadgets, or the most recent computer games, compact discs or DVDs. We compete with each other for the better job, the nicer car, and the bigger house. Food itself can become a major distraction, either for enjoyment or to avoid emotional pain.

In contrast to these worldly distractions, the soul has its own set of priorities relating to its spiritual growth and development. It can be said that, although perfection resides within each of us because of our innate divinity, this perfection, to varying degrees, has been buried and obscured by the spiritual clouds we have accumulated over the course of many lifetimes. Therefore, to actually manifest our inner perfection in the outer world, a great amount of purification is usually required.

Selflessness and Expanded Awareness

In life there can be nothing more terrible than self. This can be understood if we consider the fact that the most important part of discipline in the spiritual world is directed towards the removal of egotism. —Overcome Egotism. ET

In the process of spiritual growth, a person becomes increasingly empty of self, while simultaneously developing greater capacities for dealing effectively with the complexity of the surrounding world. On the other hand, those of us whose awareness is clouded by excessive personal desires and fears have trouble dealing with the numerous challenges that come up in our lives. This is because desire and fear distract our attention, cloud our judgment, and weaken our mental, emotional, and physical abilities. As a result, we often make bad decisions, resulting in both inner and outer conflict. Those of us who are distracted by inner conflicts are unable to find lasting peace and happiness, even in the best of circumstances. Only spiritual purification and inner discipline can bring us what our souls so deeply crave. For this to happen, we need strong determination and commitment to grow and evolve, which will restructure our mind and emotions according to a hierarchy of values, with spirituality at the top.

No problem can be solved from the same level of consciousness that created it.
—Albert Einstein

Just as a calm pool of water can reflect the nearby trees and sky without distortion, so too, can a person with a clear mind perceive and understand the world accurately. Meishusama writes, "As a person's aura becomes thinner, he becomes more liable to suffer misfortune and disaster. The reason for this is that clouding dulls the activities of the brain, so much that decisions and judgment become inaccurate and unfocused. The person becomes incapable of seeing things in their proper perspective." *(Spiritual Radiations and the Aura. ET)*

Over the course of time, if one earnestly applies oneself, it is possible to reach a level of spiritual development where suffering is no longer a foregone conclusion. The structure of human consciousness evolves and progresses gradually from simple-minded to intelligent, from selfish to selfless, and from compulsive to inwardly free. Spiritual development is like climbing a progressive series of steps on a ladder until finally reaching the highest step, whereupon one merges with the totality of God. Huston Smith, one of the world's leading authorities on comparative religion, points out that models of spiritual ascent such as this have been found in all of the world's spiritual traditions throughout the ages.

To grow and mature from childhood into adulthood, one must first develop a strong ego, one that can control emotional impulses and desires, has good self-esteem, and functions competently in the world. This is called psychological growth. After succeeding in this, one is ready to embark upon the journey of spiritual growth.

Spiritual growth, in contrast to psychological growth, is based on the lessening of ego and self-centeredness. Meishusama says that, "[I]t is the ego that blinds people." (*Do Not Tighten Your Abdomen. KW*), and also, "If you have a big ego, it will block you from receiving wisdom." (*Acquiring Wisdom. KW*)

The ego is our self-image. It is who we think we are. The ego is a mentally constructed self that sees itself as separate from others and the environment, and feels compelled to protect itself from perceived vulnerability. It takes everything personally, and thinks in terms of "me" and "mine." The ego is reinforced by the various social roles that we play, such as that of son, daughter, husband, wife, friend, student, employer or employee. This is further defined by our social status based on occupation, wealth, education, and physical appearance. The more we identify with such things, the more attached we become to our ego, and the more we lose touch with who we really are, which is deeper than mere social identities and physical attributes.

The ego is always comparing itself with others and then ranking itself accordingly. It feels superior to some and inferior to others, resulting in either pride or shame respectively. Such comparisons separate us from others and foster self-centeredness. They bind us to the ego. Whereas the more we identify with our divine spirit, the more broadminded and selfless we become

We must cultivate our souls and become strong enough to defeat our own selfishness.
—Izunome: The Movement of the Universe. KW

The more dis-identified we become from our ego image, as well as from our mind, emotions, desires, and physical sensations, the more they become objects of awareness rather than who we think we are. Surprisingly, this dis-identification does not reduce the enjoyment of life, but increases it, for finally we can stop struggling with the way things are, and become more accepting of life. This is how to become inwardly peaceful and free.

On a relative level, we have a particular name and form—our ego identity—but on a higher level we are nameless and formless—our impersonal divine spirit. Like clothing, we temporarily put on a physical body, mind and social identity, but when we die, we discard these things and return to our true nature as invisible Spirit.

During the course of spiritual development, the ego becomes increasingly transparent, with a lessening of sharp distinctions between oneself and the world around us. Old selfish patterns of behavior that were based on limited levels of awareness gradually diminish. In place of egotism, an expanded state of consciousness that is selfless, unlimited, and highly aware begins to emerge. This state does not deny our own needs and desires, but continues to satisfy them. Yet now the needs and desires of others often become more important than our own. We seek the happiness of not only our personal family and friends, but also the happiness of all beings everywhere. No one is left out, not even ourselves. The limited personality continues to function effectively, although at the core of our being there is only sublime peace and tranquil awareness. About this state, Meishusama says, "This realization is what Buddhists call 'Empty of self, full of peace.'" (*Atheism. HT*)

Evolution of Spirit through Form

Grass and trees grow higher and higher, reaching for the sky. Not a single one grows downwards. All of nature progresses onward and upward in this way.

—A New Person. ET

The driving purpose behind the creation and evolution of the universe is the transformation and expansion of consciousness, using physical matter as a vehicle for the emergence and manifestation of Spirit. All things are subject to a grand evolutionary impulse moving toward ever-greater capacities for intelligence, altruism, and love. On a physical level, there is evolution from simple structures toward those of greater organized complexity. The universe evolves from atoms to molecules, minerals, cells, bacteria, plants, insects, reptiles, mammals, and finally to humans with their highly developed brains and nervous systems. Each stage of evolution depends on the previous stage in order to advance further. According to Meishusama, humanity is now on the verge of the next stage of development.

In short, life is an active process of transforming imperfect matter into perfect matter. —The Comedy of Nutrition. ET

Each stage of development will have a greater structural and functional complexity and integration than the previous stage. The higher a life form is in terms of evolutionary development the more sophisticated will be its brain, biochemistry, and nervous system. This evolutionary trend is mirrored by that life form's greater capacity for intelligent interaction with the environment. Protozoa are limited to simple stimulus and response behavior. Plants alter how they grow depending upon the weather, soil, and competitive life forms. Insects, fish, birds, and reptiles have an advantage over plants in their ability to crawl, swim, or fly in search of food, and in their ability to flee from danger. Mammals are still higher in their evolutionary development, as demonstrated by their innate capacity for maternal love, feeling, and social bonding. Humans, in particular, with their superior intelligence, have a greater ability than other species to learn from the past and plan for the future. (Dolphins, whales, and octopuses also appear highly intelligent, although they do not seem to plan ahead much.) As described above, this grand process of evolution includes not only the external world of matter and life, but also the internal world of consciousness and culture. It is a multidimensional process that includes all things and all beings, in all realms and on all levels.

Evolution does not always move forward in a steady way. Sometimes it may stagnate, regress, or divert in another direction. And at other times it may suddenly speed up. However, over the long run, the direction of evolution is toward ever-higher levels of form and function, affecting everything physically, mentally, and spiritually.

Evolution biologist Elisabet Sahtouris states, "Nature evolves by intelligent response to crisis (not by accidents, as we've been taught)." These evolutionary stages of development are mirrored in the human triune brain, containing the reptilian brain stem, with its "fight or flight" impulses; the limbic system, with its capacity for emotional bonding; and the neocortex, with its ability to reason and conceptualize. The French philosopher Henri Bergson also promoted the theory of the evolution of consciousness. He wrote: "The more complicated the brain becomes, thus giving the organism greater choice of possible actions, the more does consciousness outrun its physical concomitant."

Humans, in particular, have evolved their consciousness through organizing themselves into larger and larger cooperative groups, such as (in ascending order), families, clans, tribes, city-states, nations, and the recently emerging global civilization of our present technological age. To function well in complex societies, people need to learn to cooperate with each other. They need to develop such positive qualities as maturity, intelligence, sensitivity, and altruism. Evolved societies require evolved individuals, just as evolved individuals require evolved societies. Each reinforces the other.

Humans have greater intelligence, capacity for empathy, aesthetic awareness, and freedom of choice than do other life forms. Especially unique to humans is our strong sense of self-awareness, which allows us to self-reflect, and to learn and grow as a result. Most importantly, we have the ability to consider how other people think and feel. This expanded consciousness gives us a highly developed social intelligence, which helps us to interact with each other harmoniously and effectively. Beyond this, not only can we observe others, but we can also interpret how they see us.

Consciousness underlies all of manifestation and is the engine driving all things toward both greater awareness and higher functional capacities. Thus, trees are more conscious than rocks; animals are more conscious than trees; and humans are more conscious than animals. According to medieval Sufi poet Ibn Al Arabi, "God sleeps in the rock, dreams in the plant, stirs in the animal, and awakens in man." Each stage of development brings with it the capacity to interact on a more complex and sophisticated level than before. All of creation is gradually evolving from matter to body, mind, soul, and finally spirit. This upward ascension guarantees the eventual liberation and salvation of all life. Together, all of us are evolving into pure Light.

This evolutionary drive is an aspect of Miroku Omikami. It is the imperceptible stillness of Spirit manifesting as the diverse activity of the world, imbuing everything with consciousness and purpose.

The Great Power of Miroku Omikami is the force generating the completion of the world as heaven on earth. —God the Creator (Miroku Omikami). MK1

Growth and Maturity

Even the greatest tree that stretches to the sky was once but a tiny sprout.
—For Youth. MK1

An infant is inwardly close to God because of its fundamental innocence and purity, but paradoxically, it also separates itself from God through its exclusive involvement with its own needs. At that early age, the child is unable to stand outside of itself or to see things from another person's perspective. They are self-absorbed and are only concerned with fulfilling their immediate desires. They have not yet developed the complex mental ability to understand the world around them, nor have they the maturity to respond to the needs of others. They are incapable of detaching themselves from their immediate moods and desires. The Swiss biologist and psychologist, Jean Piaget, claimed that a child's cognitive structure gradually increases in sophistication as the child continues to grow and mature. As each year progresses, the child's ability to mentally stand outside of itself increases, along with an increased capacity for human relatedness and empathy for others.

Although a teenager may often appear to be insecure and rebellious, nonetheless, his level of growth and maturity tends to surpass that of a child. If all goes well, by the time the teenager grows into adulthood he will have reached a level of maturity in which he is less self-centered and is more responsive to the feelings and needs of others. This progression of self-development often continues into parenthood, where the needs of one's children often take on greater importance than one's own. In short, humans are capable of undergoing a sequence of inner development that stretches from caring only for oneself, to caring for some people sometimes, to caring for everyone everywhere.

To exist is to change, to change is to mature, to mature is to go on creating oneself endlessly. —Henri Bergson

Meishusama explains such developmental growth in terms of a person's sense of justice. He says, "There are three kinds of justice: the narrow kind, which is only concerned with personal profit; the wider kind, which is concerned with one's own society and nation; and finally, the highest kind, which is concerned with all the peoples of the world. The fact is that the narrow and wider kinds are not true justice, but are false justice. For example, filial piety and loyalty to the nation and sovereign are, when all is said and done, basically selfish, and therefore forms of false justice. The reason that Japan lost World War II was that it followed its own interests exclusively. Justice must have as its aim the welfare of the whole world. The only true justice is the highest kind of justice." (*A Sense of Justice. ET*) "Narrow justice" is selfish, "wider justice" is partially selfish, and the "highest justice" is unselfish. A person who always cares for the welfare of others is advanced further spiritually than one who is always selfish. This is an easy to understand way of measuring a person's or society's level of development.

Human development does not need to stop at ordinary adult maturity because each of us has the innate potential for greater spiritual growth. Each level or phase of development surpasses and includes the abilities of the levels that precede it. One of the ways that a person's spiritual level can be measured is by how frequently he or she is able to take another person's perspective. How easily can we see things from the perspective of our friends and family members? Can we also do so with strangers and with those whom we dislike? And how often do we try to understand the point of view of those with whom we disagree? Our inability or resistance to doing so may reveal the areas in ourselves where there is the greatest opportunity for growth. Eventually our personal viewpoint needs to expand to encompass all viewpoints – our own and others, both singular and plural.

People must constantly strive for progress and evolution. This is especially true for those who have faith in God. —A New Person. ET

As spiritual growth continues, the mind develops a greater capacity for handling challenges that confront it in the world, while simultaneously expanding its self-awareness and creative abilities. The mind also becomes increasingly capable of adopting multiple perspectives – to simultaneously see, understand, and empathize with many different points of view. Hope and optimism replace anxiety and despair. Stronger ethics and higher values emerge within the person's consciousness, followed by altruism and unconditional love. The emergent recognition of our common humanity fosters the desire to be of service to others and to the greater whole. Meishusama writes about one of the psychological benefits that people derive from spiritual growth: "Their view of their own future becomes bright and clear, and their worries and anxieties disappear." *(The Strata in the Spiritual World. ET)*

Heaven and Hell

The spiritual world extends in range from the lower worlds, to the middle worlds, up to the higher worlds. These are also known as hell, purgatory (*Yachimata*), and heaven. About this, Meishusama elaborates, "The difference between these levels is a matter of radiance and heat. On the highest level, the radiance and heat are both very intense, while on the lowest level everything is dark and frigid. Yachimata lies between these two extremes, approximating the material world in this respect." *(A Description of the Spiritual World. HT)* We create our own heaven and hell in the way we live our lives. People in constant conflict with others live in their own private hell world, while those who love to make others happy and delight in their joy live in heaven itself. As Jesus Christ said, "The Kingdom of Heaven is within." Most of us currently live in various levels of purgatory, sometimes happy, sometimes suffering.

The Path to Spiritual Growth

Perfection may seem a distant hope in this imperfect world of ours, but the cultivation of one's mind and spirit so that they can gradually, step by step, approach perfection is the right action and reveals the aspirations of true faith.

—*Common Sense. ET*

There are many ways to progress in our upward reach for God. Meishusama suggests actively purifying our spiritual clouds through Jyorei, learning to always think of others first, helping people to be happy, and cultivating the appreciation of art and beauty. Studying spiritual teachings is also valuable for receiving wisdom and inspiration. In particular, Meishusama says that we can actually absorb Divine Light from exposure to his written words.

Along with these outwardly directed activities, there are inner practices as well. These consist of scrutinizing one's own fears, motives and desires; cultivating love, gratitude, and detachment; chanting sacred words of power such as contained within the Amatsunorito; and sitting in prayer or in meditative silence. Meishusama also says that, "What is important is to reconcile one's inner conflicts and to harmonize the opposite aspects of one's character. This is a very important practice for your spiritual growth." (*The Izunome Principle and Love. KW*) It is also helpful to remember that everything, both the good and the bad, is a gift from God to help us to purify, learn, and grow.

Dedicated commitment to all of these practices is guaranteed to positively transform our character and further our spiritual development. "We must improve and elevate our souls. That is, the elevation you must achieve is an elevation of character," writes Meishusama. (*A New Person. ET*)

How can we tell if we are progressing in our spiritual development? About this Meishusama says, "There is a standard against which you can measure the extent of your spiritual progress and the pureness of your spirit, and it is not difficult to grasp. It is simply the degree to which you do not like creating strife, and the amount of gentleness and modesty that you show." (*Gentleness and Modesty. ET*)

This does not mean that one cannot take a stand against hatred and aggression. On the contrary, it can sometimes be quite appropriate to intervene if we see someone being physically attacked. But in these situations, one should not return hostility with more hostility, because that would only increase the violence. What is needed is for the cycles of violence and hatred to stop completely. It is important to remember that even cruel or hateful people deserve respect, even though they do not give it to others. Whenever possible, it is best to be the peacemaker, not the avenger, and to promote universal harmony, wherever we go.

Be kind, for everyone you meet is struggling in some way. —Plato

It is not just our own personal happiness that we seek, but also the happiness of everyone. Dedicating our practice to the welfare and happiness of others purifies our desires by lifting us above our self-absorbed motives and intentions. Surprisingly, happiness comes as a gift when we do not seek it selfishly. By helping others to be happy, we find that happiness emerges spontaneously in our own heart.

Thousands of candles can be lit from a single candle, and the life of the candle will not be shortened. Happiness never decreases by being shared. —Gautama Buddha

Transformation of the World

The change from Night to Day is taking place in the following sequence: It has already begun in the profoundest recesses of the World of the Ultimate Mystery, from whence it has spread to the spiritual world and will eventually spread to the material world. —Repent, for the End of Night Is at Hand. ET

As a species, our consciousness does not seem to have evolved very far. We continue to do terrible things to each other, as well as to our environment. During the past century, in particular, through modern weapons, the level of death and destruction has increased. The collective effects of all this pain have accumulated in the spiritual world to such an extent that a great worldwide purification and transformation seems inevitable.

Nature moves in cycles—some large, some small, some fast, and some slow. There are cycles of day and night, of the moon, the four seasons, and birth and death. There are also much vaster cycles in God's plan, in which the heavenly bodies move in grand succession over eons. About this process, Meishusama writes, "Everything is in motion, perpetually following fixed criteria with absolute precision, and never an instance of delay." (*Atheism. HT*)

According to Meishusama, a long cosmic cycle of darkness is ending, and history is turning toward the dawn of a new 'Age of Light,' a world of crystalline clarity and harmony. It will be a time when the divine energy that permeates all things will begin to manifest throughout our physical world with increasing intensity. But, before this age can begin, a great cleansing and purification must occur. All that is hidden in darkness shall be exposed by Light and brought into alignment with it. About this, the philosopher Daniel Pinchbeck writes, "If the shadows appear to be getting darker, it's because the light that casts them is getting brighter."

Everything, from the largest galaxy to the smallest atom, is subject to the Law of Purification. This process of purification itself moves in cycles, and this approaching time of enormous change is the culmination of one grand cycle.

According to the Law of Spiritual Precedence, conditions in the spiritual world determine outcomes in the physical world. At dawn, on June 15, 1931, on the summit of Mt. Nokogiri, near Tokyo, Meishusama received a divine revelation that on that very day a New Age of Light had begun in the spiritual world, and that this New Age would eventually manifest on the physical plane.

The spiritual world has its own timetable. What seems a long time in the physical world might seem short in the spiritual world. Thus, how soon the effects of this change in the inner worlds will materialize in our daily lives is unpredictable. As each day passes, Divine Light becomes brighter in the spiritual realm, with a corresponding increase in its essence, the spirit of fire. Since 1931, the power of the Light has been steadily increasing in the outer world as well. The world's response to this increase has been massive purification through wars, revolutions, and other social upheavals. The intensified, purifying Light is now affecting everything, including the subjective dimension of our thoughts and emotions, as well as the objective world of matter and energy. Karma is accelerating, and we are beginning to experience the direct consequences of our thoughts and actions more quickly. When we lie, cheat, steal, or hurt others, a corresponding misfortune soon happens to us. What used to take months or years to manifest, now takes only weeks or days. Within this new environment, the only way to avoid the negative karma from past mistakes is to make amends for what you did and to change your behavior for the better.

The movement of every object is merely the result or reflection of the prior movement of its spiritual equivalent. The delay between the original spiritual movement and its eventual physical movement is decided by the size of the object in question. At the shortest, the delay is a matter of days; at the longest, the time can extend to several years. As the Age of Day approaches, however, this time-lag has been steadily decreasing, and has recently become remarkably short. The spiritual world is now in an unprecedented turmoil which mirrors the change to come, the change that will be the end of the world as it now exists. —*The Dominance of Evil Spirits. ET*

During this period of transformation, there may be cataclysmic changes, earthquakes, hurricanes, tidal waves, wildfires, droughts, tornadoes, blizzards and floods. Our civilization will suffer political turmoil, economic chaos, famine, and social dislocation. Every region of the world will be affected. Nothing will be exempt from radical change, as all of the negativity in the world is dredged up and cleansed. The corruption and lies that society is based upon will be exposed to public scrutiny. All of the suffering that this transformation causes will be part of the birth pangs of a new world. Throughout this turbulent time, many people will undergo personal transformation and spiritual awakening. The Light will shine on everyone and everything.

The Indian yogi, Paramahansa Yogananda, had similar ideas about human karma and environmental destruction. He wrote: "Nature evolves earthquakes, spitting volcanoes, and cataclysms through the accumulated wrong thoughts of men. These destructive thoughts distort the ether and throw the atomic and thermal combinations out of balance, creating natural disasters."

The extent of suffering that will occur during this transition depends upon the level of humanity's consciousness. Only those who have already been purified, both spiritually and physically, will be able to adjust to the higher frequencies entering our world. Meishusama said, "If one's spirit is pure, one can pass through this critical time with ease, no matter what form it takes." (*The Last Judgment. MK1*) Many may become ill, mentally unbalanced, or perish. The Native American Lakota medicine man, Wallace Black Elk, declared that, "In the turn of the next great cycle the sun will produce a 'fire' so powerful that it will burn the souls of the impure but the pure souls will not feel this fire." This is why Meishusama was given Jyorei to share with the world at this point in history: to help as many people as possible to successfully make this transition. People who hold peace and love in their hearts, and are genuinely concerned about the

125

welfare of others, will help to usher in this great transformation from Night into Day, and will remain relatively unharmed by much of the suffering that occurs around them.

The great changes that result will be completely unprecedented in the history of the universe. There will be destruction and creation on a scale that has never been experienced before as the corruption of the spiritual world is swept away and all is made clean. This change will inevitably be manifested faithfully and completely in our everyday world and the transformation that it will cause is beyond imagination. —*Repent, for the End of Night Is at Hand.* *ET*

Meishusama was not alone in predicting this change. Ancient myths, scriptures, and oral teachings from throughout the world have prophesized this approaching time. The Bible warns of the apocalyptic end times, followed by the Second Coming of Christ and the establishment of God's kingdom on earth. Hindu scriptures predict the ending of this current dark age, called the Kali Yuga, to be followed by the great golden age of the Satya Yuga. The elders of the Hopi tribe of northern Arizona warn us that we are now in the midst of the "Great Purification" long predicted in their oral tradition. The calculations from the Mayan calendar indicate that the world will soon enter into a higher dimension, called "The World of the Fifth Sun." Details differ from one source to another, but they agree that an approaching great purification will be followed by a golden age.

According to Subir K. Banerjee of the University of Minnesota, the earth's magnetic field has lost up to half its intensity in the last 4000 years due to a slowing of the planet's rotation.[10] Paralleling this, the earth's background base frequency, known as the Schuman Resonance Frequency, is rapidly rising from its traditional level of 7.83 hertz to much higher levels. Geologist and computer scientist Gregg Braden, in his book *Awakening to Zero Point*, suspects that this increase of frequency might be responsible for the feeling many of us have that time is speeding up. He also claims that we are experiencing an intensification of our emotions and increased difficulty remembering things because our emotional body and memory are closely connected with the Earth's magnetic field. Braden predicts that when the lessening magnetic field strength reaches zero, and the earth's base frequency reaches 13 hertz, there will be a magnetic pole shift and

10. National Geophysical Data Center (NGDC): http:// www.ngdc.noaa.gov/geomag/paleo.shtml

a reversal of the planet's rotation, which will cause extreme weather conditions, earthquakes, and social unrest.

According to Meishusama, God works out His divine plan through people. The prophesied changes will happen, but our attitudes and actions will determine how mild or harsh they will be. Therefore, each of us plays an important part in helping to usher in this new world. Each of us can promote peace in our environment and harmony with our neighbors. Together, we can usher in this Age of Light through serving God and humanity.

Meishusama was a modern prophet whose goal was to help all of humanity. He was not just promoting inner growth and healing, but also perfection of the world around us. To his mind, the inner and outer are inseparable. For that reason, he dedicated himself to healing and transforming not only individuals, but also society and the environment. People's hearts must be purified of selfishness and malice. Society must learn to take care of everyone, even those who are disliked. Government, business, culture, medicine, education, religion, and ethics—all must align themselves with higher values and principles. The earth, water, and air must be purified of pollution. The fulfillment of this ideal will coincide with a dramatic rise in humanity's spiritual level.

The world of man will end as the first buds of God's world shoot forth.

—Last Judgment. MK1

The coming Age of Day will accompany a new enlightenment within humanity's consciousness. Those who survive will have been purified and transformed in body and soul. Meishusama prophesied that even the material substance of the world will be transmuted into something resembling translucent crystal, rather than the dense, opaque matter we see today. The world that survives these changes will be permeated with Divine Light—and will literally be a "World of Light." This will be an age when people learn to honor and appreciate their individual differences, rather than feel threatened by them. Individual actions will be motivated more by generosity and kindness rather than greed and spite. Humankind stands on the threshold of a profound awakening, the dawning of a Paradise on Earth, and the fulfillment of humanity's long-held dream of universal brotherhood and peace.

After thousands of years of waiting, God's plan is now being fulfilled.

—God's Plan. MK2

127

Truth, Goodness, and Beauty

The ultimate aim of God is the creation of an ideal world of truth, goodness, and beauty, as all members of our organization well know. The aim of the devil is the complete opposite, and this is starkly obvious; it is to incite falseness, vice, and ugliness. I scarcely need to explain the nature of falseness and vice for these two foul things are well enough known to everybody. —Heaven Is a World of Beauty. ET

Meishusama's goal was to create a world embodying the primary values of truth, goodness, and beauty. These three values, championed by Plato over two thousand years ago, now characterize branches of Western Philosophy concerned with metaphysics, ethics, and aesthetics, respectively. Truth, goodness, and beauty are considered the core values from which all other values are derived, similar to the way all colors can be produced from the three primary colors of red, yellow and blue. This makes these three values fundamental to all qualities.

On an individual level, truth engages the mind; goodness, the will; and beauty, the senses. One discovers truth in facts and logic, as well as through self-introspection; one develops goodness through dispassionately serving others as well as the greater good; and one cultivates beauty through studying the arts and spending time in nature.

A person's character is made up of three critical components: thoughts, words, and deeds. Thoughts are subjective because only the thinker can perceive them. Actions are objective because others can observe them. Words, however, are "inter-subjective" because they are what we use to communicate our subjective thoughts to others through the use of speech and written text. When purified and developed to the highest level, our thoughts, words, and deeds can become significant vehicles for helping to transform the world into an ideal place embodying the values of truth, goodness, and beauty.

The ideals which have lighted my way, and time after time have given me new courage to face life cheerfully, have been Kindness, Beauty, and Truth.

—Albert Einstein

Truth

The fact that people become ill indicates that they have strayed from the Truth in some way; and the same is true for why they cannot be cured. The corruption of politics, the decadence of ideas, the increase in crime, the distress caused by tight money, inflation and deflation—all of these are caused by straying from the Truth. If we do not stray from the Truth, things will go as we wish. This is how God created the world. A society of Goodness and Beauty will be born, and humans will be able to live joyful and fortunate lives. In other words, the paradise on earth of which I speak will become reality. —The Embodiment of Truth. ET

Truth has many levels. At the highest level, Truth is the spiritual dimension that is experienced by mystics, saints, and seers. It is not an idea, but a non-verbal experience. This truth is the primary concern of theology and metaphysics. Truth, on a more mundane level, relates to the mental disciplines of logic and mathematics, and to the physical world of the material sciences. Although the highest spiritual Truth is eternal and unchangeable, its verbal expression in the world is subject to change in accordance with current cultural values, religious ideas, and philosophical theories.

On a personal level, truth is expressed through words that are honest and accurate. To be truthful includes accepting responsibility for our mistakes, not pretending to be someone we are not, and being frank about our thoughts and feelings even when expressing them may be socially dangerous. Truth is about recognizing facts and expressing them simply and clearly.

Beyond a doubt, truth bears the same relation to falsehood as light to darkness.

—Leonardo da Vinci

The opposite of truth, which is falsity, is the cause of much suffering in the world. On a personal level, self-deception (lying to oneself) contributes to most of the psychological problems we see today. The lies that we tell ourselves torture our minds and lead to errors in our behavior. Similarly, relationships based on deceit are doomed to fail. About this, Meishusama said, "To foster honesty in others, discard your own lies." (*Honesty. MK2*) Not surprisingly, most psychotherapy is concerned with helping people to become more honest with themselves and with others. Honesty and sincerity are crucial for the development of individual maturity and for maintaining healthy relationships.

In a time of universal deceit, telling the truth becomes a revolutionary act.

—George Orwell

Meishusama says that the world is suffering from "a culture of external forms," a world enamored by false glamour and obsessed with status. Recognizing what is truly important amidst a confusing swarm of stimuli is the basis for wisdom and inner peace.

Ultimate Truth is the direct knowledge of God. The more we perceive the spiritual reality within ourselves, the more we perceive it everywhere else: in people's hearts, in nature, in beauty. This is both seeing and living Truth on the deepest level, beyond the scope of the mind with its endless chatter. This spiritual reality is the meaning of Meishusama's expression, "the point within the circle." In a human being, this point is the indwelling spirit, the divine spark within each of us.

Relative truth, however, is more concrete and obvious than ultimate truth because it refers to objective facts that can be verified. One can easily look outside to see if it is raining, taste soup to see if it is hot, or listen to hear if people are talking in the next room. Relative truth lies within the jurisdiction of common sense and can be accurately measured. When a statement correlates with the facts, we say that the statement is true.

How refreshing it is to hear a person say white is white. —Honesty. MK2

According to Meishusama, nature itself is Truth—not an abstract truth, but a truth that is both felt and visible to those who are observant. He says, "In order to understand the world, to find the answer to the deepest problems, you usually need to do no more than look closely at nature." (*Impasse. ET*)

The natural world can manage itself without the need for outside intervention. Nature rejuvenates itself from within. All of creation is spontaneously evolving toward greater complexity, care, and intelligence. The wisdom of nature is vast and impersonal, yet nurtures the growth of countless life forms, each with their own unique individuality. Nature reveals a higher Truth not based on rationality or logic. When one seeks inner peace, one can benefit greatly from visiting nature where there is silence, tranquility, and beauty. When in nature, it is much easier for us to find these same qualities within ourselves.

If the pure truth had been expounded upon, human society would not be troubled by so much deep suffering as we see today." —The Embodiment of Truth. ET

Goodness

To become a person with a pure spirit, you must do good deeds and increase your accumulation of virtue even though it requires a fair amount of time and self-sacrifice. However, there is a way to raise your soul's rank in the spiritual world immediately by tens of strata. —*The Strata in the Spiritual World. ET*

Goodness is an inner quality that is revealed by our actions. It relates to morals, ethics, justice, and common standards of right and wrong. Although morality and social standards vary significantly from one society to another, some universal agreement is necessary for cooperation and harmony among peoples of the world. We can find this in such universally valued qualities as kindness, generosity, courage, modesty, honesty, and loyalty. The golden rule, "treat others as you would have them treat you," is a universal guideline for ethical behavior. To do this well requires us to place ourselves in other people's shoes and see the world through their eyes.

Goodness is action that does no harm, and that benefits others as well as ourselves. It is selfless action that contributes to the common good. Concerning goodness, Meishusama says: "Virtuous behavior is actually enjoyable. Anyone, even if he is a prominent figure in society, can and should find pleasure in avoiding the snares of dubious entertainment and vice, while spending any spare money he has toward the welfare of society, performing virtuous acts, helping those in need, turning to God, and sometimes taking his family out to the cinema, theater, or on a trip." (*The Enjoyment of Virtue. ET*) One can imagine Meishusama adding that last phrase as a humorous twist to the more lofty sentiments expressed in the earlier part of the sentence. Always advising moderation and pragmatic values, he was therefore quite sincere about suggesting recreational family pastimes.

Meishusama describes vice as, "… lying, making others suffer, and creating problems and troubles in society. The fact is, however, that far too many people care only about themselves and act without giving a thought to the problems and interests of others. This is the worst possible kind of behavior and will never find favor with God. *(To Be Loved by God. ET)*

Greed and selfishness originate from want: want of love, want of security, or lack of self-worth. A person emotionally wounded by others often internalizes his or her pain and wants to hurt others in retaliation. As the wounds accumulate, this person may become driven by anger to take revenge against all of society. Many of the criminals, who prey on others through robbery, assault, or murder, were themselves once victims of emotional or physical violence. Thus, anger breeds more anger, and violence breeds more violence.

Returning hate for hate multiplies hate, adding deeper darkness to a night already devoid of stars. Darkness cannot drive out darkness; only light can do that. Hate cannot drive out hate, only love can do that. —Martin Luther King Jr.

The only way out of this vicious cycle of pain and more pain is to make a radical break from the past and to begin acting in ways that alleviate suffering and promote happiness in others. Helping others is the essential foundation for virtuous action, and it results in greater personal happiness for both the giver and the receiver. Unfortunately, this profoundly simple formula is often ignored in our obsessive pursuit of meaningless and superficial activities.

Each time we act for the benefit of others, we accumulate virtue and our level of happiness increases. As Thomas Jefferson, a founding father of the United States of America said, "Happiness is the aim of life but virtue is the foundation of happiness."

There is no need to wait for our reward in some distant future, because with each act of charity our character improves. The truest virtue occurs when we do good without any concern for self-gain, and surrender the outcome of that deed to God. When doing so, our intentions are as important as the deeds themselves. Furthermore, acting with a gentle and loving heart produces the best outcome and is also the most rewarding to both giver and receiver. All acts of kindness and goodwill move us up in the spiritual world.

Although virtuous actions bring us closer to the Divine, there may be the possibility of acquiring salvation through grace, which does not depend upon our actions, and is unearned. The Supreme Being is full of mercy and love. The joy resulting from spiritual emancipation is the product of both good works and grace, each benefiting the other. Good behavior makes us more receptive to grace, which uplifts our spirit and thus promotes even more good behavior.

As to salvation, I would like to make it clear that true salvation of spirit cannot be brought about by humans. It is God who acts on this, and humans are mere instruments to assist Him. However, being allowed to work as one of God's instruments is truly a blessed thing. —Judge Not. KW

Beauty

The purpose of art is the elevation of the human spirit. —Meishusama

Beauty occurs when the balance and perfection existing at the highest levels of the spiritual world are expressed in the physical world through nature or art. The spiritual world, in all its varied dimensions, permeates our ordinary world, both including and transcending it. A great artist often obtains a heightened experience of reality in which the ordinary world is perceived in an extraordinary way, with greater sensitivity, depth, and appreciation. Using their knowledge, skill, and experience, artists are able to communicate this glimpse of the spirit in the physical world through music, painting, writing, and other artistic forms.

Art is the language of the heart; that is, the language of the emotional structures.
—Margaret Mead (Anthropologist)

If the artist is receptive, he or she may receive inspiration from the heights of the spiritual world. Sometimes higher beings, such as guardian spirits, may provide assistance. However, Spirit is the true source of all great art and intellectual discovery. It falls upon the artist to capture this inspiration and then translate it into works of art. About this, Meishusama writes, "When an artist is working creatively or when an inventor is trying to solve a problem, they often get ideas in what we call 'a flash of inspiration.' This is, of course, guidance provided by their guardian spirits." (*Guardian Spirits. ET*)

For a work of art to express beauty, it must contain balance, harmony, and proportion. It must also express passion, either mild or exuberant. Such art also needs unity, in which all of its various elements relate to the greater whole in which nothing is out of place or superfluous. Finally, art needs Spirit, which cannot be defined or measured, only felt.

While experiencing great art, if one is sufficiently perceptive, one will receive a glimpse of the Divine world, a world of timeless beauty and radiant Light, which brings feelings of peace, harmony, and joy. Art, like love, accepts all. Like love, it reveals the Light shining beneath the surface of all things. It is not just the world of the spirit that engages art, but also the textures, shapes, colors, rhythms, and sounds of the world around us. Art embraces the senses as well as the imagination. It is both rational and irrational. More than anything else, art demonstrates the essential unity of matter and Spirit, of passion and purpose, and of form and formlessness. By reconciling these and other dualities, art heals. It makes whole that which is fractured.

All forms of beauty, like all possible phenomena, contain an element of the eternal and an element of the transitory—of the absolute and of the particular.
—Charles Baudelaire

Nature is Spirit made manifest. It the formless becoming form. Taken as a whole, the natural world is without ego or artificial contrivance. It is God's artwork expressed in mountains, rivers, flowers, trees, oceans, and sky. Seeing the majestic Himalayan Mountains, the serene Pacific Ocean at sunset, or the multicolored Aurora Borealis in the northern sky, can be life changing. Nature's art is mostly asymmetrical, non-regimented, and non-repetitive, as can be seen in the patterns of flowing water, meandering smoke, drifting clouds, and grains of wood. The world of nature is more wiggly than straight. In nature, no two flowers are exactly the same, nor are two ocean waves, nor two frogs. Although oftentimes two or more of these may look similar, each is unique in a number of ways. Nature's beauty incorporates both individuality and universality. Each and every thing, although part of larger groups of things, has its own color, shape, movement, or sound. Nature, although inwardly still, is wild and exuberant in its many expressions. About this Meishusama comments, "Again, a flower, a leaf, the beauties of natural scenery, and every living thing from beasts, birds and fish to the last tiny insect - all show the wonders of God's works. And who can fail to marvel at them?" (*The Truth about Health, God's Way to Health. ET*)

Beauty is certainly a soft, smooth, slippery thing, and therefore of a nature which easily slips in and permeates our souls. —Plato

Practicing Truth, Goodness, and Beauty

The true, the good, and the beautiful are not just things to understand and idealize; they are also things to practice. And there are inward and outward ways to do so for each of these values.

Studying philosophy, science, and spirituality can lead one to deeper truths about reality. Also, looking within can lead one to valuable insights into one's suppressed emotions, hidden motives, and unrealized potential, as well as the divine presence at the core of one's being. An outward practice of truth would be to teach others, as teaching is one of the best ways to deepen one's knowledge and understanding of the wisdom one has learned. Another outward practice is to speak out and defend truth, justice, and fairness in one's home, workplace, community, and the world at large when needed.

Cultivating positive thoughts, harmonious feelings, and good intentions are inward ways of practicing goodness. Praying, meditating, chanting, and contemplation are other ways to inwardly connect with goodness. Whereas serving others with kindness and compassion is an outward way of practicing goodness. Ideally, such service should be done without attachment to end results, but instead by surrendering the outcome to God, trusting the Divine to handle everything perfectly.

Exposing oneself to beautiful works of art and music and spending time in nature are good ways to deepen one's capacity for appreciating beauty. While doing so, it is helpful to notice which elements within art and nature attract one the most, and then analyze why. Expressing oneself through playing music, singing, painting, drawing, sculpting, dancing, or acting are outward ways of practicing beauty.

Inner and outer go together like two ends of a pole. You can't have one without the other. To recognize truth is to want to share it; to appreciate beauty is to want to express it; and to experience goodness is to want to become like it. These are natural human tendencies. By practicing these universal values, both inwardly and outwardly, we align ourselves with the natural rhythms of life, such as those of giving and receiving, working and resting, and inhaling and exhaling. It is hard to be spiritually healthy without contributing to others, just as it is hard to be spiritually healthy without experiencing a meaningful inner life. Both are necessary to fully embody the qualities of truth, goodness, and beauty.

Interrelated Values

Meishusama often created hanging scrolls with the three Chinese calligraphy characters for truth, goodness, and beauty painted on them. A person looking at these scrolls once asked him, "Why don't you include the word 'love' in the calligraphy?" Meishusama responded by explaining, "Love comes from God. As long as truth, goodness, and beauty are fully present, then love will naturally be present there, too." So, in other words, there was no need to add love to the list because it, like many other spiritual qualities, is secondary to these primary values. All other values or qualities are embraced by truth, goodness, and beauty.

Love is a very significant quality. However, for love to be spiritual, it must be true, good, and beautiful—not false, abusive, or ugly. Love has many levels, ranging from selfish to selfless, from partial to universal, and from conditional to unconditional. The lower forms of love do not qualify as transcendent values. Only the highest form of love can be considered truly transcendent and spiritual.

The true, the good, and the beautiful are interrelated. To choose truth over falseness, and to prefer beauty to ugliness, is good. Similarly, to discover the truth about things is good because it leads to wisdom. Selflessly serving the greater good is not only good, but is also beautiful and aligned with truth. When one's actions are graceful and beautiful, they are also good and true. Meishusama described truth as "the way," goodness as "the deed," and beauty as "the heart."

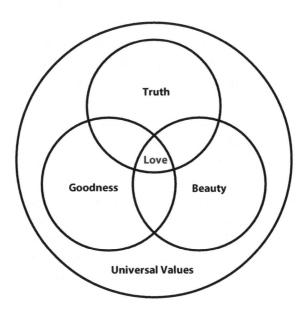

Although human civilization may at times appear to move backwards, the general trend is actually forward and upward. We admire those who demonstrate noble qualities such as love, kindness, honesty, elegance, courage, intelligence, fairness, and modesty in their behavior or outward creations because these qualities are inherently attractive. They are expressions of the core values of truth, goodness, and beauty. We all have, at some level or other, rational, moral, and aesthetic aspirations. Over time, these aspirations will inevitably drive evolution forward, both personally and collectively, as well as physically and spiritually. The path of evolution will be toward increasingly higher expressions of truth, goodness, and beauty. These values are the best standards by which to judge our progress because they are valid at all times and on all levels. Indeed, they are leading us to no less than the "World of Light." And whether we know it or not, each of us has a significant role to play in this cosmic drama of ascension.

CHAPTER 8

LIVING A SPIRITUAL LIFE

God is both immanent and transcendent. God exists within everything, and everything exists within God. The whole is within the part, and the part is within the whole. This paradoxical and seemingly dualistic nature of God is called Miroku Omikami. Miroku Omikami is that which encompasses everything. The apparent presence of opposites in the nature of God is due only to the limitations of imagination and logic, both of which cannot grasp undivided Oneness. In the spiritual life, this Oneness has the attributes of harmony and balance.

The Purpose of Life

Meishusama always cared for balance, which could be seen in both his lifestyle and in his published teachings. His great effort to elevate human souls was balanced by his natural gift for enjoying the simple pleasures in life. Rather than separating these two activities, he cultivated both simultaneously. Each supported the other, because by helping others to grow spiritually, he became happier, and by radiating happiness, he was able to draw more people to himself and thereby influence them in a positive way.

Live for today as if you will live forever and for eternity as if you will die tomorrow.
—Ibn Khaldoun (Medieval Arab Historian)

The ultimate and the immediate are not separate, but are actually one undivided whole. A delicate flower growing beside a road, a raindrop splashing on a pond, a ray of sunlight shining through clouds—all of these can reveal God's presence if a person's mind is absolutely quiet and his or her heart is sufficiently open. God, when viewed as the transcendental reality beyond this world of ignorance and suffering, can best be approached through gradual purification and elevation of the soul; whereas God, when viewed as the immanent reality existing within this world of time and space, can best be approached by living fully in the here and now, with love and gratitude.

Consequently, from Meishusama's perspective, life has not one, but actually two overriding purposes: the spiritual development of the soul, and the simple enjoyment of the present moment. One may appear distant and the other close, yet happiness and enjoyment depend, to varying degrees, upon both the sacred and the secular. Two things contribute to our sense of happiness: the soul's spiritual purity, and the amount of peace and harmony in one's surrounding environment. In the joy that comes from experiencing beauty, both the inner and the outer come together, because outer beauty can only be appreciated to the extent that one is inwardly capable of perceiving it. Thus, the higher our spiritual level, the more we live in a world of beauty.

Each of us also has two primary tasks in life: to learn to love self and others completely and unconditionally, and to help create Heaven on Earth. The first is what we must feel, and the second is what we must do. These two soul tasks support the attainment of our two life purposes because each of them helps us to grow spiritually and each contributes to our overall enjoyment and happiness in our day-to-day lives.

Spiritual Growth

The spiritual clouds that cover our soul are the chief cause of suffering. These clouds not only darken and distort our experience, but also strongly influence the conditions and circumstances of our daily life. The more we eliminate spiritual clouds and elevate our soul, the more capable we will be of enjoying the simple, ordinary things in life. "Therefore to become happy and fortunate you must make all possible efforts to purify your soul and make it light so that it reaches the highest level possible. There is absolutely no other way. As stated earlier, Jyorei purifies your soul and raises your spiritual level. This is the great significance of Jyorei," writes Meishusama. *(Jyorei and Happiness. ET)*

Through the experiences of many lifetimes, each individual soul goes through various stages of purification, accumulates wisdom, and gradually progresses toward final union with God—that loving Presence which is our ultimate source and fulfillment. Activities that create spiritual clouds, that create impurities in the body or soul, contribute to both current and future suffering. Because happiness is dependent on our spiritual level, our leisure activities should also support spiritual growth, or at least not detract from it.

Put simply, the purpose of life is happiness, and this happiness is synonymous with the inner peace and radiance that comes from a life attuned to Spirit. Despite popular opinion, happiness does not come from the pursuit of selfish preoccupations. Rather, happiness results from making a meaningful contribution to others. This is why, in the Bible, Jesus Christ says, "It is better to give than to receive." A friendly concern for others that translates into concrete action helps the soul progress upwards in the spiritual world. Through service to others we receive Toku Energy (spiritual merit), which fosters refinement of character.

Each soul evolves in its own unique way during its journey through life. The further the soul progresses on its journey, the purer it becomes. By purifying oneself, one also contributes to the purification of the world by radiating more Light to others.

God gives each individual a unique mission in this world. He gives them special characteristics and special talents. He gives them physical existence and takes it away again, and He makes us all move ever forward toward the ideal object of Eternity. Good and evil, war and peace, destruction and creation—all of these are processes necessary to this ongoing evolution.

—The Strata in the Spiritual World. ET

Enjoyment

The saints of ancient days wrapped themselves in sackcloth, but I do not.

—Art. MK1

Although spiritual growth determines our capacity for true happiness, by itself it is incomplete. If spiritual realization were the only purpose of life, we would then be encouraged to devalue pleasure as no more than a meaningless distraction from that pursuit. This point of view promotes an ascetic lifestyle that rejects the pleasures of the world, including people, art, food, and nature. This ascetic attitude differs from Meishusama's way because it lacks love, joy, and beauty.

> People commonly believe that there is no spiritual practice without tremendously painful efforts. But I disagree with putting such emphasis on the severity of the practice. The purpose of spiritual practice is not to seek

140

harshness in life, but to find a way to make our life easier. It aims to improve one's spiritual condition. This is the most essential thing that I would like you to understand, and with this understanding, continue in your practice. —*Meishusama, The Izunome Principle and Love. KW*

Meishusama was a gregarious man who experienced life to the fullest. He did not view life as a problem to be solved, but rather as a gift from nature to be enjoyed and appreciated. Meishusama was well-known for his infectious sense of humor. He had a gift for sharing delight in the comic absurdity often found within ordinary circumstances and events. Meishusama loved going to the movies, dining out with friends, gardening, visiting art museums, and attending concerts. Rather than overly dwelling on the rampant sin and corruption of the world, he preferred to enjoy the good things in it. Meishusama wanted to transform and redeem the world. *More than anything else, he wanted people to be happy.*

Those with faith should be filled with jubilation, which will allow them to fully appreciate such things as beautiful flowers and trees, carefree birds with their myriad songs, gentle breezes, distant rolling hills, and the pale glow of the moon. Such beauty is made by God to please and comfort humankind. —The Glory of Faith. ET

Desire and Oneness

To be human is to be driven by desire. Some desires are primal, such as the need for food and shelter, some are instinctual, such as the urge for sex or physical pleasure, and some are ambitious, such as goals for fame and fortune. But what all desires have in common is that they constantly compel us to seek fulfillment in the future, while ignoring the here and now. Because of this, the present moment always feels incomplete and unsatisfying. Big houses, new cars, good jobs, soul mates, long vacations, and stylish clothes—these things may bring a degree of happiness, but such happiness is usually only short-lived. We may become temporarily happy after acquiring these things, but soon enough, new desires will emerge, and we will then return to seeking new things. This is why worldly things, although enjoyable, are not sufficient for creating happiness that endures.

When we obtain the things we want, our desires tend to subside, and we become contented and peaceful for a while. But it was really the lack of desire that made us happy, not the outer thing that we obtained. Unfortunately though, when new desires emerge, we go back to being dissatisfied again.

Deep down, what all of us really seek is to become free of division, because all division (both inner and outer forms of it) causes alienation, fear, and conflict. These feelings are the underlying cause of desire. They cause us to desire positive feelings, which at their deepest source, originate from unity—not division. This is why worldly objects do not bring lasting happiness. They do not satisfy our deepest need, which is to experience a state of inner Oneness with all that is; a state in which there is no underlying division, only unqualified unity. Most of us are not conscious that this is what we are really seeking, but if we investigate deeply, it will become self-evident to us. Only when this most fundamental desire is fulfilled—the desire for unity and love—will we be truly happy.

The first peace, which is the most important, is that which comes within the souls of people when they realize their relationship, their Oneness with the universe and all its powers, and when they realize that at the center of the universe dwells the Great Spirit, and that this center is really everywhere. It is within each of us.

—*Black Elk (Lakota Medicine Man)*

The Present Moment

The ability to be in the present moment is a major component of mental wellness.

—*Abraham Maslow (Psychologist)*

By staying focused on the present, we move closer to this state of unqualified happiness. The pleasant company of family and friends, a meal of delicious food, an arrangement of beautiful flowers, and the rich sound of a live concert: these are not experiences to be dutifully endured as a means toward an end. Rather, we experience these things joyfully for their own sake, for it is the nature of joy to be fully satisfied with the present moment.

Although we encourage everyone to help create a perfect world, when this perfect world finally arrives, then what will we all do? Should we continue to search and strive for perfection? But when the world is finally perfect, there will not be anyone left in need of saving, or anything left to improve. The only thing left to do will be to relax and enjoy life. It will finally be time to celebrate!

But we do not need to wait until then to celebrate. Maybe we should start celebrating here and now instead of postponing it until later, because how can we promote joy and happiness in the future if we do not feel it in this very moment? It is hard to make others happy if we ourselves are miserable. Only joy creates more joy, just as only love creates more love.

Although purification and self-cultivation are essential for our spiritual growth, we can also grow spiritually from living joyfully in the present moment in playful activity—activity done without ulterior motives or future objectives. To be fully present, the mind must become very quiet and alert, rather than preoccupied with thoughts about the past and future. Meishusama called this the "instantaneous self," Henry Bergson's term for a state of mind that reacts immediately and intelligently to whatever arises in the moment.

Need there be a purpose to love, kindness, joy, or beauty? Is there a reason or objective to the innocent delight of a child's play? Where is the enjoyment in dancing if a goal is attached? The simple pleasure of immediate experience is often its own reward.

Everything has beauty, but not everyone sees it. —Confucius

Using activities or people merely to fulfill an objective—even a spiritual objective—is unwise. Nobody likes being treated as an object, because when we objectify people, we deny them their humanity. Similarly, to objectify our own life, or to regard our experiences as mere stepping-stones to a distant, abstract goal, is to not live fully in the here and now. Instead, it is a life lived in perpetual anticipation of the future, rather than in relaxed enjoyment of the present moment. Obsession with the future distracts us from the eternal silence that exists, unnoticed, within the present moment. This is the window through which God's Grace enters our life.

A Balanced Life

On the other hand, if mere enjoyment were the only purpose for living, then there would be no meaning or justification for higher principles. All values would have secondary importance in comparison to momentary pleasure. Kindness, loyalty, honesty, generosity, altruism, fairness, and many other human virtues would have value only because they are pleasant, not because they reflect something higher. For most people, the pursuit of pleasure would become their overriding concern.

But eventually hedonism can become empty and meaningless, not to mention exhausting. Plus, our attraction to pleasure always coincides with an aversion to pain. They go hand in hand. And since no one can control everything, then none of us can avoid experiences that cause pain. Each of us will inevitably experience suffering in one form or another during our lifetime.

However much we enjoy life, the fact remains that everything decays and falls apart eventually, including the things that give us pleasure. We all get sick and die, as well. This means that our pleasure and enjoyment will also end at some time or other, and we will then be left with nothing, not even a life purpose. This leads to inevitable frustration and suffering, rather than enjoyment.

Based on the above analysis, it should be clear that the simple pursuit of pleasure will not lead to lasting happiness. Spiritual growth needs to be added to the pursuit of pleasure in order to give life greater depth and lasting fulfillment.

These complementary life purposes, spiritual growth and simple enjoyment in the present moment, are mutually supportive. The greater the purity of our spirit, the more capable we are of being present in the here and now, and of appreciating all the beauty that is around us. Equally true is that the more capable we are of enjoying the present moment, the more we can learn and grow, and thus progress further in our spiritual development.

Only a balanced pursuit of both spiritual growth and enjoyment of the present moment can create true happiness. This balanced and moderate way of life is referred to as "Kannon's Way."

Nowadays, everything is out of balance. This includes not only the state of the world, but also that of individuals. And once balance is lost, the situation quickly leads to a dead end. On the other hand, if you remain balanced, you will do well.
—A Balanced Approach. KW

Attachment and Faith

Suffering is subdued and dispelled by putting everything in the hands of God.
—Signs of Divine Mercy. MK1

We grasp at pleasure, while running from pain. This leaves us at the mercy of change. There is no security in this way of living because everything is unpredictable. That which brings us joy today may be gone tomorrow, including our family, our friends, and even our own physical body. Everyone dies eventually. Therefore, to depend solely on transitory things for happiness guarantees suffering.

Most suffering is not caused by the actual circumstances we encounter, but by our mind. By insisting that life conform to our personal desires—our attachments—we set ourselves up for frustration, anger, and depression. In reality, life does not usually turn out exactly the way we hope. Sometimes it is better, sometimes worse. The more we cling to personal desires, the more we suffer from anxiety about the future and regret over the past.

Attachment is the underlying cause of much bitter strife and suffering visited on other people and on themselves. —Self-will and Attachment. ET

Usually our desires are driven by blind momentum, not wisdom. Sometimes our desires seek to fulfill authentic needs, other times they chase whim and fancy. Most of us have experienced times when following desires has led to disappointment and disaster. Sometimes it may be better not to get what we want.

Part of the problem is the assumption that the world is a dangerous place, full of chaos and accidents, devoid of meaning and purpose. In such a bleak world, it seems we have no choice but to struggle desperately for survival and security.

Meishusama counters this materialistic view of life by teaching that the physical dimension is only a field of effects, not causes, and that the true cause of everything is found in the spiritual world. Looking inside our minds, we will discover that everything we experience originates in our own consciousness. Nothing exists until it registers in our consciousness as a perception, thought, feeling, sensation, or intention. Our inner experience is the subjective aspect of the spiritual world and; our outer experience is the objective aspect of the spiritual world. If we do not experience something, at least hear or read about something, how do we know it exists? This question is mirrored in the Zen Buddhist "koan" or riddle: "If a tree falls in a forest and nobody is there to hear it, does it make a sound?" Everything starts with our experience. To an extent, we create our own reality by what we experience and how we interpret it. We then draw those things to us that energetically resonate with what we hold within our consciousness. Thus, the nonphysical dimension is the cause, and the physical is the effect.

Whatever you believe in intensely, your mind will materialize.
—Paramahansa Yogananda

The universe is not composed of blind forces acting upon inert matter. In reality, these forces and substances are but gross expressions of subtler realities that are not easily perceived by ordinary consciousness. Quantum physics reveals

145

that the universe is an endless ocean of particles invisible to our senses; that each particle is comprised of still-tinier particles; and that, at deeper levels, these particles are made up of pure energy. Similarly, Meishusama saw Spirit in all things. To him, the world was conscious and intelligent. The further we expand our own consciousness, the more we can perceive this conscious intelligence operating through all things: in ourselves, in others, and in all creation.

All the experiences and events in our lives have meaning, whether recognized or not. The world is fundamentally spiritual, although it may seem solid and stable when perceived by the senses. Everything is permeated by Light. Understanding this can transform cloudy skies of doubt and fear into the clear heaven of faith and trust. Instead of struggling with life, we cooperate with it. We begin to trust that life will do what is best, and will give us those experiences that are most appropriate for our spiritual growth and overall happiness.

Faith is different from belief, which is based on preconceptions. Many of us cling to various preconceived ideas and opinions for the security they offer. But hidden within these beliefs are seeds of doubt, whereas faith is free of doubt because it is based on trust in the unknown. To have faith is to let go and allow the universe to unfold in its own natural way. As Meishusama states, "The primary aim of spiritual practice must be to remove self-will and attachment from the hearts and minds of people." (*Self-will and Attachment. ET*) Not being attached to outcomes promotes inner peace, which gradually spreads outward to the world around us. Faith does not need to control life, but instead flows gracefully with the natural unfolding of events. "Thus, as the feelings of attachment are swept away, the spirit ascends higher and higher in the spiritual world." (*Self-will and Attachment. ET*)

Of course, this does not imply that we should be careless. Life is always full of challenges, so it is wise to be cautious. By preparing for the worst, we give ourselves the luxury of expecting the best. It is always good to save money, buckle our seatbelts, and to lock our doors at night. This frees us from worry, allowing us to meet whatever comes our way. Instead of blind faith, we should adopt pragmatic faith, which entails taking responsibility for the details in our lives. Humans were given intelligence in order to use it.

Faith is not unusual. To trust that we will continue to breathe throughout the night while sleeping is an act of faith. To trust the bank with our money, to trust our car to run safely, and to trust that water will pour from our faucets, are all acts of faith. Even trusting that the sun will come up each morning demonstrates faith. We could not function without trusting various things to operate correctly.

True faith encourages detachment from results, allowing us to live a more harmonious life. When we are inwardly detached, our behavior becomes relaxed rather than compulsive and stressful. Detachment should not be confused with apathy, which is motivated by resignation, fear, or laziness. Authentic detachment can express itself as either action or inaction, depending on circumstances. And, it is deep inner faith that supports this detachment.

I think that faith is the only possible way to help the world, which has lost and abandoned all its moral values. —Meishusama, Good and Evil. HT

There are times when circumstances require decisive action. However, if done with faith, this action will not come from closed-minded willfulness, but from open-minded awareness. We each need to do our part while trusting God to do the rest. Instead of doubt, we need faith. True faith puts us in alignment with the higher power that directs all things. We become agents of a higher will. However, even when we act with faith, there is no guarantee that events will turn out well (at least not according to our expectations). Regardless of the immediate outcome, we need faith that eventually all will be well. In other words, we turn the final results over to God. Meishusama says, "The key is to recognize that everything is in God's hands." (*On Removing Egotism and Worldly Attachments. KW*)

This is not simplistic 'positive thinking,' which artificially superimposes positive interpretations over negative experiences. Although a positive attitude is good, when taken to extremes, it can lead to mental blindness and the unwillingness to deal with the darker aspects of ourselves and others. With faith, however, we do not need to have an answer for everything, nor do we need for life to always go our way. We no longer demand that life conform to our personal agendas. Faith trusts that all is the way it should be, and that all is well.

To reach this state, you must have perfect trust in God, doing what you can as a mere mortal and leaving the rest up to the Divine. —The Glory of Faith. ET

Hoshi - Selfless Service

True happiness is found in helping others to be happy. —Common Sense. ET

Outwardly, at the level of physical form, we are each separate from one another, but inwardly, at the level of Spirit, we are all interconnected and part of a greater whole. The more clearly we recognize this greater whole, the more peace and well-being we experience. In particular, when our relationship to this larger totality is based on service, we align ourselves more closely with it. Each time we help someone to feel happier, all of us benefit.

Being of service to others is one of the most effective ways for us to discover genuine happiness within ourselves. In Shumei, this service is called hoshi. Volunteering to help our family, friends, coworkers, or neighbors with simple tasks is a good way to begin hoshi.

Hoshi is a selfless form of service in which we dedicate our efforts to a purpose larger than ourselves. Within Shumei, people perform hoshi in order to support the organization in its greater mission of serving humanity. Usually, hoshi consists of such ordinary tasks as sweeping, mopping, wiping, or scrubbing. It is kept simple, basic, and physical. When, as a form of hoshi, we physically clean something, we are simultaneously cleaning our soul, following the principle that the inner reflects the outer, and the outer reflects the inner. This is why hoshi emphasizes physical labor—often the simpler the better—because such action helps to purify those ingrained impulses and tendencies within us that lean toward selfish behavior. Hoshi, when done with sincerity, promotes a heart of giving.

Put the benefit of others before your own profit. —Faith Means to be Trusted. ET

When we give freely of our time and energy, we generate Toku Energy, which is the spiritual Light we receive from helping others. Toku Energy is the merit we earn from performing good deeds with an open heart. This energy brightens the aura, elevates the soul, and produces inner happiness. Actions performed with selfless intentions create an inner glow that attracts others and exerts a positive influence upon them. Toku Energy is also the basis for good luck (or good karma) because it acts like a magnet to draw positive things to us. Thus, the more Toku Energy we accumulate, the better will be our future success and good fortune. However, the best rewards come when we do not seek personal gain, but instead concern ourselves with how we can be of service to others.

To be of service to others does not necessarily require us to deny our own needs or to give up our enjoyment of life's simple pleasures. That may be true sometimes, but not always. Having fun is a healthy and natural thing to do. It fosters joy. And when we bring joy to others we find our own joy increasing as well. About service versus self-sacrifice, Meishusama says,

> Some might believe that thinking of others first leads to self–abnegation. However, though it might seem that way, what I am talking about is not self–sacrifice. Simply, the more you care for others, the more meaningful your life becomes and the more value it acquires. —*Izunome: The Movement of the Universe.* KW

Commenting even further about this, Meishusama writes,

> It is not right for one to be a sacrificial victim for the benefit of others, but it is also wrong for one to seek personal advantage by shoving others aside. The thing is, everyone's well-being should be taken into account. But you may wonder how this could be possible. And I say, "It is possible." Although ironic, to pursue one's own self-satisfaction can also help others. This is not at all difficult, so long as one remains considerate of others. People just have not noticed this fact yet. —*The Izunome Principle and Love.* KW

It is also possible to serve others in nonphysical ways. We can begin by treating people with simple courtesy and kindness. Cultivating a light and friendly attitude that brings comfort and joy to others is an outward expression of this kindness. And we should not forget to be kind to unkind people because they probably need it the most. By this simple practice, our heart begins to open, we rise to a higher spiritual level, and our capacity for kindness increases. As Mother Teresa once said, "We never know how much good a simple smile can do." *(The Joy in Loving)*

Eventually, as our desire to help others increases, our sensitivity to their inner needs increases as well. We begin to notice suffering that is not visible to the outer eye. And because of this, we become increasingly interested in helping those around us to feel better physically, mentally, and emotionally. We learn to answer rudeness with friendliness, selfishness with generosity, and hostility with kindness. We begin to radiate warmth and compassion to those in need of love, especially those who are the least lovable or who seem the least deserving. We begin to understand that they are often in great pain.

Only love can be divided endlessly, and still not diminish.

—*Anne Morrow Lindbergh*

People often help humanitarian organizations because collective efforts can assist humanity in ways that we, as solitary individuals, cannot. There is power in groups, and this power can be used for many good purposes. Spiritual organizations often engage in humanitarian work, and by dedicating their work to God, they elevate it to a higher level. They usually view their missions as ways of serving God. As Jesus said according to the Book of Matthew, "Truly I tell you, whatever you did for one of the least of these brothers and sisters of mine, you did for me."

Meishusama teaches that God has an objective: the evolution of the world into divine Light. So, the best way to serve God is by serving others, especially by doing whatever we can to help them grow spiritually. Each of us can become a humble servant of God by dedicating our lives to fulfilling the divine plan for the transformation and spiritual awakening of everyone.

Based on this understanding, hoshi can also be viewed as a way of helping a spiritual organization in its mission of spreading Light. Hoshi is a spiritual discipline, and is not to be engaged in casually, since it provides a practical path to become closer to God. It does this by helping us to transcend selfishness. We can practice hoshi by doing physical or mental labor or by donating money. Any form of voluntary service that is practical and helpful, no matter how prestigious or menial, can be considered hoshi when performed with the right attitude.

Hoshi should not be done for the sake of recognition or reward. That would make it self-serving rather than selfless. Usually it is more appropriate to give anonymously, without seeking credit for it. As Meishusama writes, "Flaunted virtue is false. Hidden virtue is true and reaches straight to God." (*Faith. MK2*) However, this does not require us to be secretive, because oftentimes in order to be effective, others need to know what we are doing.

My advice is that you do good without craving recognition. Perform good deeds even when people are not paying attention. God will return blessings to you many times greater than the value of your deeds. —On Being Humble and Flexible. KW

Hoshi serves both God and humanity. This natural balance between idealism and practicality bring both inspiration and effectiveness to the act of hoshi. No one knows what the final effects will be, and there is no need to know. What is important is that we do our best, while trusting in God to handle the final outcome. As stated by Krishna in the Hindu scripture, the Bhagavad-Gita, "Do your duty, always; but without attachment. That is how a man reaches ultimate Truth; by working without anxiety about results."

When we reach out to assist others with sincere intent, we become happier ourselves. If we perform hoshi with gratitude for the opportunity and privilege to serve God, then our soul will be filled with joy and our work will shine with excellence. Just be happy to serve. All hoshi, whether big or small, has value because it contributes to the greater good. It often comes as a surprise to people when they discover how much joy and camaraderie exists within volunteer groups. The volunteers are paid in self-satisfaction and happiness, not money. Selfless action purifies our spirit and opens us to the beneficial influences exerted by our guardian spirit. It also tends to liberate us from self-absorbed moods and preoccupations because the self is forgotten in the act of giving. Generosity reinforces a sense of abundance, whereas selfishness, by its very nature, is a miserable condition, whether we get what we want or not, because it arises from a belief in scarcity.

I slept and dreamt that life was joy. I awoke and saw that life was service. I acted, and behold, service was joy. —Rabindranath Tagore (Indian Poet)

We are naturally motivated to serve others when we see ourselves in them. As our consciousness expands to include others, we begin to find that their sorrow becomes our sorrow, and their happiness, our happiness. An unexpected benefit of this expansion of consciousness is that we now have more reasons and opportunities to be happy than we previously did when we were only looking out for ourselves. More and more, we find that when we help someone feel happier, we also feel a corresponding increase in happiness ourselves. As a result of this, we feel less isolated and cut off from others, and instead, feel more connected to them. This is why it is better to give than to receive—because giving is receiving. By acting generously, we find happiness, which is what each of us is fundamentally seeking. Therefore, pray to God to use you, body and soul, in service to the greater good. Holding this intention in your heart will re-order your priorities accordingly, and will gradually purify your being and lead to a state of undisturbed joy. Through selfless giving, we discover that, as the philosopher William James stated, "We are like islands in the sea, separate on the surface but connected in the deep."

In the conventional way of thinking, there is the role of the giver and the role of the receiver. But from a higher perspective, this and all other dualities fall away and there is only the transcendental Oneness of God, which includes all beings and all things in its all-encompassing totality. Thus, to serve others is to serve God, and to serve God is to serve one's very own self. From a higher perspective, there is no separation, but only unity. Everything partakes of God's love, which is the same love that can be found deep within one's own heart.

Living a life of selfless giving is the highest expression of hoshi. When this becomes constant, then all of our actions are forms of hoshi, because giving is now an established way of life. Like Kannon Bodhisattva herself, we have become a pure instrument through which God's wisdom and compassion can effectively manifest in the objective world.

Since receiving a new life, his eyes have become gentle, his face radiant and bright.
—Faith. MK1

The Instantaneous Self

A direct, undistorted perception [is] the only true perception, and this is a function of the instantaneous self. —Henri Bergson. ET

The natural world has a pattern, an order that varies constantly according to the seasons, the weather, and the time of day. The nature of this pattern is similar to the movement of water in a stream or the clouds in the sky. Although the natural world cannot be adequately defined in words, it is, however, possible to attune oneself to its nonverbal rhythms of ebb and flow by living fully in the moment.

Unlike man, nature is unselfconscious. It is devoid of anxiety about the future. Hawks, bears, and rabbits do not worry about tomorrow's meal or the following day's shelter. For them, to be concerned about immediate danger is enough. Beyond that, each day takes care of itself. They also do not concern themselves with what others think of them, and thus remain free of shame, guilt, and embarrassment.

Letting go of our preoccupations with the past or future gives us the clarity to respond appropriately to whatever challenges come our way. What works well one moment may not work well the next because each situation is different. Consequently, to apply an old solution to a new problem may be ineffective. Being in the present moment allows us to respond appropriately to whatever arises in our lives. Writes Meishusama, "The 'instantaneous self' is a state of consciousness that allows a person to react at the instant when he sees or hears something. It is not hampered or distorted by preconditions, prejudices, preconceptions, or other obstructions; it is just like the spontaneous reaction of a child." (*Henri Bergson. ET*)

Infants live in a state of pure experience, unmodified by recurrent thoughts or accumulated memory. There is a profound wisdom in their innocence and vulnerability. As Jesus Christ said, "Unless you change and become like little children, you will never enter the Kingdom of Heaven."

As adults, we too often regret the past and worry about the future, and as a result tend to miss the essence of life, which only occurs in the here and now. Nothing we do can change something that has already happened in the past. Guilt, remorse, and grudges over past events only poison our present experience. These feelings are unproductive and futile. Similarly, fretting about what might happen in the future is also unproductive and futile because, no matter how much we worry, we cannot control the movement of the stars. Anxiety is caused by the obsessive desire to avoid pain, yet ironically, this anxiety is itself a form of pain. Instead of protecting us from harm, chronic worrying actually harms us right now.

True happiness is to enjoy the present, without anxious dependence upon the future, not to amuse ourselves with either hopes or fears but to rest satisfied with what we have. —Seneca (Ancient Roman Stoic philosopher)

The extent of our bondage to both the past and the future is determined by the amount of spiritual clouding within us that dulls our perception and confuses our judgment. But the Light of awareness has its own innate power to dispel darkness. Each time we choose clarity and awareness over blind reaction we move closer to the Light and closer to our own inner freedom.

Only when we let go of our personal concerns and agendas can we fully live in the present moment. The "instantaneous self" is capable of responding uniquely to each situation because it does not operate based on old conditioning and prejudices. When living in a state of openness and alertness, we are able to immediately grasp vast complex details in the surrounding environment and then coordinate and prioritize them into meaningful patterns. The appropriate response then emerges from within us naturally before the mind has a chance to interfere and disrupt things. This natural unconditioned response reflects a deeper intelligence than behavior generated by ideas and habits.

Contrary to what most do, it is not practical for you to always act according to pre-conceived ideas. The ability to spontaneously adapt yourself to the environment is the key. And yes, for this to be possible, difficult though it may be, you need to refine your soul. —Yielding in a Dispute. KW

When practicing any form of martial arts, it is vital for practitioners to quiet their minds and allow their bodies to act spontaneously without any mental interference. Trying to plan and calculate the next move only slows us down. This is because the body is much faster than the mind. The body can respond almost instantly to a person or situation if the mind does not get in the way. Thinking about the future only distracts the martial arts practitioner from the immediate situation. In addition, as soon as he begins to visualize his next move, he immediately telegraphs his plans to his opponent, thereby allowing his opponent to outmaneuver him. Only when he acts spontaneously can he surprise his opponent. So, to be truly effective in martial arts, he must not focus on any specific thought, situation, or person. His attention should not be preoccupied with anything in particular. It must be silent and alert and keenly aware of everything within the surrounding environment. The martial artist needs to see without looking, feel without fixating, and move without trying. The instantaneous self always acts in this way: smoothly, effortlessly, and efficiently.

Similarly, the body can operate more effectively when either playing a piano, typing, or driving a car if the mind does not try to control or interfere with the process. Our hands, fingers, and feet are capable of rapidly performing numerous movements across the keyboard without the need for any mental oversight. In activities such as this, we need to let go and trust our bodies. Then our consciousness will be able to guide our physical movements perfectly. Not only does behaving this way make us more effective, but is also brings us greater peace of mind.

From the perspective of a spiritual vantage point, the whole or true nature of things is always apparent. —Seeing from a God-Centered Viewpoint. KW

Each moment and each situation is different from that which occurred previously. Everything is constantly changing—nothing stays the same. None of us is immune to this constant change, because we are always changing, too. Old thoughts and opinions, because they are based on the past, can only offer us old solutions. Only by living fully in the present can we perceive clearly what is needed in each and every situation, and then respond quickly and appropriately. Spirituality is less about having mystical visions than it is about taking care of everyday affairs effectively and harmoniously.

If the mind is made blank and receptive, however, the new ideas can be absorbed with little trouble. —Henri Bergson. ET

A quiet mind allows us to easily recognize "the point within the circle," which is the most significant factor within a situation or problem. With this knowledge, we can then adjust our behavior and make the most appropriate response. By relinquishing our conditioned mind, we allow Spirit to act through us, unimpeded. This requires the discipline of surrendering our thoughts to God and maintaining a relaxed but alert consciousness. In our awareness of the present, the physical and the spiritual come together as one. The Sufi poet, Rumi, declares: "Past and future veil God from our sight; burn up both of them with fire."

Our chronic thinking distracts us from the present moment. Indeed, the more we get lost in thoughts, the more we tend to react compulsively rather than spontaneously. Compulsion is not freedom—it is bondage. Anger, frustration, impatience, jealously, embarrassment, fear, and greed are compulsive reactions, not spontaneous responses. They cause us to either overreact or underreact.

Cultivating the "instantaneous self" strengthens our higher nature, freeing us from excessive influence of our instinctive spirit, which tends to mostly chase pleasure and avoid pain. The instinctive spirit has no real freedom because it is dominated and controlled by desire, whereas our divine spirit is fundamentally free because it remains untouched by events and circumstances.

Waiting for future fulfillment is the opposite of living in the present moment. Even when the anticipated future finally does arrive, we will not enjoy it if we are already chasing the next object of desire. Living obsessed with the future is inherently frustrating because life can only be enjoyed in the here and now, not later. As the Buddha said, "Life can only take place in the present moment. If we lose the present moment, we lose life."

Both past and future are merely imaginary thoughts in the mind. When the mind's endless chatter subsides, we find ourselves grounded in the present, and a deeper spiritual awareness is then revealed to us within this inner silence. To develop this profound awareness, we need to frequently interrupt our thinking and pay attention to what is currently happening both around us and within us. At first we may be able to do this for just a few seconds at a time, but with practice the length of time can extend further. The reason we used to ignore this silent space between our thoughts was because, like the air around us, it is formless and continuously present. What usually attracts our attention is the opposite: form or movement. A deliberate effort, therefore, must be made to turn our attention around. Eventually, this awareness will seem even more real than the world around us. This should not be surprising since awareness is no less than our divine spirit shining out from within.

When we rest in silence, the mind is unable to superimpose rigid boundaries between self and other, good and bad, or spirit and matter. Mental distinctions and judgments fall away, and what remains is an undivided presence. Our awareness then expands to embrace everything, and in this openhearted expansion we find true inner peace.

Only a silent mind is capable of finding deep inner peace, which is the real source of inspiration and creativity. Eckhart Tolle, in his book, The Power of Now, describes this source as that which is "[N]one other than the power of your presence, your consciousness liberated from thought forms."

The Point in the Circle

As people tend to see things from the perspective of outward appearances, they usually don't grasp the true essence of things. People usually judge by the outer shell. This is very dangerous. —Seeing from a God-Centered Viewpoint. KW

We currently live in a time of superficial fascination with outer appearances and external forms. This way of seeing things is shallow. By focusing only on appearances, we fail to see the deeper significance of things, and this prevents us from acting wisely. Meishusama compared this spiritually impoverished condition to an empty circle—a circle without a central point. People who walk through life in such a superficial manner lack a sense of inner direction or meaning. They lack inner depth.

The world we live in is of course spherical, but a sphere alone is empty, nothing more than a lifeless ball. To put this in human terms, a person who is empty is not alive, but if a soul enters into the emptiness at the center of his being, he becomes alive and is capable of action. The soul is like the point in the circle. —*The Point in the Circle. ET*

Much of the art that is produced today is devoid of soul. This art has no depth of feeling or experience. Rather, what we see is cleverly constructed forms, which, although initially pleasing to the eye, soon become boring. Such art lacks the ability to touch people deeply, or to inwardly transform them, because it has no spiritual center. In other words, it has no point within its circle.

Similarly, the purpose of food is to nourish us and to give us pleasure. But unfortunately, much of the food that we buy at restaurants and supermarkets, although superficially pleasing to the taste buds and the eyes, weakens and poisons us through lack of nutrition and the presence of toxic chemicals.

Merely punishing a child when he or she misbehaves will not produce lasting results if we do not help the child to understand how his or her behavior adversely affects others. Children need loving support rather than harsh punishment because such behavior by us only sets a bad example for them. The same applies to reforming criminals. In Meishusama's words, "If the means and methods of correcting bad behavior are not aimed at the innermost part of a human being—the soul—they are shallow and worthless. It is clear to me that if people's souls are pure, they will not do anything immoral even in a society devoid of laws." (*Kannon's Heart and Kannon's Way. KW*) The human soul is the point within the circle.

Children have never been very good at listening to their elders, but they have never failed to imitate them. —James A. Baldwin (American Psychologist)

Doctors typically prescribe drugs that only suppress the symptoms of a disease of illness, but do not address the underlying cause. At best they may provide short-term relief from pain and discomfort. When we suppress things, they tend to build up over time and get worse, not better. This is why medicine often causes illness to eventually return even more virulently than before. This approach to medicine offers no real benefit. It is a false promise. A more intelligent approach to health would be to investigate the root cause of an illness and then treat it appropriately. How else can a real cure be found? This root cause of illness is the point within the circle.

This is a clear sign of the nature of the society in which we are living—a society that only looks at the surface appearances in the material world, and does not perceive the vital underlying reality of the spiritual world. —*A Sense of Justice. ET*

To find the point in the circle requires the ability to perceive the purpose or intention of a thing. It is a matter of recognizing what is essential, and not being distracted by what is unessential. Armed with this knowledge, one can then take action that is both intelligent and practical.

The question is not what you look at, but what you see. —Henry David Thoreau

When listening to people, it can be useful to ask, "What are they trying to say? What is the point they are trying to make? What is their real motive? And how can I help them?" These questions prompt us to see beyond people's external appearances or behavior, and to see how they truly think and feel. Through this inquiry, we gain a glimpse of their very soul—the point within their human circle.

When working or playing, it is best to put your heart fully into the activity. Otherwise, not only will the quality of your work or activity suffer, but also the experience itself will become boring and meaningless. It will have no life in it— no point within its circle.

Spirit is invisible to the outer senses because it lies deep within all things. It is the central point within the circle, the secret power that animates all things.

Spirit is also that which drives the evolution of all of creation. As Meishusama phrased it, "The basis of this movement, the still point at the ultimate center, is the Divine Intention." *(The Nature and Behavior of Evil Spirits. HT)* A life without awareness of Spirit lacks depth and is devoid of real happiness. Visionary scientist and futurist, Willis Harman, wrote, "Most of us are living at the periphery of consciousness while intuition invites us into the center."

As your intelligence and spiritual perception deepens, you gain the capacity to discern the essence of things without having to rely solely on sensory observation or logical analysis. And with increased awareness, irrelevant details become less distracting or important. You become capable of instantaneously understanding the entire pattern of a problem, and of going straight to the heart of the matter. Additionally, your ability to perceive beauty increases, as does your sensitivity to the feelings of others. About people who have reached this level, Meishusama writes: "Their intelligence and spiritual perception deepen tremendously, and they become able to grasp more clearly the reality of things and situations." *(The Strata in the Spiritual World. ET)*

All of Meishusama's teachings and efforts were directed toward the spiritual upliftment and redemption of the world. This redemption will be accomplished by ridding humanity of its spiritual clouds, and by revealing the main point of life, as well as of art, medicine, politics, science, and the natural world. This is the point within the circle of life, and is what humanity was put here to discover. Some might prefer to call this point "the meaning or purpose of things." Others might call it "the spirit or soul." And some might simply call it "love."

As I often say, the world is only ninety-nine percent complete. It is waiting for a final touch to bring it to life. If we put the point in the circle, this will be the final touch that transforms the whole world. To put it another way, the power of one small touch of good will destroy all the evil in the world. To bring Truth into this world of vanity and emptiness will be like adding one point to a circle smeared and obscured with blackness, and the power of this one small point will dispel the blackness and reveal pure white. In other words, we will give the world back its soul. We will revive this civilization that for so long has been like a corpse and bring to birth the New World. —*The Point in the Circle. ET*

CHAPTER 9

KANNON'S WAY (Dynamic Balance)

I advocate a faith in Kannon that is not only different from popular beliefs about Kannon, but has many significant principles completely opposite to theirs. This faith requires no excessive dedication, and places the highest importance on gratitude as a way of responding to the daily blessings we receive. This type of Kannon faith never encourages extreme asceticism. It understands that self-imposed, severe practices often lead to great personal suffering. Because of its heavenly character, Kannon's Way is not related to practices that invite suffering. In this regard, Kannon's Way is a moderate form of spiritual practice. —Avoid Asceticism. KW

Life exists because of balance. Living cells require a balanced ratio of sodium and potassium to function correctly. Every living organism depends upon a proper balance between anabolism and catabolism—creative and destructive metabolic forces—to maintain its health and vitality. Plants and animals require a moderate range of weather conditions—neither too hot nor too cold—to survive. Ecosystems, both large and small, depend on numerous mutual co-dependencies to sustain themselves. Introducing just one new species into an environment can disrupt or destroy the delicate balance of the entire system.

The universe is in constant motion and change. To survive and prosper, we need to constantly move and change as well. Similarly, water that sits still for too long becomes stagnant, while water that moves and flows stays fresh. The water in a river, by constantly bending and turning, eventually reaches the ocean. We also need to bend and turn like a river if we wish to achieve our goals and objectives. Overall, we will always do well if we use nature as our guide.

The movement of the universe, proceeding in harmony without deviation, embodies Kannon's Way. —Progressing Upwards. KW

Kannon's Way is a way of living that embodies flexibility, balance, and moderation. People with such characteristics are patient, tolerant, and easygoing. They value peace and harmony, and also enjoy laughter and excitement. They are like a fresh spring breeze, both soothing and invigorating. They tend to go unnoticed by others because they do not push and pull at the world. They seek the path of least resistance. In many ways, they are the true peacemakers of the world.

Kannon's Way teaches how we should act as true human beings, and I believe that all humanity can eventually get there. People are meant to evolve and to reach a higher level. —Izunome: The Movement of the Universe. KW

Key Principles

Daijo and Shojo[11]

As is commonly known, in Buddhism a distinction is made between daijo and shojo. These concepts, however, still leave room for an expansion of their meaning.
—The Daijo Way. KW

Meishusama borrowed two words from traditional Buddhist terminology, shojo and daijo, and redefined them to encompass two fundamental principles that apply to all things. Shojo is the principle of inwardness and daijo the principle of outwardness. Shojo is fire, which burns upwards; daijo is water, which flows laterally. Shojo is the inclination toward spiritual growth; daijo is the inclination toward service to others. Shojo unites individuals with God; daijo unites people with people. The former is driven by the desire for truth and freedom; the latter is motivated by generosity and love. Freedom without love is joyless and uncaring; love without freedom is deluded and emotionally binding.

On a mundane level, shojo represents conservatism, and daijo represents liberalism. Shojo is analytical and detail oriented, whereas daijo is holistic and focuses on pattern recognition. Shojo looks at the trees, whereas daijo sees the forest.

A shifting balance always exists between shojo and daijo. It can be a stable balance, an uneven balance, or a destructive balance. Living things require a harmonious balance that supports their overall safety and comfort. In the Chinese

---

11. The term *Daijo* traditionally refers to Mahayana Buddhism, which means "large raft." *Shojo*, on the other hand, refers to Hinayana Buddhism, the original form of this religion. Hinayana means "small raft." The implication is that Mahayana is the greater vehicle, one that can carry more people to salvation, while Hinayana is considered elitist and severe.

religion of Taoism, this changing interplay between polar opposites is explained by the principles of *yin* and *yang*.

Kannon's Way is a manner of thinking and behaving that promotes peace and harmony in one's environment. The shojo way leads to wisdom and the daijo way leads to compassion. When we incorporate both of them into our lives, they lead to spiritual growth and personal happiness. The inner spirit of Kannon is often referred to as Izunome, which is the point at which the spirit of water intersects with the spirit of fire.

Two great civilizations had emerged, the vertically inclined Eastern, and the horizontal Western. To express it in different terms, Eastern civilization is characterized as shojo, and Western is daijo by nature. —Creating the World of Light. KW

There are many aspects to shojo and daijo, and they are not always reducible to clear cut definitions. Shojo and daijo can be understood as personal attributes or even forces of energy. To better understand this, below is a list of some shojo and daijo traits.

Shojo	Daijo
Strict	Lenient
Vertical	Horizontal
Fire	Water
Sun	Moon
Masculine	Feminine
Principled	Tolerant
Yang	Yin
Inward	Outward
Salvation through effort	Salvation through grace
Exclusive	Inclusive
Analysis	Synthesis
Conservative	Liberal
Distinctions	Similarities
Elitist	Egalitarian
Individual	Universal
Narrow	Wide
Uniting with God	Embracing others

Meishusama feels it is important to have a healthy balance between these two polar opposites. He writes, "Shojo draws distinctions between good and evil, and tends toward commandments and precepts; its virtues are easily understood by people. Daijo, on the other hand, draws no distinction between good and evil, and tends toward liberalism. Its virtues are correspondingly difficult to perceive." *(Daijo and Shojo. HT)* These two principles are not in opposition to each other but instead are complementary.

Although you are well accustomed to the terms "daijo" and "shojo" and think you know exactly what they mean, you cannot depend on only one without the other. Instead, you have to act according to the principles of both at the same time. So, the way you act should be neither exclusively shojo nor exclusively daijo, but shojo in conjunction with daijo. If instead you think you have to stick only with daijo, this restrictive thought instantly deviates you from daijo. The very idea that you have to be daijo automatically makes you shojo. —*Daijo and Divine Wisdom. KW*

Conflict of Opposites

All strife is the result of the illusion of separateness caused by the mistaken perception that life is composed of fundamental dichotomies. This perception divides people into "us" and "them." The more separate we feel from something, the greater its potential threat to us. We are conditioned to view conflict as a struggle between two opposing sides where one must win and the other must lose. We make distinctions between good and evil, and then project these judgments onto others. Our side is usually seen as morally superior, while the other side is judged as immoral and corrupt. We feel that we are right and they are wrong. Choosing sides only increases the distance between people, increasing conflict rather than lessening it. Emotionally-based judgments that generate anger and resentment are the true source of most conflicts. Then, we twist logic and facts in order to justify our position at the expense of the other person.

These conflicts are all based on the logic of extreme opposites, an emotionally polarized position that does not recognize any middle ground. Such dichotomies leave little room for compromise or reconciliation and can actually reinforce the very thing we wish to defeat. This principle is summarized in the popular adage, "What you resist persists."

Commenting about the contrasting opposites of good and evil, Meishu-sama writes, "Surprisingly, one who is labeled as being evil sometimes does exceptionally good deeds, while one who seems good often turns out to do the opposite." (*Judge Not. KW*) In other words, we should not be too swift to pass judgment on people or circumstances because things are not always what they seem to be.

Co-Dependency of Opposites

The shojo faiths, which emphasize only the benefit of the individual, and the daijo faiths which sacrifice the individual, are both mistaken and not complete. In order to achieve complete relief, both the world and the individual must be equally helped.
—*Creating the World of Light. KW*

Opposites are mutually dependent. A valley cannot exist without the mountains that surround it. A tree cannot grow its branches upwards without its roots growing downwards. A conversation cannot happen without talking and listening. The bottom of a wheel cannot move upwards without the top of the wheel moving downwards. In order to walk, the right leg must cooperate with the left. Buyers need sellers and sellers need buyers. Harmony supports melody and melody supports harmony.

The principles of shojo and daijo are complementary, not mutually exclusive. Neither one is right or wrong, nor better or worse. Together, they create a natural balance and an integrated whole. Understanding this principle of the co-dependency of opposites helps to reduce feelings of hostility toward our opponents because we begin to recognize their necessity within the larger scheme of things.

The co-dependency of opposites is also apparent in the extremely small world of atoms, which need space to separate them from each other. Neither atoms nor space are recognizable without the other.

Similarly, the vast realm of outer space is only recognizable in contrast to the planets, stars, and galaxies that inhabit it. And without empty space to separate these celestial bodies from each other we would not be able to see them because everything would be fused together into one indistinguishable clump. Thus space defines form, and form defines space.

From the infinitely small to the infinitely large, everything depends upon everything else, and each of us is part of this vast interdependency. We support the universe and the universe supports us.

Good and Evil

Do not be overcome by evil, but overcome evil with good.
— *The Bible (Romans 12, 21)*

Like beauty, the concepts of good and evil are capable of being viewed in many different ways, depending upon the person, religion, or culture. Although everyone has a sense of right or wrong, they do not all agree with each other.

Good and evil, and the moral codes that go with them, can be viewed from five different levels: individual, cultural, universal, evolutionary, and divine:

1. At *the individual level*, what is good for one person may be bad for another. For instance, if someone buys a used car, and soon afterwards it breaks down, the buyer may think the seller is an evil person who knowingly deceived and cheated him. On the other hand, the seller may feel he sold the buyer a good car that was in excellent condition, and therefore did no wrong. Each of us sees things differently based on our individual perspectives.

In conflicts, it is often hard to tell who is truly the good one and who is the bad one. Meishusama says that, "God needs a variety of people to play out His divine drama, just as with dramas penned by humans. The divine drama would be incomplete if the cast were made up solely of thoroughly good characters." (*Judge Not. KW*)

None of us like to think of ourselves as the bad one. Somehow, humans manage to justify everything they do, no matter how bad it may look to others. Each of us plays the roles of good person and bad person at one time or another. It is important to remember that, although we may feel we are the good one, to our enemies we are always the bad one.

2. At *the cultural level*, morality is often colored by limiting beliefs and prejudices. What one culture considers good, another culture may consider evil. Our world is full of diversity. For instance, some countries may think it immoral for women to expose any skin other than their hands and eyes. By contrast, other countries may consider it cruel to force women to hide behind excessive clothing. Also, some societies believe in corporal punishment while others do not. Which one is right? Meishusama comments: "Only God can truly distinguish good from evil." (*Being Daijo. KW*) Nonetheless, how we behave is important, so we must always do our best to do discern right from wrong, and good from evil.

3. At *the universal level*, behavior that is compassionate and supportive of life tends to be considered good. Whereas, behavior that is deliberately cruel and

destructive tends to be considered evil. These views transcend culture. They relate to universal values and the welfare of everyone everywhere. About this, Meishusama advises that, "The world is a rope braided from good and evil. Do not swerve from following the good." (*Good and Evil. MK1*) In order to act wisely, it is vital that we always try to see the big picture.

4. At *the evolutionary level*, good and evil are seen as necessary learning experiences that further our spiritual growth. Meishusama writes that, "God uses evil as a whetstone to polish our body and soul." (*Refining Body and Soul. KW*) This is how the Law of Karma operates in our lives. For instance, the harm we cause others may generate forces that eventually cause similar things to happen to us. This is best expressed in the popular saying, "What goes around, comes around." Learning how others feel expands our consciousness and helps us to improve our behavior. Considering the consequences of our actions helps us to become less self-centered, wiser and more compassionate.

5. At *the divine level*, all is one. Good and evil are seen as two sides of the same coin, different yet inseparable from each other. God is beyond the world of good and evil, but also part of it. Everything is ultimately part of the Divine Play, and therefore beyond the dualistic concepts of good and evil, and right and wrong. This becomes obvious to us when we look beyond duality.

Once, when speaking with his students, Meishusama took three cigarettes and arranged them in a triangle to illustrate this idea. He explained, "The two bottom points of this triangle represent these two opposite deities. One is the deity of good and the other is the deity of evil. Placing the two deities like this, God at the upper point proceeds with His cosmic drama here on earth. There is no good or evil in God himself. In God's eyes, good is indistinguishable from evil. This idea is also expressed in the familiar saying, 'Good and evil are as one.' From this perspective, we humans cannot grasp the true nature of good or of evil." (*Judge Not. KW*) In other words, God is absolute unity, beyond good and evil.

As you can see, it is not always easy to distinguish good from evil. Cultural conditioning and personal agendas usually distort our judgment. To accurately distinguish between the two, we must purify the soul, calm the mind, and set aside personal agendas.

Yet, life also demands action. Injustice must be corrected, the weak and innocent must be protected, and the greater good must be promoted. We cannot avoid making choices, and even though many will inevitably be wrong, nonetheless it is important to do the best we can while praying for guidance. The more sincerely we seek guidance, the better we get at discerning right from wrong and good from evil.

The line dividing good and evil cuts through the heart of every human being. And who is willing to destroy a piece of his own heart? —Aleksandr Solzhenitsyn

Dynamic Change

The world is complicated and continually changing. So, we constantly have to come up with new approaches. There should be differences in how you act from one day to the next. —Progression Upwards. KW

All of life is constantly changing, and this mutability sustains the existence of everything. There is a time to sow and time to reap. Winter flows into spring, which later flows into summer, and then fall. These cycles of change can also be seen in our personal lives which begin at birth and progress through the phases of growth, maturity, decline, and death. After a period of time spent in the spiritual world, the soul returns into a new body and begins the process all over again.

Life is not opposed to death, and winter is not opposed to summer. They evolve into each other through perpetually recurring cycles. Life works best when we accept and adapt to these cycles of change rather than resist them.

Change often feels threatening. Quitting one's job, moving to a new city, ending an old relationship or starting a new one—any of these can turn out badly. So, rather than take risks, we often seek the security of predictable situations.

Nothing stays the same. When we observe our minds, we discover that our thoughts are constantly changing from one moment to the next. Similarly, the breath within our lungs constantly changes with every inhalation and exhalation. Even our most dependable relationships change and evolve over time, whether we want them to or not.

Living things are always moving and evolving, whereas dead things stay the same. Life differs from rocks, which sit quietly and immobile. Instead, life resembles a rushing stream, twisting and turning, splashing and swirling about, always changing from one moment to the next.

To embrace change is to embrace life. The more we can approach life with wide-eyed wonder, the more every second becomes new and exciting. This is how we find inner peace and fulfillment.

The movement of the universe, proceeding without deviation, embodies Kannon's Way. —Progression Upwards. KW

Holism

You cannot separate the mind from the body, nor the individual from society.
—Gabor Mate (Psychiatrist)

The parts affect the whole and the whole affects the parts. Sick societies create sick people, and sick people create sick societies. Conversely, healthy societies create healthy people, and healthy people create healthy societies. Similarly, the mind affects the body, and the body affects the mind. We cannot solve problems by ignoring how things affect each other.

The whole is greater than the sum of its parts. An orange is more than just skin, rind, pulp, juice, and seeds. It is a unified pattern that integrates all of these individual parts together. A car is more than just the engine, wheels, transmission, brakes, and seats. Only when all of these components are built and assembled correctly will it run properly. A person is more than just a collection of skin, bones, nerves, and internal organs. It is the harmonious synergy of all of these various elements that guarantees a healthy, functional body.

From a vertical perspective, a person has many levels to his or her being, such as physical, emotional, mental, and spiritual. Together, these make up the totality of that person. From a horizontal perspective, a living being cannot be separated from its environment. If we pull a plant out of the ground and leave it on a rock, it will surely die. Similarly, if we deprive someone of oxygen, that person will not survive for long.

The totality of a creature includes not only its many levels of experience, but also its social and natural environment. Everything belongs within a larger context, both vertically and horizontally. The more clearly we can see the total picture, without leaving anything of significance out, the more effectively we can promote balance and harmony both within ourselves and throughout the world around us.

Attitudes and Behavior

Non-Dual Awareness

As our faith deepens, the ability to see things from the opposite perspective should be cultivated. —Progression Upwards. KW

Pairs of opposites arise from the narrow perspective of the individual perceiver. Evaluations of hot and cold are based on comfort level. One person's gain is often another person's loss. Near and far are relative to one's location. Pain and pleasure go hand in hand. As soon as we take a particular stance or position, the pairs of opposites come into play.

The most fundamental pair of opposites is that of self and other. Our typical experience is that of a separate being apart from the world around us. On the levels of body and mind we are indeed separate from others, as well as from the environment in which we live. However, on the level of Spirit, we are all One. This is because Spirit is formless and has no boundaries that can differentiate it from the forms arising within it (such as ourselves and the environment). But, until we know and feel this underlying unity of opposites in a very tangible way, we will continue to live as if we were separate from everything.

Non-dualism is the recognition that pairs of opposites are co-dependent and inseparable from each other. Consider the following pairs: can up exist without down or big without small? What is dark without light or inside without outside? Could we recognize good without comparing it with evil? Does beauty have meaning without ugliness for contrast? Each half of these pairs is only recognizable through comparison with the other, and therefore depends on the other for its very existence. This is the logic of "both" rather than "either/or."

Opposites are often relative, and therefore, difficult to determine. An ant travels fast in comparison to a snail but slow in comparison to a grasshopper. At what point is fast considered slow, or slow considered fast? We may think we are standing still, yet the earth is traveling at enormous speeds through space in relation to the sun and the other stars. So, how can we determine motion or stasis? A yacht is huge in comparison to a speedboat, but is tiny in comparison to a luxury liner. So, how can we define big or small? What one person considers hot weather another considers cold. At what point does cold become hot or hot become cold? It depends on the standard by which we measure it. So much of our judgments are relative to one's position, preconceptions, and subjective values.

Do individuals make deliberate choices, and are they personally responsible for their actions? Or do genetics and social conditioning determine their behavior? In other words, is there fate or free will? Based on the principle of non-dualism, these opposites can be seen as two sides of the same coin. Neither fate nor freewill is the complete truth, but is only a one-sided point of view. Meishusama teaches that everything is determined by the conditions in the spiritual world where there is no sharp distinction between fate and free will or between thought and action.

To cultivate Kannon's Way, it is important to look at the other side of any polarity or conflict that comes our way. This requires inner stillness and active listening. There are always two sides to everything. When faced with an interpersonal conflict, take a moment and imagine how it must feel to be the other person or group. Temporarily suspend identification with your own position so that you can understand the other person's point of view. Only after understanding and sympathizing with both sides of a conflict is it possible to act intelligently and promote the greatest harmony for all concerned. With practice, you will begin to see the whole picture, undivided and complete, and eventually attain the union of shojo and daijo within your own character.

Expanded Perspective

One of the largest problems we humans face is that of people judging each other. It is completely wrong to be judgmental of others. When people judge others as either good or evil, God simultaneously judges them. Before passing judgment upon others, judge yourself and deeply reflect upon yourself. When the urge to judge others arises, stop and deeply reflect upon yourself. It is completely wrong to call others either good or evil. —Judge Not. KW

The tendency to ignore the big picture contributes to short-sighted judgments and foolish decisions. Actions that appear evil may actually end up doing good, and actions that appear good may end up doing evil. According to Sigmund Freud, "Neurosis is the inability to tolerate ambiguity." Healthy, mature people realize that life is made up of shades of gray, rather than only black and white. In truth, there are degrees of uncertainty in most everything.

We may generously give money to a homeless man, only to later discover that he used the money to get drunk and then beat his wife. Or we may chop down a forest to build homes for our community and then watch in horror when a rainstorm hits this now barren land and washes everything out to sea. In both cases, what we thought were good actions turned out to be bad. We never know when our best intentions may end up hurting others. From our initial perspective, what we did seemed good, but from the victim's standpoint, what we did would be considered bad. Gain and loss depend upon one's personal perspective.

Eventually, from the ashes of a forest fire comes fertile soil, followed by new growth. To the burnt trees, the fire was bad, but to the regenerated forest that came later, it was good. Similarly, one person's gain is often another person's loss. From loss comes gain, and from gain comes loss.

With the approach of winter, plants and trees begin to die. Yet, without the harsh snowfalls of winter, the rivers would dry up in summer, causing agriculture to fail and people to starve. Everything goes in cycles: sometimes creating abundance, and sometimes creating scarcity.

Oftentimes, good people are driven to do bad things out of desperation. They may steal to eat, or lie and cheat to survive. And sometimes people feel compelled to hurt others because they themselves have been hurt in the past. There is an old French proverb that says, "To know all is to forgive all." By suspending judgment, we give ourselves time to collect all the facts, some of which may contradict our earlier beliefs. It should be no surprise to discover that there are at least two opposing points of view to any conflict. Instead of choosing sides, we need to gain insight into the feelings and motives of others. The best way to do this is by putting ourselves in their shoes and trying to see things from their perspective rather than expecting them to behave according to our own values and standards. By doing this we can become true peacemakers rather than promoters of conflict.

Helping others without distinguishing between good and evil is the true meaning of Kannon's unending compassion. —Infinite Compassion. MK1

Detachment

It is easy to see that almost everyone in society is afflicted by both self-will and attachment. These two are as closely related as brothers. When people examine problems that appear complicated and fail to find easy solutions to them, almost always it is because of this combination of self-will and attachment.

—Self-will and Attachment. ET

Everything is transitory, including our family, friends, homes, possessions, money, and careers. Each of us grows old and dies, and our hopes and dreams will be left behind. Nothing stays the same. Our possessions wear out, our bodies decline, memories fade, and even long-term relationships change over time. To cling to these causes needless suffering because no matter how tightly we cling we will not slow down the passage of time.

To find happiness, we need to cultivate a measure of detachment. Detachment is an acceptance of all that arises in life, both pleasant and unpleasant. The more we cultivate detachment the less our happiness is held hostage to life's events.

However, detachment is not the same as suppression. Suppression causes us to block sensitivity and awareness so that we become deadened. For instance, some people take psychiatric drugs to manage painful feelings such as guilt, anxiety, and depression. Such drugs suppress symptoms, but do not eliminate the problem. People who are medicated in this way tend to be cut off from their feelings. Their emotional responses are stifled and their sensitivity is reduced, therefore not only do they feel less pain, but also less joy.

Detachment is not the inability to feel. Rather, it increases sensitivity to the richness of life, thereby making one more sensitive to other's feelings, as well as art and beauty. This results in a greater enjoyment of life. Detachment frees one from compulsively dwelling on the past or future. It is not that those who are detached do not experience life's unpleasant realities or enjoy its pleasures, but that they do so without denying one, or grasping at the other too tightly.

Detachment is not that you should own nothing, but that nothing should own you.
—Ali ibn abi Talilb (Sufi Poet)

To be effective, one must cultivate detachment. Excessive attachment to goals can cause one to push too hard, thereby provoking an equally hard resistance from others. Excessive attachment to objects causes us to worry about losing them. And when we cling too hard to people they tend to pull away. Meishusama gives this example:

If one person is too pressing and passionate, the other person will often be repelled. Ironically enough, the attachment of one person cools the affections of the other. Indeed, many of the things in this world are steeped in irony, with results that vary from the pleasant to the painful. What you must recognize is that the most important single cause of success or failure is the degree of your attachment. As I often say in such cases, "Aim for the opposite effect of the one you want." In other words, the truth of truths is the irony of ironies. —*Trust in God. ET*

People who are detached still care about peace, harmony, and beauty, and want everyone to be happy. However, when trouble inevitably does arise, they have a balanced reaction to it, because attachment has been replaced by trust in a Higher Power to handle everything perfectly.

This trust allows us an inner distance from our problems and the problems of others. The more we cultivate detachment from the dualities of pleasure and pain, gain and loss, and praise and blame, the more we are able to see life's changes through the eyes of God. Freed from self-centered involvement with life, we will find that the world does not revolve around us any more than the universe revolves around the earth.

Beyond the narrow boundaries of our personal lives, the whole world becomes our concern. In a sense, the world becomes our extended body, with each part essential to the proper functioning of the whole. From this perspective, the vicissitudes of our individual lives take on less importance. Our minds become clear, our hearts peaceful. The happiness of others becomes our happiness. Another's smile becomes our own.

I have made the utmost effort to rid myself of self-will and attachment, and, as a result, have found ease from the sufferings of heart and mind, and have enjoyed constant success in the affairs of the world.

—*Self-will and Worldly Attachment. ET*

Flexibility

If you become flexible enough to adapt to different situations, people, and times, then you will avoid running into dead ends. —A Balanced Approach. KW

Adapting to changing circumstances requires flexibility of character. Some-times we need to change not only what we do, but also what we think, as new information reveals itself to us. This requires openness and humility on our part. If we become attached to our previous position because of pride or stubbornness, we cannot continue to learn and grow. Inevitably, we will begin to make mistakes because of our ignorance. In the *Tao Te Ching*, Lao Tzu says, "A blade of grass bends in the wind and survives, but an oak tree resists and breaks." Different people may require different treatment, and our response to each person must be unique. Sometimes we must be lenient and sometimes strict, sometimes we should speak and sometimes remain silent. In his dealings with people, Meishusama would vary his teaching depending on the person or the situation. This allowed him to be effective wherever he went.

There are often cases where I feel it challenging to pick the right approach, either daijo or shojo, and must alternately switch from one to the other depending on necessity. Although it is difficult, I can still find joy in searching for the best way to deal with some particular thing. —*Maintaining Moderation. KW*

Sometimes, when raising children, we need to be strict, and at other times lenient. If people are being selfish and unkind toward others, we may need to confront them, while at other times it may be better to respond with love and understanding. There are times when we need to hold people accountable for their actions and other times when it is important to investigate the circumstances and conditions influencing them. Sometimes, we can walk forcefully with a strong purpose and at other times we can relax and enjoy the scenery. Sometimes we act shojo and at other times daijo. Each moment and circumstance is different and requires a unique response. This dynamic range of possible responses is one of the features of Kannon's Way. It is the practical principle of adaptability and moderation.

We also need to learn to be flexible in our timing. Not pushing headlong into things before circumstances become favorable, nor hesitating for so long that they become unfavorable, are the keys to success. We need to wait for the right moment. Meishusama writes, "When I plan to do something new, I never rush to make a final decision. Instead, I take enough time to see the thing objectively and from various angles, and repeatedly deliberate upon it to ensure that it is not only right, but also beneficial in the long run for the well-being of society. Having completed these mental processes, I then wait for the right opportunity. However, most people do not have the patience to wait for the best time. They start a project before it is obviously feasible. So they get stuck in the gap between their blueprint and their miscalculations, then hurry to recover, only to make the situation worse. Finally, they end in failure. To repeat, what is essential here is to be patient until the right time comes." (*Wait for the Right Moment. KW*)

Even if we have the right ideas, the right methods, and the right people, if our timing is off, we may fail. Meishusama advises:

> From this we learn that nature teaches us the significance of time, and nature itself embodies truth. For this reason, whatever you plan, it is extremely important to have nature as your guide. Learning from the principles and processes of nature is essential to success. Since the spiritual healing and non-fertilizer growing methods that I advocate, along with other things, have their foundations in this principle, almost no failures occur when using these methods, and the hoped for outcomes always come about.
>
> —*Wait for the Right Moment. KW*

Meishusama illustrates this flexible approach to life with the analogy of steering a car while driving on a curved road. To manage the turns, we need to constantly adjust the steering wheel from left to right and right to left, always moving forward. Meishusama writes, "Above all, you should adjust your way of speaking to your listener. Speak suitably to an elderly person, speak gently to a lady, speak philosophically to an intellectual, and talk common sense to an ordinary person. If you do so, your listener will become interested in what you are saying and will listen with pleasure and appreciation." (*Henri Bergson. ET*)

Persons embodying a true balance of shojo and daijo will be fluid in their behavior, sometimes demonstrating masculine qualities and at other times more feminine qualities. Spirit is beyond gender and is quite capable of acting in whatever manner is appropriate at the time.

In our understanding of the world, it is not right to conclude that two times two always equals four. It is essential to understand that there are things beyond reason. This is particularly true in the case of faith. In practicing your faith, you should learn to judge things by results, by how things actually turned out. And, depending upon the situation, you can be flexible and change your approach to best deal with things. This is Kannon's Way. If you hold true to this principle, I believe you cannot fail. —*Be Flexible in Your Judgments. KW*

Moderation

In this world, everything is easy if one observes moderation.
—*Spiritual Cultivation. MK2*

People who are unbalanced often swing from one extreme to the other, reacting with panic, rage, or despair at the drop of a hat. Or, they may become overly elated, throwing caution to the wind and acting with reckless abandon. Many bounce back and forth from elation to depression, from starvation diets to gluttony, or from overblown idealism to deflated cynicism. The middle ground seems to always elude them. Although intensity can add richness and depth to our experiences, when taken to extremes, it causes discomfort or pain and can even be destructive.

Everything should be done in moderation, and faith is no exception. If you become too passionate in your faith, you might end by burning up. But if too passive, you might end being frozen. Ideally, things should stay in balance between hot and cold, like the warm water suitable for an enjoyable bath. That is moderation. The world up to now has not taken this seriously and has not tried to achieve a general level of moderation. People now go to extremes, either too hot or too cold. But Kannon's Way can teach them the path of warm water at just the right temperature. —*Izunome: The Movement of the Universe. KW*

It is best to find a middle path. Be neither too generous nor too cheap, neither too open-minded nor too opinionated, neither too aggressive nor too passive, and neither too strict nor too permissive. When cooking a delicious meal, the taste should be neither too sweet nor too bitter. When driving, the speed should be neither too fast nor too slow. It is best to wear lightweight clothing during hot weather and heavy clothing during cold weather. And during conversations with others, it is best to balance one's talking with one's listening in a natural flow of give and take.

A person practicing Kannon's Way seeks balance and moderation at all times and will not overreact with too much emotion and excitement, nor will they under react with too much rational analysis and indifference. Regarding this, Meishusama writes, "When people try to solve a problem, they generally tend either to get lost in emotion or to solve the problem through reasoning. However, we need to care about both the emotional and rational aspects of problem solving at the same time. If we strive to seek a solution that involves both, there is a greater chance that we will arrive at a place of freedom and assurance." (*A Balanced Approach. KW*)

Just as the ability to walk down the street depends on the balance and rhythm between the right and left legs, so too does a person seek balance between action and inaction, depending on circumstances. They do not become proud with success or shamed by failure. When complimented, they remember their faults and, when criticized, remember their virtues. This inner practice of remembering the opposite side of things keeps them balanced and undisturbed despite the ups and downs of life.

Nowadays, everything is out of balance. This includes not only the state of the world, but also that of individuals. And once balance is lost, the situation quickly leads to a dead end. On the other hand, if you remain balanced, you will do well.

—A Balanced Approach. KW

Although we may find ourselves in the midst of conflict, it is not always necessary for us to choose sides. If we always cling to our shojo principles, we may become intolerant and aggressive. If we indiscriminately adopt too much daijo, we can become overly permissive and passive. Recognizing that most things come in pairs, and are mutually dependent on each other, provides us with the wisdom needed to resolve most conflicts.

The person who is not biased toward either side of a conflict listens to both sides with sympathy and objectivity. These people win the trust and confidence of all concerned and are truly the peacemakers in the world.

Being able to see all points of view allows us to compromise and to find the most effective solution. This is another sign of moderation. An intelligent person will take into account all the various factors in a situation before taking action. When we go to extremes we usually ignore some important facts or concerns. We risk being thrown off balance by our blindness, making it difficult to respond effectively to new developments. This tendency to ignore the obvious is caused by attachment to personal preferences. If we find ourselves acting in extremes, we should ask ourselves, "What am I missing that is important?"

To practice Kannon's Way, one never does things partially, nor does one go to extremes of action. —Kannon's Way. KW

Common Sense

The most important thing we must do is to ensure that faith and its expression do not become separated from the dictates of common sense. —Common Sense. ET

Common sense is the ability to recognize the obvious and to then follow through with effective action. This requires that one not be clouded by emotions, preconceptions, or personal agendas. Such clouds usually lead to poor decisions because they block one's ability to be well informed. Just as a car driver needs a windshield free of dirt and grime to see the road clearly, so too does one need an open mind and an untroubled heart to see reality clearly. Only then can one make sound judgments and then act intelligently.

More often than not, what people consider common sense is actually preconceived ideas and habitual ways of doing things. A reporter summarized Albert Einstein's thoughts on this matter as, "Common sense is the collection of prejudices acquired by age eighteen." This is actually close-mindedness rather than common sense. It is not practical, but impractical. Just because most everyone does things in a particular way, does not mean it is right. Unfortunately, true common sense may not really be so common.

Never be swayed by fixed ideas or preconceptions. —True Faith. ET

Common sense is a very practical attitude that values simplicity and useful results. It is the ability to use one's senses to recognize obvious solutions even when others fail to notice them. Common sense is the opposite of shojo dogmatism, which fails to see concrete reality because of its attachment to abstractions. When one has common sense, one maintains an open mind and trusts one's senses and takes note of the facts. One prefers simple, down-to-earth solutions to most problems.

Mostly we notice common sense when it is absent rather than when it is present. How often have we seen people make terrible mistakes when there was a much better option available? Occasionally, though, we are dazzled by someone's brilliance when that person solves a problem that no one else was able to do. Frequently the solution turns out to be so simple that it should have been obvious to everyone, yet somehow was not. These are the times when we appreciate common sense for the rare gift that it is.

There is a popular story, although partially true, nonetheless still serves to illustrate the use of common sense. Back in the early days of space exploration, neither the Russian nor the American astronauts were able to record scientific data on paper because their ballpoint pens failed to operate in zero gravity. The American solution was to spend millions of dollars to invent a special pen that could function in weightless space. The Russians, however, simply switched to using a wooden pencil. The American's made use of science and technology. Their solution was brilliant, but wasteful. The Russians, however, made use of common sense. Their solution was simple, easy, and inexpensive.

Every matter that relates to Kannon's Way, without exception, must accord with common sense. —Against Asceticism. KW

Common sense can be summarized as the ability to notice the obvious rather than be distracted by what is irrelevant or inconsequential. To have common sense is to not be confused by complexity. Such clarity of mind is then followed by practical action.

Our conduct also needs to be consistent with Kannon's Way. When we act, it is very important to locate our heart within the binding knot that connects vertical with horizontal. In a way, this connecting point is common sense, and this is the underlying reason that we set a high value on common sense. However, in our society, people who abide by common sense are seen as mediocre, and those who deviate from it tend to be seen as special. We should keep this in mind. For it is a fact that the reputations of those who are monomaniacal are ephemeral, and those people never accomplish anything truly great. As history clearly shows, eventually, by their very nature they invite their own failure. *—Vertical and Horizontal. KW*

Compassion

I imagine the soul of a saint who from compassion prays for his foes.
                                                                    —Courage. MK1

Conflicts arise when people confront the variety of opinions, values, and objectives that others hold. How can we accommodate everyone when there are differences of interest? Whose needs are the most justified? Whose views are correct? People with closed hearts and minds see only differences and struggle with others because of their limited perception. Peace and harmony demands that we look for what we have in common. As the Taoist sage, Lao Tzu, wrote,

"People rivet their eyes and ears upon differences amongst them. The sage, with childlike innocence, sees one humanity in all."

We make better, more informed decisions when we listen to all points of view. By doing this, a consensus is reached that does not foster hostility or opposition. Each point of view is regarded as one of a variety of colors in a large palette. Although an artist's colors may vary, the substance of his paint does not. The purpose of this substance is to express beauty. The more colors we value, the greater the possibility of creating art that has richness and depth. Peace is created when everybody feels acknowledged and appreciated. It is important to honor differences, while striving for unity.

It is vital that the future superpowers of the world avoid trying to spread their own colors on other countries and instead try to make those other countries brighter and more beautiful. This kind of policy will follow God's Intensions and bring about an ideal world. —*God the Artist. ET*

When opening our hearts to others, we see everyone as part of our family. We see the good in them despite their outward behavior. We are less likely to fight with them because it would be like our right arm struggling with our left or our mouth yelling at our ears. Once we recognize the common humanity we share with others, we can no longer dismiss their needs and desires any more than we can dismiss our own. Instead, people are embraced as extensions of ourselves.

If someone behaves badly, pause before passing judgment. Be big hearted enough to give them the benefit of the doubt. Assume they meant well, rather than intended to hurt. By assuming this, most conflicts are prevented. Remember, each of us thinks our behavior is justified, no matter how it appears to others. If someone throws a valuable possession of yours away, find out if they were trying to be helpful, rather than inconsiderate and mean. What is valuable to one person might be trash to another. Even if people intend to hurt, this often is because they were hurt earlier, and so want others to also know what it feels like. This does not excuse their behavior, but it can remind us of when we may have felt and acted the same way. An open heart begins with an open mind. By listening, by communicating with kindness instead of reacting with anger, most conflicts are avoided. This is the heart of compassion.

Take the case of a thief. If you take the shojo approach to reforming him, you will attempt to persuade him by taking him to task. The daijo approach is first to get close to him, and then, when the opportunity arises, to point out that what he is doing is not really profitable and is causing him more anxiety than it is worth, and in this way, guide him from inappropriate to proper behavior. —*Daijo and Shojo. ET*

Compassion for others is essential, but so is compassion for oneself. Only when we are compassionate to both others and ourselves will there be universal compassion. The pursuit of spiritual growth can be burdensome and unhappy if we hold extremely high ideals and then judge ourselves harshly against them. This harsh self-judgment saps our inspiration, depletes our life-force, and hinders our progress. Therefore, it is important to be gentle with ourselves and remember that no one is perfect. Placing our imperfections and virtues in a balanced perspective is the best way to support our spiritual growth. We are happier when we balance a dedication to personal growth with an easygoing humor and self-acceptance.

Although there are great benefits to be gained from self-improvement, it is equally important to accept ourselves as we are. This is the basis of self-love. Only when we accept ourselves—both the good and the bad—can we accept others as they are. The purest love accepts people as they are, rather than holding idealized expectations of how they should be. This type of love treats everyone with tolerance and kindness.

Kannon's Heart is the actual embodiment of Kannon's great compassion, which is acquired when one adopts that heart as one's own. Kannon's Way is to act from this heart. —On Kannon's Heart. KW

Humility

If you stay on the path with neither a selfish nor egotistical heart, your life will be blessed with success and will flourish.

—Izunome: The Movement of the Universe. KW

Meishusama put great emphasis on humility. Humility has to do with our sense of self-worth, how that sense arises, and consequently, how we see ourselves in relationship to others.

Those who lack humility live in a painful inner world of insecurity and low self-esteem. They feel that their personal attributes—being intelligent, attractive, successful, or more skilled in a variety of ways—define their worth. They judge themselves by these attributes, and feel that others judge them the same way. Thus they are always compelled to compete, striving to elevate themselves above others, to be "better than" or "best." They see others as competitors for status and admiration.

God greatly dislikes human self-conceit.
—Humbleness, Courtesy, and Self-restraint. ET

A humble person's sense of self-worth is not based on personal attributes or accomplishments, but on the recognition that we all have an innate self-worth, irrespective of what we do or have. Humble people are aware of the inner needs and desires we all share—the need to love and be loved, the desire for happiness, freedom, security, meaning, and purpose. This gives them affinity with and empathy for others. They understand that at our core, we are all the same.

If you let pride into your heart and turn your back on God, you will crumble when the crucial moment comes. —Poems of Inspiration. MK1

When we think we are better or worse than others we reduce everyone, including ourselves, to mere two-dimensional egos instead of multi-dimensional human beings with genuine thoughts and feelings.

If we do something exceptionally well, it is fine to appreciate our accomplishment. This only reflects healthy self-esteem, which is different than pride. But these accomplishments do not make us "qualitatively" superior to others.

Showing off one's achievements makes one look vain and egotistical. Modesty is best expressed by leaving one's achievements unknown.
—Izunome: The Movement of the Universe. KW

We can only be humble when we lack the internal tendency to identify ourselves with specific qualities, including shame, guilt, vanity, or pride. Even the inclination to identify oneself as one who is humble negates true humility. To be humble is to not identify with anything in particular. It is to be selfless.

Humble people radiate purity and innocence. Identification with our personal attributes on the other hand, is a type of spiritual cloud that obscures our Divine Spirit. When we are truly humble, our Divine Spirit shines through in brilliance, without effort or self-consciousness. To find true happiness, we must be satisfied with not standing out, with being, just one among many. Humility and selflessness leads to contentment.

Though I am no more than a grain of sand on the shore, please accept this token of my Makoto. —Harmonize with God's Will. MK1

Humor

An environment where you can enjoy things with cheerful laughter, and where you can make others laugh in the same way, will naturally lead to a heavenly state. In this way, laughter contributes to the resolution of disputes and to the creation of a peace-loving atmosphere. And to establish peace on earth, it is necessary to eradicate conflicts. —Roundness. KW

Understanding that life is ironic and full of unexpected contradictions encourages a humorous attitude toward our experiences and brings joy to our hearts. Humor is based on incongruity and surprise. It arises from the sudden perception of two things that do not really belong together, such as a team of military generals caught wearing ballerina tutus, or flames coming out of a showerhead. The greater the discrepancy between what is expected and what actually happens, the funnier the result. Oftentimes there is a dark or negative component to humor, such as when a dignified person slips on a banana peel and falls on the floor, or when someone's pants fall down while they are giving a speech.

One of the reasons we find such things funny is because we see ourselves in them. Because similar things have happened to us (although usually in a less exaggerated manner), we can identify with the victims and their reactions of anger, frustration and embarrassment. Such dramatized situations can help us to recognize our own foolishness. It also reminds us that we are not the only ones who suffer cruel indignities.

Man plans and God laughs. —Hebrew Proverb

Life is ironic. Despite our best efforts, things rarely turn out the way we expect. Life is too full of surprises for that to happen. One may wonder if there is some tormenter hiding somewhere in the sky who actually enjoys giving us mismatched pairs of socks and leaky umbrellas. Yet, one must ask why it is that we get so angry when annoying things happen to us, but find it funny when similar things happen to others. Maybe it is because we do not take other's misfortunes as seriously as our own. As the American humorist, Will Rogers, once said, "Everything is funny as long as it is happening to somebody else."

If we could give up our incessant demands for life to turn out the way we want, then maybe we could find a bit of humor in all the imperfection that exists around us. The difference between drama and comedy is in the level of personal involvement in the story. The less involvement, the lighter the story tends to be. Often, with the distance of time, we are able to laugh at a painful incident that earlier we took very seriously. When we make jokes about ourselves, people usually laugh. When we make jokes about others who are not present, people will often laugh as well. But when we make jokes about those who are present, they will usually not laugh but instead be offended.

Humor depends upon one's ability to stand back and experience things from a distance as if watching a bad movie in which everyone is acting out of character. Laughter arises spontaneously when we look at things from this kind of detached perspective.

Life is far too important a thing ever to talk seriously about it. —Oscar Wilde

We can use laughter to neutralize the frustration and hurt that life sometimes brings. It can be beneficial to take a moment and imagine that your life is a comedy and that you are eating popcorn while watching it. See how silly you look with that frown on your face and your fists pounding on the table. Then ask yourself, "What's so terrible about a flat tire, a burnt pot of rice, or a bad haircut?"

A sense of humor is the reward we receive for relinquishing our heavy chains of expectation and attachment. Humor can bring pleasure and enjoyment to the most trivial of things and, most importantly, frees us from morbid self-preoccupation.

Laughter is the source of good health for everyone. —Meishusama

Meishusama was renowned for his great sense of humor. A friend who came to visit him one evening ended up leaving with a stomachache because of the non-stop laughter. Meishusama's jokes ranged from the ironic to the absurd and from satire to slapstick. He commented that most religions were sadly lacking in humor, but that heaven was full of laughter. Even during the depths of war and government oppression, he was still able to find things to laugh about.

> Laughter creates fun and relaxation. Unless we create an atmosphere in which people can share laughter openly, the door to the heart cannot open. Arguing and finding fault in others only helps keep that door closed. We need to become increasingly good-humored and magnanimous. A generous-hearted person has a bright glow about them, and without brightness we cannot open the doors of Heaven. —*Opening the Door of Heaven. KW*

Laughing at ourselves when things go wrong may not change the circumstances, but at least we will not suffer internally. That is one of the most significant benefits of humor. Humor actually transforms darkness into light. Humor does this by acknowledging darkness rather than by ignoring, denying or repressing it. Some of the best jokes come from fear, pain, or anger. Bad circumstances offer some of the best opportunities for making good jokes because humor thrives on darkness. Humor accepts negativity while simultaneously liberating us from the suffering that usually accompanies it. Humor helps us find happiness in sickness, poverty, and strife, as well as in health, wealth, and peace.

He who tickles himself can laugh when he pleases. —Danish Proverb

Malicious humor, however, derives from a closed heart. People use sarcasm to ridicule others so as to cover up their own shortcomings. If people expand their consciousness, they would see themselves in others rather than judge them. Their laughter would be a sign of friendship, not animosity. It would express sympathy. This type of humor has a healing effect on everyone.

Humor delights in the incongruities of life. A funny joke has the miraculous power to transform a catastrophe into a vehicle for personal liberation. Humor widens our perspective so that we see things within a larger context. It helps us accept our day-to-day existence with a light heart and an even mind, and promotes an easygoing tolerance of others by bridging our mutual differences. According to Meishusama, laughter is one of the best ways to deal with adversity and abuse: "Once you learn to deal with slanderers by laughter, your character is guaranteed to improve." (*Responding to Slander. KW*)

Laughter disrupts the logical mind, with its narrow opinions, judgments, and agendas, and brings acceptance and freedom. It helps us to simply enjoy the here and now. When we laugh from our hearts, we become like children, full of innocence, wonder, and delight.

Laughter is flowers in heaven. —KW

Summary of Kannon's Way

The popular Buddhist deity Kannon is the embodiment of boundless and infinite compassion. The teaching on Kannon's Way describe how to act and live in a world that naturally promotes peace, harmony, and compassion. Kannon's Way is at the heart of Meishusama's philosophy.

Key Principles

Non-dualism: Opposites are not separate from each other. Each is co-dependent and could not exist without the other. Common examples make this easy to see: up/down, big/small, man/woman, life/death, good/evil, true/false, and so on. Each opposite has its part in a larger, integrated whole.

Order: Everything in nature has a certain sequence: spring follows winter, day follows night, from a seed comes a sprout, and then a plant. Correspondingly, from the spiritual comes the physical. On a personal level, when making decisions, first there is an intention (whether conscious or not), then a plan, and then action.

Dynamic Balance: Life is constantly changing and fluctuating between opposing forces, yet it maintains an overall equilibrium throughout this process. Life works best when we learn to harmonize with these cycles of change.

Holistic: The whole is greater than the sum of its parts. A person is more than just a collection of bone, blood, and tissue. He or she is all of these and more. The individual includes a mind and a spirit as well as a physical body. The more we perceive things as part of a larger whole, the more health and harmony we promote.

Attitudes and Behavior

Inclusiveness: Recognizing the intrinsic value of all beings, we allow them to express their various points of view, despite how different those might be from our own.

Non-judgmental: By understanding that we usually do not see the big picture, we learn to put ourselves in other people's shoes and try to see things from their perspective, rather than expecting them to behave according to our values and standards.

Moderation: Avoid extremes by being neither too generous nor too stingy, neither too open-minded nor too opinionated, neither too assertive nor too passive, neither too strict nor too permissive. Finding the middle ground is the goal.

Common Sense: Common sense means paying attention to the obvious, taking into account all factors, keeping things simple, and looking for practical results. Trusting one's native intelligence and judgment is a sign of common sense.

Compassion: To be compassionate, one sees the good in others, has empathy for their pains and joys, and treats them with warmth and kindness.

Flexibility: It is a skill to be able to modify one's behavior to suit a variety of changing situations and people. With flexibility one can sometimes be strict, sometimes lenient, sometimes serious, sometimes humorous, sometimes cautious, sometimes bold. Being adaptable requires flexibility.

Gentleness: Kannon's Way encourages being polite, mild-mannered, and considerate rather than pushy and aggressive.

Open-Mindedness: Being receptive to new ideas and behavior rather than being closed-minded or opinionated is consistent with Kannon's Way.

Tolerance: Living the Kannon's Way life includes recognizing that no person or group holds a monopoly on truth and that some truths, even those considered universal may, in fact, not be. Respecting the differences of others brings us closer to peace and harmony.

Fairness: Treating people equally and evenhandedly, each according to his or her own needs, is part of Kannon's Way.

Relaxed Manner: The manner in which we live our lives can reflect Kannon's Way by: not being overly excited or stressed by situations, not forcing things, and remaining calm and even-tempered.

Humility: Authentic humility means knowing that we are just one among many, like a blade of grass in a field. And although each of us is unique and significant, none of us is better or worse than any other. Humility also includes not identifying with one's accomplishments as well as behaving modestly.

Deference: Using deference, we allow others to shine more brightly than ourselves, and sometimes we allow them to win arguments and have their way. We can also allow others to speak more often than we do.

Being Natural: Following Kannon's Way means to act naturally rather than in a contrived or artificial manner. It means to be authentic. It also means to harmoniously align oneself with the forces of nature.

Humor: Humor makes life enjoyable. By accepting that things might not turn out the way we expect, by viewing our own misfortunes as cosmic jokes rather than tragedies, and by delighting in unexpected reversals, contradictions, and exaggerations, we are following Kannon's Way. It is good to take things lightly.

Practicing Kannon's Way

Everyone thinks of changing the world, but no one thinks of changing himself.
—Leo Tolstoy

It can be said that ideals are valuable only to the extent that they can be successfully accomplished in life. After reading and understanding the significance of the qualities of Kannon's Way, the next step is to practice them. But as with most things, it helps to know how.

Should we make an effort to be loving, kind, humble, detached, moderate, flexible, practical, and humorous? And if we are serious about this, should we try hard? For many things in life, the harder we try, the better the results. But with attitudes and feelings, that does not always work. Emotions are unpredictable forces beyond our control. It is usually easier to control our outward behavior than our thoughts and feelings.

When we try to control our feelings, it usually backfires. The same is true for trying to control others. Nobody likes to be controlled, and this is true whether the controller is someone else or even oneself. Just as we can hold our breath for only so long before exhaling, it is also true that we can control our behavior for only so long before reverting back to our old ways. This is especially so if there are underlying motives or needs that we are unaware of that are driving our behavior.

When we try too hard to eliminate negative emotions such as anger, contempt, irritability, arrogance, hostility, or impatience, it only tends to make them stronger. As Sigmund Freud and other psychotherapists have pointed out, what we repress, like the contents in a pressure cooker, tends to build up force. Then, sooner or later, the emotions will erupt with even greater intensity than before.

Also, when we struggle to change, we create an inner conflict between our current behavior and our ideals. This conflict does not create peace and harmony, but rather its opposite. A conflict-ridden person is as likely to create peace and harmony in the world as darkness is likely to produce light.

What is important is to reconcile one's inner conflicts and to harmonize the opposite aspects of one's character. This is a very important practice for your spiritual growth.
— The Izunome Principle and Love. KW

The secret to successfully practicing Kannon's Way is openly revealed in the very qualities it prescribes. The practice must be done with gentleness, moderation, and flexibility. If we try too hard, we create inner conflict rather than change. Conversely, if we try too little, nothing will improve. Kannon's Way is the middle way, not the extreme way. Here are some ways to practice Kannon's Way:

1. Pick one positive quality at a time to work on. For instance, if the quality is non-judgment, then imagine what that feels like. Practice holding that feeling in your mind throughout the day, for a week or more, until it becomes a part of you. Also, repeatedly visualize acting that way. Don't force it, but instead be gentle with yourself. Eventually you will find that you have successfully incorporated this quality into your life.

Or if you prefer, pick someone whom you feel embodies this quality, and at the appropriate times ask yourself, "How would this person act if he or she was in

this situation?" The answer (or image) should come to you immediately. Then do
what you can to emulate this person.

2. Try to see things from other people's perspectives so that you can understand
why they do what they do. When you put yourself in their shoes, it becomes
hard to judge them when they act poorly. Instead, you will begin to understand
why they do what they do, even when it seems unwise. This can help to not hold
a grudge against others when they hurt, annoy, or offend you. There is an old
French saying that, "To know all is to forgive all."

3. When someone is acting annoying or inappropriately, ask yourself if you have
ever done anything similar to that. If so, you then have little justification for
condemning them. As the psychotherapist Carl Jung said, "Knowing your own
darkness is the best method for dealing with the darknesses of other people."
Sometimes seeing all the ways that you actually differ from your own ideals is
the best way to attain them. After all, it is hard to change that which you are not
aware of or do not understand. (This particular exercise can be quite humbling.)

4. Surrender your negative thoughts, emotions, and behavior to God, the Supreme
Power. Of course, this kind of surrender also cannot be forced. Surrendering is
the opposite of force. First you must ask yourself, "What do I prefer, to hold onto
a negative feeling, or to feel happy?" You can choose either one or the other, but
not both. However, you can only surrender things when you are inwardly ready.
So, do not push yourself. If you are sincere, the time will come.

Our emotional nature is like a child. It responds best to attention, affection,
and acceptance. On the other hand, when you force things, it provokes an equal
but opposite resistance. In Gestalt Therapy, this is called "The Law of Reversed
Effort." Under threat, the child may obey you out of fear, but inwardly will resist.
And when you are not around, the child may revert back to his or her old ways.
The child won't change inwardly. And if you are even more forceful, you may
create a monster out of the child. Children grow up better with love and gentle
guidance than with threats and excessive control. This applies to our emotions as
well.

Whenever you find yourself acting judgmental, rigid, dogmatic, intolerant,
uptight, harsh, egotistical, artificial, or extreme, rather than immediately trying to
suppress what you see, stop and take a deep breath. Stay present with the current
feeling rather than trying to change it. Look for the underling motive behind the
thought or behavior. Ask yourself, "Is this how I really prefer to behave at this

moment? Do I really want to impact others with this type of behavior, or would I prefer to act according to my ideals?" If the latter, then gently focus on whatever Kannon's Way quality you most wish to adopt. Make this positive quality the light that guides you through the darkness.

Of course, always do what you can to be polite and kind to others, but also examine your thoughts, motives, and feelings. Allow the contrast between whatever negative traits you discover and your heartfelt ideals to co-exist with each other. Do not judge what you see, nor rush to change your current feelings, because feelings are not responsive to coercion. To force change is to deviate from Kannon's Way. Instead, be gentle with yourself. You deserve to be treated with kindness.

The more you treat yourself with this kind of gentleness, awareness, and acceptance, the more these very qualities will become a part of you, and the more they will transfer into your treatment of others. This kind of change cannot be forced; it can only be allowed. Similarly, authentic love is never based on effort, but on sincerity. Forced love, on the other hand, is always fake. Learn to uncover the authentic love that already dwells within you.

Remember, Kannon's Way is not a path of aggression, but of gentleness.

Ultimately, truth exists without disciplines. If people can truly embrace ONE teaching that encompasses everything, then their hearts can penetrate the inner spirit of all disciplines. This allows people to follow their disciplines naturally, without effort. Kannon's Way helps people find this single teaching. This is how it works: Kannon Bodhisattva, a manifestation of God, is symbolized by the figure One—the ultimate dimension of divine unity. —Freedom Beyond Discipline. KW

A Life Filled with Joy

The more liberated from spiritual clouds a soul becomes, the more it is capable of dancing to its own internal rhythms rather than blindly conforming to the outer dictates of society. Such souls trust their own internal wisdom rather than the beliefs and opinions handed down to them by society. They are free of self-conscious doubt and thus behave in an easy and natural way. They intelligently adapt to circumstances rather than unconsciously react to them. There is often a lighthearted playfulness in their behavior. Such souls are able to express the freedom and joy of Spirit itself while simultaneously maintaining an inner balance and harmony with all people and all things.

I tend to work playfully. So, when engaged in a task, there is never any struggle. For me, my work is like a luxurious hobby. Among the many images of Kannon is the Yugyo[12] Kannon, and the spirit of this Kannon suits me best. When I carry out tasks in this spirit, I can do a much better job. On the other hand, when I feel I am struggling with a heavy burden, and am all tired out doing things I am reluctant to do, then things do not go as I wish.

This light-hearted approach is the opposite of what people used to believe was best, and I see that most of my students also share this outdated view. When they work too passively or too strenuously, their efforts inevitably turn out badly. For example, when you are asked to visit someone who is sick to give them Jyorei, if you go with the spirit of joy, the person will begin to recover, and that good result will encourage you to continue helping him or her. In this way, both you and the person will enjoy the results. So, the more joy you find in what you do, the better the result will be. *—Work with Joy, Not Pain. KW*

With each new step along the path of spiritual growth, our awareness expands and we gain new knowledge and insight about ourselves and others. At each step, it is important to accept and embrace this new knowledge and insight, as this will help us to integrate it. Then, we are ready to proceed to the next level of spiritual development. In this way, we build our own spiritual ladder, one step at a time, toward the final destination of subjective Oneness with God and all of creation. The end of the journey is not a final step on the ladder, but an embracing of the entire ladder itself. And it is not we, as individuals, who embrace the ladder, but the universe itself that embraces the ladder through us. This is an example of Kannon's unconditional love for all things.

If we truly understand the principles of Kannon's Way and learn how to live according to them, spiritual clouds will not accumulate at all. At the same time, one will become a person who constantly gains toku energy. Not only will one be free from sickness and misfortune, but also be blessed with health, longevity, and prosperity, not only for oneself but also for one's family and friends. Finally, one will be able to live a life filled with joy. —The true cause of sickness is found in the soul. KW

---

12. *Yugyo* means to act or behave with a light heart and enjoyment, free from attachments to results and suffering.

CHAPTER 10

JYOREI

If we can only find a way of curing sickness then it is inevitable that cures for poverty and strife will follow. And if these are achieved, then humanity will have found the basic conditions necessary for happiness. —Jyorei and Happiness. ET

Divine Light

Jyorei is Divine Light. It comes from Spirit, not matter. Jyorei is different from physical light, which consists of minute particles of energy called 'photons' traveling at enormous speeds through empty space. Jyorei is coherent patterns of energy that bring order out of chaos and harmony out of discord.

This Light extends throughout the cosmos, infusing all things with its sublime radiance. Without this Light, nothing could exist. It is the Light that gives expression to the clouds in the sky, the fish in the sea, and the thoughts within our minds. It is the mysterious energy that animates our heart, our lungs, and our breath.

Although divine Light is everywhere, most of us cannot sense it because it is invisible and intangible. This Light exists within us as well, yet we usually do not notice it because of our inner darkness. Because the Light of Jyorei is weightless, it can help us to feel lighthearted; because it is transparent, it can help us to perceive clearly; and because it is bright, it can guide us through darkness.

When we share Jyorei, we access and focus this energy for the benefit of others. Through receiving the blessings of Jyorei, our spiritual clouds—the root cause of all suffering—are dispelled. Jyorei promotes health and spiritual growth, which leads to greater happiness.

God, appearing in the form of the deity Kannon, gave this divine power to Meishusama to heal and awaken as many people as possible. They, in turn, were often encouraged to share it with others so that the blessings could spread still further. Jyorei is now being shared with people throughout the world, in the six continents of Asia, Africa, North and South America, Australia, and Europe. Thus, as one candle lights another, the world grows increasingly brighter until every corner is set ablaze in brilliant Light.

All the darkness in the world cannot extinguish the light of a single candle.
—Hasidic proverb

The appearance of Jyorei in the world today coincides with a higher frequency of spiritual energy entering our world at this time. We are approaching a new age in which the element Meishusama calls the Spirit of Fire is growing stronger, promoting increased miracles of healing and spiritual awakening.

The advent of Jyorei in the material world is, of course, a harbinger of the ideal world to come, for Jyorei is at the very heart of the Age of Day.
—The Strata in the Spiritual World. ET

Jyorei and Purification

The fundamental cause of unhappiness is spiritual clouding. And there is a sure means of clearing this clouding of the spirit, which is Jyorei.
—Jyorei and Happiness. ET

In ancient times, before books and organized belief systems, people did not need to be convinced of the existence of a higher power exerting a profound influence in their lives. They intuitively knew this. For many, life revolved around Spirit: the deeper their connection with it, the greater was their inner peace and harmony. But in our modern world of cell phones, fast cars, cable television, computer games, and the Internet, this connection with the sacred dimension seems to have become lost. Thus, it is no wonder that so many people nowadays find their lives so empty and meaningless. They suffer from a poverty of the soul that cannot be healed by endless entertainment or by the compulsive accumulation of more and more things.

Increasingly, people are coming to realize that the answer to their deepest problems comes not from large bank accounts, long vacations, or small bottles of pills. Many are now turning to various forms of spiritual healing, meditation, and prayer for help with their physical and emotional problems. Others are turning to psychotherapy or counseling. Not only do these practices offer relief, but they also provide a direct experience of something beyond the ordinary world. Amongst these various practices, Jyorei is drawing special attention from people because it incorporates healing, meditation, and prayer into one simple, but powerful process.

Jyorei, in Japanese, means "purification of the spirit." It is a simple, yet profound healing technique in which spiritual Light is directed to people for their overall health and happiness. Through the experience of Jyorei, we enter into communion with the silent presence of God, and then allow this presence to move through us. The energy of Jyorei dispels the spiritual impurities within people's souls and also eliminates the physical toxins that have accumulated in their physical bodies. These "spiritual clouds" are the true cause of human suffering. This does not imply that people's souls or spirits are polluted, but only that they are covered up, just as the sun might be covered by clouds in the sky. Removing these clouds does not cause the sun to shine brighter; it merely reveals that which was hidden. What then begins to emerge from behind the spiritual clouds is our divine spirit, which is innately peaceful and happy, just as the sun is innately warm and bright.

Methods that purify the spirit through the five senses are, in a sense, indirect, and since they are physical methods directed to the non-physical spirit, the results are relatively ineffective. On the other hand, Jyorei, as practiced in our organization, works directly on the soul, purifying it and filling it with Light. The results are incomparably superior to those of any physical method. This is proved by the fact that Jyorei can heal diseases, which are considered incurable by various conventional approaches, in a short period of time. — *Sermons and Precepts. ET*

There is more to healing than repairing broken bones. It is about mending broken hearts and calming agitated minds. Most importantly, it is about renewing the spirit. Although Jyorei is most often introduced to people as a form of physical or emotional healing, its primary purpose is spiritual growth. Through spiritual growth, we eventually arrive at a heart full of love, joy, and serenity.

Strife, poverty, disease, and other forms of suffering arise from excessive clouding within the spiritual world. Each of us creates spiritual clouds by our flawed attitudes, beliefs, and behavior.

According to Meishusama, all suffering is a form of purification, and all purification results in a discharge of toxins and negativity. The more we

JYOREI

eliminate these spiritual clouds, the better off we will be. However, not all types of purification are equal. Some are more beneficial than others, and some can be unpleasant, if not downright painful. Other types of purification can be pleasant or joyful.

A functional distinction can be made between two kinds of purification: Reactive Purification and Proactive Purification. Both can be unpleasant, but each has different causes and results. Reactive Purification is caused by life-denying experiences, such as exposure to environmental toxins or our own negative thoughts, emotions, or behaviors, whereas proactive purification is caused by life-affirming experiences such as Jyorei, appreciating beauty, eating healthy food, or performing good deeds. Although both forms of purification discharge accumulated toxins and negativity, *Proactive Purification is more beneficial than Reactive Purification because it prevents the generation of new spiritual clouds. Both eliminate the bad, but Proactive Purification also promotes the good.*

Reactive Purification does not tend to improve things long-term because it only discharges surface-level toxins, not deep-seated ones. It also does not prevent new toxicity from occurring. Reactive Purification can sometimes be quite unpleasant. For instance, a flu infection will often discharge some toxins from the body through phlegm, runny nose, diarrhea, sweating, or vomiting, but it does not usually produce significant improvement to one's overall health. At best, Reactive Purification will release just enough toxins from the body so that one does not become overwhelmed by them, but not much more.

On the other hand, Proactive Purification, such as that caused by Jyorei, is usually mild. It tends to discharge greater amounts of toxins from the body than does Reactive Purification, and also lessens the tendency to generate future toxicity. For instance, the more we release built up anger, the less likely we are to get angry in the future. Also, the more we release emotional pain, the less likely we are to use addictive drugs to suppress it. Oftentimes, Proactive Purification is either unnoticed or can actually be quite pleasant, producing feelings of comfort, serenity, and well-being. Over time, not only does Proactive Purification improve physical and emotional health, but it also fosters spiritual growth. *Because of this, it can be said that all suffering is a form of purification, but not all purification is a form of suffering.*

These days it is almost impossible for us to avoid all forms of toxins and to avoid generating new spiritual clouds. Therefore, it is advisable to receive Jyorei on a daily basis. The Proactive Purification caused by Jyorei is similar to taking a daily shower or to washing one's clothes frequently. Both Jyorei and showering make one look and feel better. However, if one neglects to do one's laundry regularly, one's shirts and pants may become so dirty that some of the stains will fail to come out no matter how hard one scrubs. Similarly, if one neglects to generate Proactive Purification regularly, one may accumulate so much mental and physical toxicity that it becomes embedded in one's mind and body. The more one experiences Proactive Purification, the freer of toxicity one becomes, and therefore the less suffering one is likely to experience.

There is no need to endure the suffering of Reactive Purification if one simply avoids exposure to physical and mental toxins and refrains from engaging in negative actions. The suffering occasionally caused by Proactive Purification, on the other hand, is but a minor discomfort when compared with the increased health and happiness it can produce in the long run. Therefore, a wise person will always choose Proactive Purification over Reactive Purification.

The key to understanding Meishusama's teachings is this distinction between these two types of purification. *It is better to purify ourselves of spiritual clouds in a painless or pleasant way rather than through unnecessary suffering.* One of the best ways to promote Proactive Purification is through helping others. Fortunately, the practice of Jyorei is especially well suited for this purpose. Making others happy can also be a great source of personal satisfaction and fulfillment.

Often, healing people's physical illness is the first step towards promoting happiness in them. The next step is the healing of their mental and emotional problems. At other times the reverse is true, and the person's inner nature will be the first to improve. The Greek philosopher Plato said, "If you want to heal your body, you must first heal your mind." The body and mind are interconnected, and each affects the other. Oftentimes, problems originating in the mind or from past lives must be healed before conditions in the physical body can be addressed. Although the true source of these problems lies in the spiritual world, most people are looking for immediate, tangible relief from their pain rather than abstract explanations. Nevertheless, it is important to understand that the real healing is actually occurring on a spiritual level.

Jyorei strengthens the divine spirit's influence over us while simultaneously purifying the corrupting influences of the instinctive spirit, thereby lessening the latter's excessive control over us. The instinctive spirit is basically narcissistic and selfish by nature, subject to greed, lust, and aggressiveness. As the spiritual body becomes cleansed, the instinctive spirit resumes its rightful place as the servant of the physical body, not its master.

Spiritual purification opens us up to the beneficial guidance of the guardian spirit, bringing us increased inspiration and good fortune. It promotes inner harmony between the divine spirit and the instinctive spirit, and supports the soul's progress in its journey towards greater spiritual awareness and happiness.

Not to commit evils, but to do all that is good, and to purify one's heart—this is the teaching of all the Buddhas. —Gautama Buddha

Spiritual growth occurs through the purification of thought, feeling, and intention. Through the power of Jyorei, the desires that we hold within us become less negative and compulsive. As selfishness and immaturity are transformed into greater concern for the welfare of others, we begin to relate to others in a more positive manner and begin to see the world as a friendlier place. This is the opposite of alienation and separation, which cause anguish to the soul. Spiritual growth expands our awareness into greater and greater levels of perceived unity. We begin to feel a kinship with everyone and everything. We see that there is no need to exclude others from this kinship because of personal judgments or animosity.

Meishusama says, "If you do not make others happy, you can never be happy yourself." *(About Myself. ET)* This simple motto does not advocate trying to subserviently please other people all the time, but rather to open our hearts to others, and to feel their pain as our pain, and to feel their happiness as our happiness. If we have an open heart, then how can we be happy when those around us are miserable? This sensitivity generates spontaneous feelings of empathy for others as well as the altruistic motivation to help them.

As the Light within us increases, we also begin to recognize its presence in others. This perception is the basis of love. Love helps us see beyond our outer differences by revealing our common humanity. Love unites us and makes us care about each other. As the Sufi poet Rumi wrote: "Love is the bridge between you and everything."

Love is the true motivation for practicing Jyorei. There is never a charge for Jyorei other than donations based on gratitude. These donations, when given, go to support Shumei's altruistic activities, not the Jyorei giver, who offers it freely. The only personal gain the giver of Jyorei receives is the satisfaction derived from helping others.

199

The act of helping others purifies our soul and raises our spiritual condition to a higher level. When we serve the greater good, we receive Toku Energy, which benefits us in the spiritual world. Toku Energy is the Light that comes back to us because of our good deeds. Of all the possible ways we can help others, to help them spiritually is the best because its effects are the most enduring. Everything else, such as houses, cars, and people, comes and goes. When we die, only our spiritual wealth can be taken with us. Jyorei is one of the simplest, yet most profound, ways to help people spiritually, as well as to help ourselves.

I have not only perfected a way to dispel clouds by focusing this spiritual radiation on a specific part of the body, but I have also created a special way to increase the power of everybody's radiations. —*Natural Power. ET*

Jyorei is a unique healing method in that it is very easy to learn and practice. The primary requirement for practicing Jyorei is an altruistic concern for helping others. It does not require any special breathing techniques, concentration, visualization, mantras, or difficult bodily postures. Jyorei also does not require faith, nor does it depend on the innate power of the person giving Jyorei. Its blessings are not earned; they are given. Jyorei is a gift from God and Meishusama to all of humanity.

If you light a lamp for someone else, it will also brighten your path. —Buddha

The Practice of Jyorei

Jyorei bathes the soul in Divine Light and instantaneously awakens the spirit. As this transforms people in a way that we can describe as "effortless," it obviously relegates sermons and precepts to a position of secondary significance.
—The End of Suffering. ET

A Jyorei session is usually conducted with two people, one giving, and the other receiving. If both are qualified to give Jyorei, then afterwards they can trade places, so that the former giver can then be the receiver, and vice versa. When transmitting this energy, we simply raise our arm to project healing Light out of our hand. When our arm gets a little tired, it is time to switch hands. It's best to not feel stiff or strained, but to keep our arm and hand very relaxed and loose. No effort is required. Regarding the importance of relaxing while sharing Jyorei, Meishusama writes, "The more we reduce our physical tension the more effective it becomes." *(On Forcing An Argument. KW)* It is more a matter of allowing the energy to move through us, rather than feeling that we are doing something special to make this happen. The Light of Jyorei is not our personal possession; we are merely voluntary conduits for its expression. This energy comes from God (or Spirit), with assistance from Meishusama, and it is our privilege to be allowed to share it with others and to work for the betterment of humanity.

As human beings, there are generally two ways that we can give to others: either through kind words expressed by our mouths or through generous actions performed by our bodies. Jyorei, however, comes from neither of these two sources, but originates from a third source: the eternal Spirit that transcends all things. Jyorei is one of the very few ways that the average person can give to someone on a spiritual level without relying on words or physical actions to do so.

As mentioned earlier, Jyorei is given using the arms and hands only. There is no need for talking or verbal prayer, which would only distract from the session. Some people can feel the energy traveling down their arms and out their hands as it radiates to the person in front of them. But even if the givers feel nothing, they know in their hearts that the transmission is occurring.

The best way to give Jyorei to others is with a quiet mind and an open heart. The more love and concern you have for the person in front of you, the better, as this strengthens the connection between the two of you. Let go of your various worldly concerns, and focus on the present. If distracting thoughts come up, just surrender them to God. Stay focused on the act of giving Jyorei, without effort or strain. Especially, let go of the need for particular results. Who are we to say how a person should benefit? The soul of a person may need to experience a particular sickness or problem in order to learn an important spiritual lesson from it. About this Meishusama says, "Consider the possibility that your struggles might have a deeper meaning, and that they are part of a necessary process arranged by God for your spiritual growth." *(On Removing Egotism and Worldly Attachments. KW)* Instead of telling the universe what to do, it is better to trust in Divine Intelligence to know what is ultimately best for everyone. Our job is simply to be a lens for focusing Light on the world, and that is all. Remember, the main point when sharing Jyorei is to relax and allow.

If the success of our efforts depended on us, we might fall short. But this action is divinely inspired and is much greater than any one of us. Therefore, we need to put our egos aside while giving Jyorei. Successfully doing so is much like blowing away the clouds in the sky, revealing the bright sunshine of Spirit that was formerly hidden. The sunshine of Jyorei is waiting for the chance to break through the cloud cover so that it can light up the world around us.

Some of us may feel that Meishusama is guiding and assisting us in the transmission of Jyorei. This feeling can help us to relinquish personal credit for the effects of Jyorei by acknowledging either Meishusama or God as the true giver of Jyorei, rather than us. We are merely the physical instruments being used by them for the healing.

Love and compassion are two of the most powerful ways of opening the heart. They help more Light to pass through us when sharing Jyorei. Meishusama describes two kinds of love: "Love is of two fundamental kinds: one is God's love and the other is human love. God's love is truly daijo, since it is unconditional and eternal. Human love, by contrast, is essentially shojo, which usually leads one to care only about oneself, one's friends, and one's own race. Because of its limited scope, the pursuit of this kind of love can produce evil results. If you understand this, you must constantly follow the Daijo Way within your own life. More specifically, when you give Jyorei,[2] you must always keep your heart aligned with God's love. If you do, good fortune will surely follow. Go with God's love and extend this absolute love to others, and you will be a person whom everyone feels comfortable talking with and being around. Then, your actions will never fail to bring success." (*Being Daijo. KW*)

People can give Jyorei even when they are sick, depressed, or angry, but it is best to bring as much purity as possible to the Jyorei session. Sick people, however, find that by sharing Jyorei with others, they themselves become healthier. Those with emotional problems also find more inner peace and happiness from sharing Jyorei. Some people feel that the act of giving Jyorei benefits the giver more than the receiver. This adds a new perspective to the words of Jesus Christ, who said that, "It is better to give than to receive."

When we hope for something, we often find that it is impossible to bring it about, but once we have almost forgotten about it, things suddenly go the way we wish. Even the giving of Jyorei follows the same pattern. The more eager one is to heal the patient, the less effective the cure is. When, however, one does not let such thoughts enter one's mind, but simply gives Jyorei as a matter of course, or when one does not know whether the patient is curable or not, but gives Jyorei anyway, the cure is unusually easy and effective.

—*Trust in God. ET*

Attachments block the Light. Even attachments to the results of Jyorei, although altruistic, can reduce the flow of energy. To thoroughly align ourselves with divine power requires detachment, which comes from faith and trust in a higher power. Although good intentions are valuable, the attachment to a desired outcome is not. Trust and allow divine intelligence to work through you. About this Meishusama writes, "It is absolutely necessary for us to do everything we can with all our effort, while simultaneously trusting in God to do what is best." (*Maintaining Moderation. KW*)

When receiving Jyorei, it is best to have an attitude of openness and gratitude. Simply quiet the mind and open the heart. This does not add to the Jyorei energy, but rather puts one in a more receptive state. Although a spiritual orientation may be helpful, the results are not dependent upon it. Even people who fall asleep while receiving Jyorei, benefit from it. This is also true for those who might be unconscious or in a coma. Neither the giver nor the receiver needs to believe in the power of Jyorei for it to work. This healing through divine Light can even be effective with people who are skeptical or disbelieving, and can also benefit animals and plants. Each individual has different personal beliefs, attitudes, and needs, and our intention is to always respect those differences.

The procedure is this: the recipient is normally seated from two to four feet from the person giving Jyorei. First, Jyorei is directed to the forehead. Next, the recipient is asked to lower his or her head, and then Jyorei is directed to the top of the head. These areas of the body are especially sensitive to spiritual influences, and from there the energy will travel down to whichever part of the body needs healing.

Some may wonder why we do not direct energy to other parts of the body, especially to those areas where there is pain or dysfunction. Although it does not hurt to do so, usually this will merely treat the symptoms of a problem, not the cause, thereby resulting in only short-term benefits. For example, a stomachache might be caused by food poisoning, an ulcer, emotional stress, a pinched nerve, parasites, a spiritual disturbance, or even a physical injury. These problems, in turn, may have still deeper causes on a physical, emotional, or spiritual level. In other words, diagnosis can be complicated and difficult. Although it is important to know the cause of a problem so that we can deal with it on a practical level, this knowledge does not usually affect how we give Jyorei. We do not usually send energy to the stomach when someone has a stomachache because that would only be dealing with the secondary effects, not the root cause. Instead, we usually direct energy to the forehead and the top of the head. Just as the nutrition in food (when swallowed through our mouth) will go to wherever in the body it is needed, so too, Jyorei (when directed to these two vital spots) will go to wherever it is most needed within a person.

It is important to remember that Jyorei is divine energy, and that it works on many levels, not just the physical. Jyorei intelligently interacts with our whole being to guarantee the best outcome. Most importantly, Jyorei clears up the spiritual clouds that underlie all problems. And as these clouds dissipate, our awareness expands, allowing us to discover what is contributing to our problems and then to know what to do about them. For example, sometimes we need to improve our diet, eliminate toxins from our homes, get more exercise, become more considerate of others, change jobs, or get more sleep at night. There are also times when Jyorei produces seemingly miraculous healings, without the need for any change on our part. Jyorei both weakens the bad and strengthens the good. It works in more ways than we can imagine. Therefore, our job is not to diagnose an illness or problem, but only to share Light with compassion and trust.

The forehead area (sometimes referred to as the Third Eye Chakra) gives us access to the frontal part of the brain, including the pituitary and the hypothalamus glands, which are located deep inside the brain, directly behind the bridge of the nose. The hypothalamus is a cluster of brain cells that sort out messages to and from the rest of the body, and responds accordingly through the pituitary gland, which in turn produces the specific hormones that the body needs. These hormones are then circulated in the blood to the body's organs and tissues, including other endocrine glands. The hypothalamus is currently considered by many to be the master gland of the entire endocrine gland system, which is responsible for regulating many of the essential biological processes in the body. Thus, when we direct Jyorei to the forehead and the area behind it, the rest of the body is affected. Most significantly, directing Jyorei to this location also awakens inner spiritual perception and mystical consciousness.

The top of the head (sometimes referred to as the Crown Chakra) gives us access to the pineal gland, which is located in the central part of the brain, just behind and above the pituitary and hypothalamus glands. The pineal gland produces and controls various hormones and neurotransmitters, such as melatonin and serotonin, which influence many important physiological activities, including our moods and energy levels. Thus, when we direct Jyorei to the top of the head, we are affecting another area vital to our general health and well-being. Transmitting Jyorei to the top of the head causes the energy to flow downward, thereby purifying and healing the entire body in the process.

Together, these two points promote homeostasis and balance within the body. Receiving Jyorei on the forehead emphasizes purification of the spiritual body, whereas receiving Jyorei at the top of the head has a greater healing effect on the physical body. Of course, spirit and body are interrelated, so each affects the other to a large extent.

The usual amount of time spent during a Jyorei session is just five minutes, although longer sessions are also beneficial. However, long the session, we cannot judge or quantify Jyorei based on duration because Jyorei is spiritual in nature, and Spirit transcends time.

When you give Jyorei to someone, always keep your heart aligned with God's love. If you do so, good results will surely follow. —Being Daijo. KW

The Experience of Jyorei

What joy to have my life renewed. What greater joy to heal with Jyorei.
—Reception of Ohikari. MK2

The power of Jyorei can often be experienced through one or more of our five senses. In recalling a healing session, recipients often report feeling heat in various parts of the body or all around it. Other common experiences include: tingly sensations on the skin, feelings of gratitude or joy, subtle pressure in the head, calming of the breath, weightlessness of the body, subtle lights of various colors, faint inner sounds, the smell of flowers or incense, or deep inner peace. Some people even report spiritual visions of Meishusama or Kannon Bodhisattva.

If a person feels a bit sleepy or tired after receiving Jyorei, it may be because their body is redirecting its own internal energy to assist in the healing process. This may be similar to the tiredness one feels after eating a big meal; it is temporary, and will soon pass after the digestive process is complete. Such tiredness, after Jyorei, is a good sign because it indicates that a deep cleansing and healing is occurring within the body. Therefore, during these times, it might be helpful to lie down and rest for a while.

When people start receiving or giving Jyorei they often notice dramatic changes in their lives. The more often they engage in Jyorei, the more dramatic the results can be. Jyorei frees us from future suffering by purifying us of internal toxicity. Meishusama views all purification as an opportunity to learn and grow. It provides us with the opportunity to re-evaluate our lives and to seek inner guidance. Rather than resisting or complaining about our various hardships or pain, it is better to keep in mind that this discomfort is only temporary, and inevitably leads to greater health and happiness. Knowing this, it is better to feel grateful for the purification. Gratitude has a way of transforming even the most difficult of situations into something of inexplicable beauty and value.

Our blood can be viewed as a physical manifestation of the soul. Because of this direct link, when Jyorei is used to purify the soul, it also purifies the blood. On the physical level, as the body becomes free of toxins, the immune system gets stronger, and other biological processes move to a deeper state of balance, harmony, and vitality. Meishusama writes, "The spiritual clouding we are talking about also has a physical equivalent or expression, and this is poisoning of the blood and the accumulation of purulent matter in the body." *(Spiritual Clouds and Sickness. ET)*

Meishusama often refers to Jyorei as purification by the spirit of fire, and when people are receiving it they feel heat. This heat can be a sign of physical healing, as the body will often raise its internal temperature in order to subdue harmful viruses or bacteria, such as when we have a fever, or to flush internal toxins from the system, such as what happens in a sauna. Jyorei also appears to activate the lymphatic system to further facilitate detoxification. Often people who have received numerous Jyorei sessions will experience powerful elimination symptoms such as runny noses with dark, thick discharges, skin rashes, tremendous sweating, boils, diarrhea, and even pus oozing out of their skin. These symptoms are usually the result of medicines, environmental pollutants, and other poisons that the person has ingested or been exposed to in the past. Sometimes physical toxins can also be inherited from a person's ancestors. Meishusama explains that symptoms such as these are the outer effects of inner lumps of accumulated toxins melting and discharging from the body.

A useful distinction can be made between the symptoms of sickness caused by purification (proactive purification) and sickness caused by environmental pollutants such as contaminated food, bacteria, parasites, venom, pollen, smog, radiation, chemicals, or polluted water (reactive purification). Although both types of sickness can be considered forms of purification, one is favorable, and the other is not. Purification caused by Light leads to greater health and happiness, whereas purification caused by toxins only slows down the gradual descent into ill health. With the former, it is good to appreciate the healing we are receiving, whereas with the latter, it is good to isolate and identify the cause of the discomfort, and to avoid further exposure to these substances whenever possible. This is a common sense and practical approach to dealing with sickness.

Sometimes one can help reduce the discomfort of purification by drinking plenty of water, which helps to flush toxins out of the internal organs and the lymphatic system. Additionally, as common sense tells us, eating foods with lots of fiber can assist in pushing sluggish toxins out of the digestive tract.

The lymphatic system is one of the body's most important means for eliminating toxins and metabolic waste products. But unlike the bloodstream, which is constantly circulating throughout the body because of the pumping action of the heart muscle, the lymphatic system depends on physical movement (including breathing) to carry these toxins out of the body. Therefore, some light physical exercise, such as walking, can be helpful. An added benefit of exercise is that it stimulates the bloodstream to carry active components of the immune system to where they can attack and eliminate viruses, bacteria, and other pathogens. In general, it's important to pay attention to the current needs of one's body, and to care for it wisely in order to go through one's physical purification smoothly and effectively.

Although many people feel or perceive such sensations as heat, pressure, vibration, or light when receiving Jyorei, it is not necessary to feel anything to benefit from the healing sessions. Some people never feel any immediate sensations from Jyorei, but nonetheless still benefit from the increased health and spiritual growth that it promotes. The important thing to look for when evaluating Jyorei is its practical effects in one's life.

Experiencing the various miracles produced by Jyorei gives people the opportunity to re-evaluate their beliefs about life. One may ask, "Is there a higher power or intelligence somewhere that has the ability to dramatically affect our lives?" This is the beginning of faith, which can inspire one to transcend one's limited conditioning and to step into a larger life, a life dedicated to spiritual values and to serving the greater good.

Testing out new things before coming to conclusions about them is often wise. Therefore, a little skepticism is welcomed. Cynicism, on the other hand, may not be so helpful. Such an attitude not only closes the door to new experiences, but also drains the joy out of our lives. During the healing session, if we can keep our hearts and minds open, then the full benefits of Jyorei will enter our being unobstructed. Jyorei is a form of non-verbal prayer in which peace, love, and joy are the means of prayer as well as the end result. To feel grateful for the Light is to fully participate in this prayer. This prayer is not one of ritualized words, but of silent communion with the sacred dimension of existence.

Sickness that purifies body and soul is a gift from God. —Sickness. MK1

Jyorei can be given anywhere and is not dependent on either the immediate surroundings or on a person's personal beliefs and attitudes. Nevertheless, these can still influence the effectiveness of Jyorei. The following is a list of the factors that can sometimes, to some degree or another, affect the power of Jyorei:

1. Spiritual level of the giver (The higher the level, the better, although only God can judge a person's level).

2. Attitude and intention of the giver – ideally gratitude, love, altruism, detachment, selflessness, humility, attention, and so on).

3. Attitude of the recipient, including physical and emotional needs (the more receptive the better).

4. Strength of spiritual cords between the people exchanging Jyorei (strong cords create openings for more Light to come through).

5. Number of people exchanging Jyorei together (the more the better).

6. Type of Ohikari the giver is wearing. (*See the following section "The Ohikari."*)

7. Proper arm posture and hand gesture (should be loose and relaxed, and focused in the right direction).

8. Physical environment, ideally clean, quiet, beautiful, and at a high vibration. (The best place is near a Scroll of Light, which contains calligraphy by Meishusama.)

9. Duration of session (sometimes longer is better).

10. Particular circumstance (sometimes crisis can create opportunity).

11. God's Grace, which cannot be predicted or measured.

While it is helpful to consider the above factors, one should not obsess over them. These are merely listed as helpful guidelines. What is most important is to be grateful for the divine blessings that Jyorei offers.

Although the Light of Jyorei is always the same at its source, our attitudes and receptivity greatly affect the power of its transmission. Because we are the physical transmitters of this energy, we have a sacred obligation to be as clear a conduit as possible. Letting go of self-preoccupation, distracting thoughts, and attachment to results allows the Light to move through us unimpeded. The more humility, purity, and love we bring to the session, the more both the recipient and we ourselves will benefit. Jyorei will be stronger and more effective when one embraces these positive attitudes.

It is important to realize that the higher the spiritual level of the source, the finer and subtler the radiations will be. This is a basic principle. And although radiations from the human body are all extremely powerful, their strength varies according to the individual more than one can imagine. Along with this, as the radiation becomes stronger, the power of Jyorei increases. —*Natural Power. ET*

Furthermore, the thicker the aura of one who gives Jyorei, the better will be the healing results of his cures. And, as one helps more people through Jyorei, one will receive more gratitude and appreciation, one's aura will become even thicker, and the results of one's healing will climb to new heights of splendor. —*Spiritual Radiation and the Aura. ET*

People are attracted to Jyorei for a variety of reasons. Some are looking for relief from their suffering, whereas others are more concerned with helping people. For the former group, Jyorei offers comfort and healing, and for the latter group. Jyorei offers a wonderful way to be of service to their families, friends, and associates. Both, however, receive internal purification, spiritual growth, and greater personal happiness from sharing Jyorei.

Jyorei is the Light that will unify the peoples of our world and heal their aching hearts and troubled minds. It dispels spiritual clouds, which are the invisible influences that cause our suffering. As the clouds obscuring the soul are dispelled, the radiations of the spiritual body begin to increase in strength and power. Meishusama states, "The true object of our attention should be the soul, not the body." *(Natural Power. ET)*

Humans are fundamentally patterns of vibration. Some are refined and harmonious, whereas others are less so, depending upon their level of purity. Jyorei raises a person's personal vibration to positive, Light-filled levels. If we wish to improve the quality of our lives, then this is what we must do.

At the deepest level, sharing Jyorei strengthens our inner spirit. The stronger and more radiant our spirit, the happier and more positive we become, and also the more capable we become of helping others. With progress, we become increasingly motivated to create love and harmony in our environment. Our aesthetic sense becomes more developed and we become more sensitive to the conditions of the world around us.

It is important to remember that God is using us as an instrument to help heal and transform the world spiritually. As Meishusama says, "Human beings do not have the power to perform even a single miracle; only God can perform miracles." *(Religion is Inseparable from Miracles. ET)* There is no better way to realize a perfect society than by purifying the spiritual bodies of more and more individuals. The more people that actively share Jyorei, the sooner will our world transform itself for the better. Each of us can make a difference in the lives of those around us. Anthropologist Margaret Mead said, "Never doubt that a small group of thoughtful, committed citizens can change the world; indeed, that is the only thing that ever has."

The Ohikari

When I take a brush and write, the writing on the paper is vibrant with life. If this paper is folded and put around someone's neck as an Ohikari, their feelings become radiant, and miracles start to happen. —The Savior of the World. HT

For an individual to give Jyorei, it is first necessary to attend a series of formal introductory classes, followed by an initiation into divine energy. At this time, there is a brief ceremonial reception of an Ohikari, which is a sacred silk amulet that is worn around the neck. Inside the Ohikari is a reproduction of one of Meishusama's hand-painted symbols for Light, written in Chinese calligraphy. Each Ohikari carries Meishusama's blessings and healing power within it.

Something is considered sacred when it carries a high spiritual vibration, communicates spiritual wisdom, or symbolizes a spiritual quality. Each of us has a spiritual dimension deep within our being, and wearing the Ohikari helps remind us of this dimension.

Wearing an Ohikari reinforces the connection we have, through powerful spiritual cords, with Meishusama and God. It is through these cords that we receive the power of Jyorei as a gift from God and Meishusama. The Ohikari is symbolic of the Light that each of us carries within the center of our being. Meishusama writes, "The Light given out through me is carried instantaneously to the inscription of each and every Ohikari by spiritual cords. Similar to a central broadcasting station that sends out radio signals to any number of receivers, my spiritual body radiates Light waves through spiritual cords." *(The Principles of Jyorei. ET)*

Many have reported a sense of spiritual protection while wearing the Ohikari. The powerful vibrations emanating from it can help to raise our level of awareness, strengthen our intuition, lift our mood, and draw good fortune to us. To wear an Ohikari is a great privilege.

We need to take special care of the Ohikari. How we treat it is an outer reflection of the care and respect we give to our soul. In our busy lives, it can be easy to ignore and neglect our spiritual life. Taking thought to be careful with our Ohikari reminds us of our connection to the spiritual world and of the need to think and behave in ways that enhance our spiritual condition.

Life is not a chain of haphazard events, but is essentially an intelligent reflection of the conditions in the spiritual world. Our relationship to the Ohikari is more profound than our relationships with ordinary objects. What happens to the Ohikari is a reflection of our life at that time, and by association, our current inner condition. There are no accidents. For instance, if we discover a foreign element, such as a strand of hair, inside of the outer pouch of the Ohikari, it may reflect a spiritual impurity within us that requires our attention. Similarly, if we were to accidentally drop the Ohikari, it may reflect a certain carelessness about our spiritual life. In these cases, the Ohikari is acting like an outer reflection of an inner condition that needs to be examined. It can also point to problems we are having with our personal relations or with our finances. Or, we may be carrying an emotional burden within our hearts that needs to be addressed.

If something unfortunate happens to the Ohikari, the owner of the Ohikari is advised to consult with the person designated to support his or her spiritual growth. Through dialogue with this person, the Ohikari owner can receive help in unraveling the hidden meaning of this incident, and also in discovering ways to improve the current situation.

The conditions and circumstances surrounding our Ohikari often have great meaning and significance. What initially can appear as a problem may actually be an important message from the spiritual world offering us spiritual guidance (if we can interpret it accurately). If ever there is a need to purify our Ohikari, it may signify that our soul also needs extra purification. It can also be an encouragement to discover God's Will or to resolve to do better in some area of our lives. Incidents of purification are gifts from the spiritual world for which we can be grateful. They are opportunities to change our destiny for the better, and often these incidents can lead us in the direction of greater peace and harmony.

A special donation is requested to provide for the initiation into Jyorei and to thereby receive an Ohikari. The choice to begin sharing Jyorei is a momentous decision to live a life of generosity and service to others. It is a choice to look beyond one's own personal needs by focusing on the needs of others. Many have discovered that genuine happiness does not come from the selfish pursuit of personal desires but actually comes from the act of giving. They begin to experience a joy and fulfillment that is untouched by the daily circumstances in their lives. The initiation donation is a concrete expression of this commitment to giving.

The Nature and Source of Jyorei

Be like the flower; turn your face to the sun. —*Kahlil Gibran (Poet)*

There are several organizations in the world other than Shumei who also study the works of Meishusama and who also practice Jyorei, each with different approaches or different techniques for directing energy. In this book, we are expounding on Jyorei as practiced by Shumei, which puts greater emphasis on a person's attitude and consciousness rather than on elaborate techniques and procedures.

Although there may be positive benefits from using the more elaborate Jyorei procedures, there are also advantages to Shumei's simpler approach, which humbly relies on the highest power in the universe to effect change. Our human intelligence is quite limited in comparison with that of our Creator, and therefore, by putting our trust in this Higher Intelligence, we do not need to concern ourselves with having to diagnose people or to create customized healing procedures for them. By surrendering our personal will to Divine Will, we become aligned with the ultimate source of Jyorei, which is also the ultimate source of life itself.

Interest in spiritual matters is becoming increasingly popular in modern society. Among the topics of interest, the subject of spiritual healing is drawing special attention, perhaps because it is experiential as well as practical. Some of the more popular forms of spiritual healing are Reiki, Chi Kung, Mahikari, faith healing, and laying on of hands. Although these techniques all deal with transmitting energy, there are also some fundamental differences between them.

Within the electromagnetic frequency spectrum there are many different types of energy, such as microwaves, X-rays, gamma rays, radio waves, ultraviolet rays, infrared rays, and cosmic rays. What they have in common is all are forms of pulsating energy. Yet scientific instruments can detect significant variations in the qualities and functionalities of these types of energies.

Light is something invisible that, through vibration, makes all things visible. To see something, we must shine light on it. But the light itself remains invisible, no matter how bright it is. We can only know light by what it does, not by what it is. Despite all the scientific explanations, light's fundamental nature is still a mystery cloaked in brightness.

Our eyes can only see light indirectly by its reflection off of physical objects. Along with the familiar spectrum of colors that most of us can see, there are also other colors that we cannot see, such as infrared and ultraviolet. These latter two colors differ from the colors of the visible spectrum because they vibrate at different rates of speed. Similarly, it would be hard to transmit radio and television signals using X-rays or gamma rays because both of those are the wrong frequencies of energy for broadcasting these signals. Again, these examples merely stress the differences between various types of energy, regardless of whether they are physical or spiritual in nature.

From the highest perspective, it can be said that everything, including the energies of the electromagnetic frequency spectrum, originates from Spirit. Meishusama writes, "The true nature of spirit is the fundamental source of all energy and the directing power behind the creation, movements, activities, and changes of every single thing in this infinite universe." *(Natural Power. ET)* Spiritual energy emerges directly from pure Spirit, whereas physical phenomena emerge only indirectly from Spirit, with many intermediate causes or sources in between. In other words, the things of this world have many levels of origination, depending on how dense, complex, or artificial they are. For example, although sunlight, like all things, ultimately comes from Spirit, its more immediate source is the sun. The sun is the material source of sunlight, and Spirit is the immaterial source of them both. In the case of water from a faucet, the local river is the relative, or material source, whereas Spirit is the ultimate or immaterial source. The purer the spiritual energy, the closer it is to Source, and therefore, the more it mirrors the qualities of Spirit.

Some people have asked whether Jyorei and Reiki are similar or possibly even the same energy. Both are described as originating directly from Spirit, without any significant, intermediate sources in between (such as the sun, which is the intermediate source of sunlight, or a kitchen faucet, which is the intermediate source of tap water). In truth, everything originates from Spirit, but this does not make Reiki and Jyorei identical, just as it does not make apples and oranges the same, either. As a glass prism refracts light into a spectrum of diverse colors, so too, does Spirit manifest in a variety of energies and forms. Before hitting the prism, the light is pure and undifferentiated, whereas afterwards it takes on various qualities of this world, such as color and shape. At the level of appearances, there is always diversity, whereas at the level of Spirit there is none. Also, many people who have experienced both forms of healing report that the energies of Jyorei and Reiki feel different from each other.

Not only does the type or quality of energy used by Jyorei and Reiki differ from each other, but so, too, do their techniques. According to our understanding, Reiki practitioners visualize various symbols while transmitting energy, plus they are allowed to touch the recipient. Jyorei does neither. Also, the set of points on the body that Reiki directs energy to differ from those that Jyorei focuses on.

The ideal motive for sharing Jyorei is the pure desire to alleviate suffering and to help make the world a better place. Jyorei practitioners are altruistic, with a strong desire to help humanity. They never charge money for their services, unlike many other healers. Jyorei is always given freely and unconditionally.

Despite the various differences between Jyorei and other forms of spiritual healing, many Reiki practitioners and other types of healers are also dedicated to serving humanity, and therefore we support them in their mission.

Since Jyorei tends to heal and strengthen everything, one might wonder if it also does so to the harmful bacteria and parasites within the body. Although Jyorei is universally beneficial, it does not appear to empower harmful microorganisms within the body, such as parasites, yeast, bacteria, or viruses. Jyorei might possibly strengthen these organisms if they were to be isolated in a laboratory Petri Dish, but not when inhabiting someone's body. This is because life is an evolutionary process promoting a hierarchy of increasingly complex biological structures: cells are composed of collections of molecules, internal organs are composed of colonies of cells, and bodies are composed of groups of internal organs. The needs of the larger and more complex structures generally supersede the needs of the smaller and simpler structures. Thus, the body, being the largest organism within this biological hierarchy, makes use of Jyorei to strengthen itself and to inhibit harmful microorganisms while simultaneously promoting the growth of friendly microorganisms. In most cases, the smaller become subservient to the larger, not the other way around. Similarly, the interior organs, as they become stronger, begin to work more harmoniously with each other to support the overall functioning of the body.

Meishusama claimed that he received the power of Jyorei from Kannon, the Japanese name for the popular Buddhist deity of compassion, who instilled a mysterious orb of golden Light within his abdomen. (Some refer to this deity by the Chinese name of Kwan Yin.) This was the immediate source of power for Meishusama and his disciples. Jyorei is a gift from Kannon to Meishusama and to humanity.

I have in my body a Sphere of Light usually about two inches in diameter. This has been witnessed by many individuals. Infinitely powerful Light waves are given out by this Sphere. The fundamental source of the Light energy of the Sphere is to be found in the spiritual world. The Orb of Kannon constantly and infinitely replenishes this Sphere's Power with Divine Light rays that are directed at me. This is the power of Kannon, the Superb Power, the *Myochiriki*, as it is often called. This Sphere is the same as that borne by Nyoirin, or the Wish-fulfilling Kannon. — *The Principles of Jyorei.* ET

Kannon can be viewed as an outward expression of God, specifically God's power of compassion. An analogy would be the flames at the perimeter of the sun that are distinct from the sun itself while simultaneously remaining an integral part of its overall body. The flames are a part of the sun but not the sun itself—the same but different. Understood in this way, Jyorei can be described as originating from both God and Kannon, who are inwardly the same although outwardly different. Although there are numerous images of God, the reality all of behind them is identical. It is the mind's identification with various names and forms that creates the illusion of multiplicity.

Although the source of Jyorei is a divine mystery beyond human understanding, the way it functions can be partially explained in terms of the three symbolic elements: fire, the power of heat and expansion; water, the power of fluidity and movement; and earth, the power of coldness and contraction. The energy of Jyorei is primarily composed of fire, which melts and dissolves toxins, and secondarily of water, which flushes the liquefied toxins out of the body. When one gives Jyorei to another, its power first passes through the physical body of the giver and then penetrates the physical body of the recipient. Through this process, the element of earth, which is inherent in the human body, is integrated with the energy of Jyorei, resulting in the combination of the three elements of fire, water, and earth operating in dynamic unison. The earth also symbolizes the solid, tangible results that can be felt in the mind, in the body, and in one's interpersonal relationships.

When these three elements are mixed together, power or energy is created.
—The Spirits of Fire, Water and Earth. ET

For most of us, these various subtle distinctions are not so important to focus on. What is significant is the spiritual source of Jyorei—the boundless wellspring of energy that is beyond our limited world of observable phenomena. Jyorei comes from the infinite vibration that is Spirit itself.

The Effect on Humanity

This world can be liberated by performing genuine works of healing.
—Meishusama IV. MK1

According to Meishusama, our minds are interconnected with others through numerous spiritual cords. Taken together, this results in one huge interwoven field of consciousness—the collective consciousness of all of humanity. Developmental biologist Rupert Sheldrake, author of *A New Science of Life: The Hypothesis of Formative Causation*, refers to these fields as "morphic fields," or "form-generating fields." They are the collective memory and intelligence of individual species. According to Dr. Sheldrake, each species of plant or animal has a unique, nonphysical memory bank that feeds it the information necessary to survive and reproduce, and which is the real source of their instinctual knowledge and behavior. The morphic field is what informs fish about how to swim upstream, beavers how to build dams, and birds how to flock together in perfect formation. This field can be viewed as the biological equivalent of an electromagnetic field, one that determines the form and inherited behavior patterns of various species.

Dr. Sheldrake postulates that when a large enough percentage of a particular species learns a new skill or acquires new knowledge, it then automatically (through morphic resonance) becomes available to the entire species. Through this psychic networking, individual races and species are able to learn, grow, and adapt to changing circumstances. Morphic fields are the habits of nature, which evolve over time. This principle has popularly been referred to as "The Hundredth Monkey Effect." Following this logic a step further, if enough people, beyond a certain threshold, evolve to a higher spiritual level, then possibly the entire human race may rise up to that new higher level as well.

In the entire process of cosmic evolution you see a spiritual process as well as a material process. You can't separate the two.
—Rupert Sheldrake (Evolutionary Biologist)

Every time a person is healed of negativity or is raised to a higher level of consciousness, that person exerts a positive effect on the mental and behavioral aspects of this morphic field. Thus, as each individual progresses, so too does everyone else. The Light from Jyorei, through its beneficial influence on millions of people, and therefore on this field, may be helping to purify and uplift all of humanity. In Meishusama's terminology, we could say that everyone benefits from Jyorei, either directly or indirectly, through the spiritual cords that link us all together in an invisible web of relationships. Therefore, Jyorei is not just a gift to individuals, but also to humanity as a whole.

At its highest level, Jyorei is an experience of Oneness. When we give with love and receive with gratitude, we touch everyone through our shared collective awareness. Love and gratitude, empowered by divine Light, are capable of dissolving the inner barriers of alienation and separation that have troubled humanity for countless millennia. Through Jyorei, we can each help in the transmutation of this world into a realm of radiant beauty and Light.

CHAPTER 11

NATURAL AGRICULTURE

The principle of Natural Agriculture is an overriding respect and concern for Nature.
—A Great Agricultural Revolution. ET

Fundamental Principles

Meishusama developed the principles of Natural Agriculture through his own personal experience of farming in the late 1930's. The reason that he started farming was originally to help farmers who at that time were experiencing dire hardship and poverty because of poor harvests. Many had to abandon their farms and move to the cities. The condition of the farmers was so devastating that Meishusama could not overlook it. He felt compassion for their suffering, and wanted to find a practical solution. At first he wanted to find ways to help farmers increase their crop yields and reduce the general food shortage. Later, he searched for ways to prevent the toxic chemical residues in food left over from pesticides, as well as to improve the food's overall nutritional quality.

Natural Agriculture is a spiritually based form of food cultivation that does not use chemicals, fertilizers, or manure, and pays special attention to the farmer's spiritual relationship to the environment. As such, it is both a spiritual discipline and a practical vocation. The expression that "some gardeners have a green thumb," because of what appears to be their natural talent for growing things, could also apply to practitioners of Natural Agriculture. The attitude of the farmer plays an essential role in the quality of his or her crops. Especially important is the emphasis on love, respect for nature, and gratitude.

Since his early stages of farming, Meishusama maintained a firm belief in the power of nature. A proper relationship between the growers and nature was essential to healthy food. This relationship is based on gratitude. Three principles—love, gratitude, and respect for nature—are at the foundation of the

Natural Agriculture movement. These principles arise from our realization of our fundamental Oneness with all things, including nature.

Philosophical Overview

Contemporary View of Nature

I believe that people are meant to live in harmony with nature.
—Progression Upwards. KW

Based on his experiences with medicine earlier in life, as well as his later experiments with fertilizers, Meishusama came to have serious doubts about the mentality of controlling and suppressing nature—whether illness in the human body or insects and disease in plants. He felt this tendency to control was contrary to the principles of nature because such control caused more harm than good. Humankind had lost its way in its over-reliance on technology to dominate nature. As a result, nature, as well as humanity, suffered the consequences of this misdirection.

Meishusama would agree with the popular English philosopher, Alan Watts, who ironically suggested that the bulldozer could be the most appropriate symbol for the modern era. Bulldozers level the mountains and fill in valleys, treating the natural habitat as no more than worthless dirt to be pushed around for our convenience. In our rush to increase consumption, modern man has managed to desecrate the land, air, and water. We use technology to dominate nature for the sake of shortsighted goals, while ignoring long-term environmental effects. Our bulldozers shove around massive amounts of earth to create monotonous housing tracts, leaving behind chopped-up landscapes. Natural beauty is sacrificed for the sake of "progress."

Our scientific power has outrun our spiritual power. We have guided missiles and misguided men. —Martin Luther King Jr.

Our contemporary mentality, influenced by nineteenth century mechanistic scientific models, still tends to view the universe as essentially unintelligent. This model conditions us to experience the universe as something dominated by chaotic forces with no concern for life, consciousness, or beauty. According to this model, the universe was created eons ago by a spontaneous explosion known scientifically as the "Big Bang." Much later, life supposedly originated in a freak accident. Intelligence is considered to be the lucky result of "natural selection," or evolutionary adaptation to hostile circumstances. It is no more than a subtle byproduct of physical matter.

The psychiatrist Stanislav Grof says this about such theories, "The probability that human consciousness and our infinitely complex universe could have come into existence through the random interactions of inert matter has aptly been compared to that of a tornado blowing through a junkyard and accidentally assembling a 747 jumbo jet." Such a world appears inherently hostile to all life forms, especially to humans with any sensitivity or thoughtfulness. This outlook encourages us to develop an adversarial relationship to the world and to use whatever technological power is at our disposal to dominate nature for our own safety and survival. Humans are thus left feeling anxious about their existence and alienated from nature.

The Intelligence of Ecological Systems

We do not weave the web of life—we are merely a strand of it. Whatever we do to the web, we do to ourselves. —Chief Seattle

An alternate view holds that the universe is inherently conscious and intelligent, with love at the foundation of its existence. We humans are likewise inherently conscious and intelligent, all the way down to the cells in our bodies, with love at the core of our being. Not only humans, but also all the other creatures in our environment contain this innate intelligence and love. Elizabeth Sahtouris, an evolution biologist and futurist, calls this "a living universe." In her book *Biology Revisioned*, she writes: "The dynamic dance of nature is ever conscious at every level, from the tiniest particle to whatever its currently largest configuration, or holon, is."

The earth's ecosystem is composed of chains of smaller, local ecosystems, all interrelated with each other. Each of these local ecosystems is composed of a fantastic variety of life forms, from birds, animals, and insects to trees, grasses, and plants. All are subject to multiple influences, such as sun, rain, wind, soil, and temperature. Nothing exists independent of anything else. A profound intelligence harmoniously orchestrates the diverse elements within each of these ecosystems so that they live in balance. This is not an outside intelligence, but an inner one. It is part of nature itself. This same intelligence regulates the circulation of our blood, and the digestion of our food.

We are not separate from nature, but an expression of it. The natural environment is teeming with life, from the smallest microbes and fungus to giant whales and sequoia trees. We share this world with the animals, birds, and fish; it does not belong to us alone. All of nature is sensitively alive, and responds to kind thoughts and actions.

This interpretation of the natural world is supported by fieldwork on animal behavior conducted by the Russian naturalist and political theorist Peter Kropotkin. Based on six-years of research in Siberia, he concluded that animals in the wilderness bond together in social groups for their mutual survival. In his book *Mutual Aid: A Factor in Evolution,* he writes, "They [hamadryas baboons] have been observed working together to accomplish shared goals and even risking their lives to save members of their own group. In some species several individuals will combine to overturn a stone in order to search for ants' eggs under it. The hamadryas not only post sentries, but have been seen making a chain for the transmission of the spoil to a safe place; and their courage is well known." Kropotkin's view on nature starkly contrasts with that of Charles Darwin and his theory of evolution, who describes animal behavior as based on ruthless competition for survival. This view is commonly summarized as, "survival of the fittest." Kropotkin, in his writings, gives ample examples of intelligent, altruistic behavior amongst animals. His description of nature is one of harmony and cooperation, where self-sacrifice and sharing form the basis of life in all its diversity.

Nature teaches us a multitude of things in this way. In order to understand the world, to find the answer to the deepest problems, you usually need to do no more than look closely at nature. —Impasse. ET

Environmental Degradation

In order to understand the larger purpose of Natural Agriculture activity, we need to note the grim state of our world. Our biosphere is sick. The entire planetary ecosystem, handed down to us from generation to generation, is being relentlessly destroyed. There are over one hundred thousand chemicals in the environment today that did not exist a hundred years ago. Well water, streams, and even deep underground aquifers are increasingly polluted from the poisonous runoff of agricultural chemicals such as organophosphates and n-methyl carbamates. And the petroleum industry's more recent use of fracking is polluting the ground water even more. Air pollution is everywhere; not only in giant cities such as Los Angeles, Beijing, Cairo, and Mexico City, but also in regions that have burning rainforests and in areas near factories and oil refineries. Massive amounts of topsoil are being lost each year, and it takes hundreds, perhaps thousands of years to recreate just a few centimeters of it. Every day, approximately 35 to 150 species of life (mostly insects and plants) become extinct. Global warming is melting the icecaps. Rainforests are being destroyed at a furious pace, and the micro-plankton at the bottom of the food chain, deep within the oceans, are dying off. Because forests and micro-plankton create so much of the oxygen on the planet, the future looks grim.

Not only is our surrounding environment deteriorating, but our inner biology also is being traumatized. Hundreds of millions of people are suffering from hunger, mostly because of direct and indirect problems in the existing marketing system. The alarming rate of increase in American degenerative diseases indicates that something is wrong. According to the American Cancer Society, almost one out of four deaths in the United States is due to cancer. (*Cancer Facts and Figures 2005.* www.cancer.org) Heart disease, diabetes, arthritis, multiple sclerosis, Parkinson's disease, and numerous other chronic illnesses are increasing without any potential cures available. At best, drugs manage these afflictions and lessen suffering on a short-term basis. We need to ask the question, "Are the toxins in our environment causing these diseases?"

Only after the last tree has been cut down; Only after the last fish has been caught; Only after the last river has been poisoned; Only then will you realize that money cannot be eaten. —Cree Indian Prophesy

The Impact of Modern Agriculture

Conventional agriculture was designed for mass-produced, single-crop production, heavily dependent on toxic chemicals and the exploitation of cheap labor. Because of its massive use of toxic pesticides, chemical fertilizers, and animal manure, as well as slash and burn practices in forests and jungles, the single crop practice causes environmental degradation. If modern agriculture continues its current practices, in the near future the global environment will become unsuitable for many species, including human beings.

In anticipation of the future crisis resulting from degrading environmental conditions, we need to alter the way we grow most of our food and end the destructive cycle endangering the world's entire ecosystem. Beyond agribusiness, the overall global market system perpetuates the existing food production system. This economic system also must change.

We use the most powerful chemical fertilizers, pesticides, and herbicides to force the land to yield large quantities of crops. This process has had the very unfortunate consequences of polluting the land, depleting the topsoil, and producing food that has less and less nutritional value as each year passes. As far back as 1936, an official document by the United States Senate *(Document No. 264)* warned that the soil used to grow fruits and vegetables was seriously deficient in needed minerals. For the last seventy years nothing has reversed this trend, and so it is frightening to ponder the current level of deterioration.

Another crisis is the alarming loss of honeybees throughout the United States. According to scientists, the domesticated honeybee population has declined by about 50% in the last 50 years. This is dangerous because bee pollination, which most farmers depend on, is responsible for as much as 30% of the U.S. food supply. Similar conditions are occurring in many other countries. The conclusion drawn by most scientists is that pesticide usage, which continues to increase dramatically, is poisoning the bees. Unless something is done soon to protect the honeybee population, many fruits and vegetables may disappear from the food chain. We appear to be approaching an emergency situation in our food supply that will soon affect everyone, both rich and poor alike.

The prevailing trend in our civilization continues to destroy the natural environment and our physical bodies. Advanced technology worsens the situation instead of improving it. People turn their backs, both consciously and unconsciously, to the plight of Earth. Most adults do not have a clear picture of the link between the environment and human life. We have come to a point where we must look at modern agriculture in a larger context. With this understanding, we can take immediate and decisive action to reverse this negative trend.

Hidden Costs of Modern Farming

In the future, the time will come when there is a mountain of food in front of us but we cannot eat it. —Meishusama

The organic movement and Natural Agriculture originated as a response to our basic right to live healthy lives. Their alternative food production processes are beginning to shift the trend from large, transnational agribusinesses to local-economy oriented businesses. Because of the recent success of the organic movement, critics are appearing who warn us of dire consequences if chemical free farming continues to gain popularity. They label organic farmers as starry-eyed idealists generating mass starvation by replacing conventional farming with "primitive" natural farming, which they claim is inefficient and less productive.

Although modern mechanized farming has been successful in terms of crop yield, its prices do not reflect the hidden expenses from pollution, such as waste management and environmental "clean-up" projects, not to mention health risks to both consumers and farm workers. One way or another, we all pay for these hidden expenses. The cost of dealing with farm pollution is paid for in the form of higher taxes. Because the public indirectly pays, farm pollution is considered a hidden form of subsidization. When we include the increase in medical expenses and lost productivity brought about by farm pollution, the overall cost to society is compounded. If these "external" costs were reflected in the actual prices consumers paid, the financial inefficiency of modern agriculture would be exposed. David Suzuki, scientist and environmentalist, sums up the viability of organic farming:

According to a landmark 21-year study recently published in the journal *Science*, organic farming can produce good yields, save energy, maintain biodiversity and keep soils healthy. The study took place on 1.5 hectares (3.7 acres) of land in Switzerland, using four farming methods and several different crops. Crop yields, on average, were 20 percent lower using organic methods, but they required 56 percent less energy per unit of yield. Organic plots also had 40 percent greater colonization by fungi and microbes that help plants absorb nutrients, three times as many earthworms and twice as many pest-eating spiders.

Guy Dauncey, an environmental activist and author, compares conventional and organic farming productivity:

In 1998, the Rodale Institute in Kutztown, Pennsylvania, published the results of a 15-year study that compared three ways of growing maize (corn) and soybeans; a conventional chemical rotation method, an organic system involving crop rotation and legume crops, and an organic system using cow manure. The yields were similar for all three systems, debunking the myth that organic methods cannot feed the world.

We commonly think that modern farming methods have been a huge success because, over the past century, they have drastically reduced the percent of the American population directly involved in farming. Large-scale agriculture would supposedly free people to contribute to society in other ways, thereby adding to the overall productivity of the economy. While it is true that the number of small family farms has shrunken enormously during the past 100 years, it has been estimated that the actual percentage of people employed in the total, combined agricultural support industries has remained almost identical. By this measurement, the real increase in productivity has been questionable.

Long ago, farms were more self-contained and provided local regions with most of their food. They did not require the enormous infrastructure of specialized modern agriculture to run their farms efficiently. Now food travels an average of 1,500 miles from farm to table. This requires a massive energy consuming transportation system that delivers food that is neither fresh nor nutritious. When we take into account the millions of people employed in supportive industries, such as farm equipment, agricultural chemicals, specialized production facilities, accounting, and distribution, we discover that the independent farmer has been replaced by a gigantic agricultural industry.

Millions of small, independent farmers have been replaced by a handful of giant farming corporations. Instead of being eliminated from the farming industry, however, former independent farmers have found less gainful employment in other agriculture-related industries. Consequently, there has been a migration of population from small farms to mechanized industry, accompanying a massive transfer of wealth from individuals to corporate ownership. In light of these alarming facts, the true value to society of modern farming needs to be reassessed.

If we calculate the devastating cost of pollution, soil depletion, and inferior food quality resulting from modern agriculture, we might ask, "What is the worth of having lost so many of our traditional family farms, the bedrock of our rural society?" In exchange for the supposed efficiency of modern farming industries, great numbers of small towns have shrunken or disappeared because of the transferring of unemployed farm labor from rural areas to large cities.

In stark contrast to modern, mechanized, chemically driven farming practices, the organic movement in agriculture values local production, chemical-free farming, and a healthy environment. The basic tenet of organic farming is that food grown by natural means is safer than chemically grown fruits, vegetables, and grains, as well as more nutritious.

Genetically Engineered Organisms

Another threat to farmers and consumers are GMO (genetically modified organism) crops that have been genetically altered whereby genes from the DNA of one species of plant or animal are extracted and artificially forced into the genes of an unrelated plant or animal. They are unnatural. Some GMO crops are engineered to produce their own pesticides, or are designed to withstand heavy spraying of toxic pesticides, especially glyphosate (Monsanto's Roundup™). These toxins are then transferred to the animals and humans who consume them. The environment also suffers from these harmful chemicals.

DNA is complex, and current knowledge and understanding of it is very limited. Side effects of GMO technology are unpredictable. Live trials have produced sick, sterile, and dead livestock, with damage occurring in almost every organ. Also, many people have reported allergic reactions, digestive problems, lower immunity, and illness from consuming GMO foods.

Despite biotechnology industry promises, GMOs have not offered in-creased crop yield, drought resistance, or enhanced nutrition. Instead, they are producing super weeds and super bugs that have learned to withstand the pesticides used by or produced by these crops. Genetically engineered crops have contaminated nearby fields through pollen drift and seeds carried by birds. This is especially threatening to organic and Natural Agriculture farmers.[13]

The Practice of Natural Agriculture

Purpose

Look deep into nature, and then you will understand everything better.
—Albert Einstein

Natural Agriculture teaches us how to grow sufficient, healthy, and delicious food. The purer the condition of people, animals, plants, and soil the greater their well being. Eating pure food helps the body release toxins and gain strength. When we spend time either gardening or walking in the woods, we feel purified and rejuvenated by nature's beauty and sanctity. Nature exists within our own bodies

---

13. This entire GMO section is based upon information gained from http://responsibletechnology. org.

as well as our surroundings, and by learning to trust nature, we learn to trust ourselves. This overall trust promotes a harmonious relationship between the external world and us, and is a key to inner peace.

One purpose of Natural Agriculture is to promote love for humanity and respect for nature, both essential to creating an ideal world. Some other purposes are to foster gratitude, restore unity between people and nature, and awaken the sacred dimension in life. On a physical level, the movement aims to improve health by producing delicious and nutritious foods. Interestingly, Meishusama claimed that if an exclusively materialistic person correctly practiced Natural Agriculture, he or she would eventually become spiritual.

From a spiritual perspective, Natural Agriculture is seeking to produce food that contains a powerful spiritual essence and life force, which can often be tasted as a vital freshness. A healthy condition can be attained from achieving a balance between body, mind, and spirit; and this will be brought about when we have a proper relationship with nature, of which our body is an extension. Natural Agriculture offers a practical opportunity for people to discover their essential relationship with nature and to directly experience a sense of wonder at the miracle of life.

Principles of Nature

Nature itself embodies truth. For this reason, whatever you plan, it is extremely important to have nature as your guide. Learning from the principles and processes of nature is essential to success. Since the spiritual healing and non-fertilizer growing methods that I advocate, along with other things, have their foundations in this principle, almost no failures occur when using these methods, and the hoped for outcomes always come about. —Wait for the Right Moment. KW

Natural Agriculture is based on a number of assumptions and principles concerning nature and its relationship to the farmer. The understanding of these principles forms the backdrop of the farmer's relationship to nature.

1. **God created nature and exists within nature.** Humans are not separate from nature or God.

2. **Nature is perfect.** It does not need to be changed or improved upon by us.

3. **Nature is beautiful.** Nature is God's artwork.

4. **Nature is abundant.** It provides us with everything we need for life and enjoyment.

5. **Nature is truth.** This truth is revealed through studying nature and its various processes.

6. **Nature seeks balance.** Sun, rain, wind, trees, grasses and animals—all move toward balance and harmony with each other.

7. **Nature evolves.** All of creation is constantly evolving to higher levels.

8. **Everything has a purpose.** Each and every living thing has an inner drive towards growth and evolution, eventually leading to the realization of Heaven on Earth.

9. **Everything consists of spirit, mind, and body.** Everything has the ability to perceive, feel, and react. In this sense, the natural world is conscious and intelligent.

10. **Everything is composed of fire, water and earth.** The invisible force that animates all living things expresses itself through a complex mixture of these three spiritual elements.

11. **Nature is holistic.** Everything is connected to everything else. Nothing exists by itself. The whole is greater than the sum of its parts.

12. **Nature is regenerative.** Everything in nature goes through a cycle of creation, sustained existence, and disintegration, after which its various components are recycled back into the larger whole in order to support new creations.

Meishusama did not list these principles as such, although they are clearly implied in his teachings on Natural Agriculture. And the people who practice these truths may not intellectually understand them, but they intuitively comprehend them in their hearts.

The Heart of the Farmer

Plowing in the sunshine, painting when it rains, I happily tend my garden on this late spring day. —Meishusama VI. MK1

Natural Agriculture offers an alternative to our destructive lifestyles by cultivating humility and reverence toward nature. The Natural Agriculture farmer views nature as his partner, not as his adversary. Rather than dominating the land, he cooperates with it.

Only with profound humility can we learn how to live and work with the natural world. In this regard, we have much to learn from the indigenous traditions of people living for uncounted millennia in harmony with the environment. "Nature teaches us everything," says Meishusama. (*A Great Agricultural Revolution. ET*) This same idea was also stated around the same time in history by the Austrian naturalist and inventor of vortex technology, Viktor Schauberger, whose motto was, "Study nature and copy nature." If we observe nature with an open heart, we will begin to discover its innate beauty and divinity. This view of nature as sacred closely echoes that of the Eastern traditions of Taoism and Shinto, as well as those of Native Americans.

By paying close attention to the leaves and soil, the insects and birds, the wind and rain, and the sun and sky, we grasp the interconnection of everything. The growth of a tree affects the sunlight below it, and the movement of the wind determines which crops become pollinated. Observing these phenomena reveals the hidden unity within nature, inspiring awe.

Nature will reveal itself if we will only look. — Thomas Edison

The Natural Agriculture farmer's occupation is more a vocation than an ordinary business. He or she must possess the physical means, diligence, training, and intelligence of conventional farmers, and also a spiritual capacity. Such farmers improve the spiritual well-being of others as well as of themselves. Also, they must love what they do because we are only present in the here and now when we love what we're doing. Along these lines, the Japanese farmer and philosopher Masanobu Fukuoka states in his book *The One–Straw Revolution: An Introduction to Natural Farming*, "Just to live here and now—this is the true basis of human life."

Of course, one should not be misled into thinking that Natural Agriculture farming is easy. It may be hard work. Weeding, plowing, and harvesting can be tedious and exhausting, but so too can many other activities that people voluntarily engage in, such as recreational sports, musical performances, physical exercise, and dancing. On the plus side, physical exertion tends to pull us out of our mind, with all its attendant anxieties and preoccupations, and brings us back to our senses so that we can more fully appreciate the natural beauty of the surrounding environment. When we become peaceful and quiet inside, we begin to truly see the beautiful shapes and colors of the plants and trees, smell the subtle but rich aromas of the earth and its diverse vegetation, and hear the sweet songs of birds in the trees and the gentle rustle of leaves in the wind. The practice of Natural Agriculture is not only practical; it is also a meditation on beauty. And as the effects of this meditation sink deeper into our hearts, we may find that many of our physical discomforts do not bother us so much anymore, and feel more like passing clouds in the sky. We may also find that touching the soil helps to ground us so that the inner tree of our spirituality can take root and grow toward the heavens above.

To forget how to dig the earth and tend the soil is to forget ourselves.
—Mahatma Gandhi

We must learn to pace ourselves so that, although we work hard, we do not overexert ourselves to the point of pain and exhaustion. It is important to feel happy, not miserable, while gardening because our moods affect the growth of the crops we cultivate. We live in a conscious universe in which everything affects everything else. All of nature, including the soil, the weather, rocks, plants, and insects, respond to our thoughts, intentions, and feelings. What we project outwardly determines what comes back to us. So, if we want a happy world, we need to radiate happiness.

There is another important thing I would like to stress here. Up until now people have believed that conscious reflection of thought and will, which functions as reason and emotion, was limited only to animate beings. To our very surprise, however, even inorganic beings have the same ability; and not to mention soil and plants, which do as well. *—NA*

As documented in the book, *The Secret Life of Plants* by Peter Tompkins and Christopher Bird, plants attached to biofeedback devices in laboratory experiments have demonstrated the ability to respond to a human being's thoughts and feelings. By extension, it is quite probable that the bacteria and microorganisms in the soil will also respond to the farmer's inner state of consciousness. Not only are we all intimately connected, but also from a higher perspective, we are all One.

We are not separate from our environment, for it is what feeds, clothes, and shelters us. When the hills and valleys, forests and meadows, lakes and streams are gone, replaced by endless housing tracks, parking lots, and shopping malls, how will this affect our souls? Do we need the beauty of the natural environment for our basic sanity and happiness? The raw material for creating and maintaining our physical bodies comes from the land. In this regard, we are quite literally not only a product of, but also an expression of, our natural environment. What we do to our environment comes back to us in the food we eat, the water we drink, and the air we breathe. The ecological sciences confirm this basic unity of the organism and the environment, which includes plant, bird, animal, and man. Albert Einstein wrote; "A human being is part of a whole—the universe. Our task is to free ourselves from the delusion of separateness—to embrace all living creatures and the whole of nature."

The Natural Agriculture farmer presumes the existence of an innate intelligence within nature, one fundamentally benign and life sustaining. The more one studies the natural world, the more wisdom is discovered there. As a result, he is incapable of dominating the environment, but instead, is in conscious relationship with it.

The plants that yield the highest quality food are usually grown by people with love in their hearts. The intensity of love that farmers pour into their plants greatly influences the growth that follows. —*Warm Hearts Attract People. KW*

Only when one subject relates to another subject is love possible. This is different from an object-to-object relationship, in which each ignores the inner awareness of the other. When we relate to others as objects, there is no need to be kind or considerate. Objects can be used as means to an end, whereas subjects are ends in themselves. We can ignore our impact on things but not on conscious beings. Within all things there exists a "point within the circle," an inner awareness. By acknowledging and honoring this awareness within the soil and plants, the farmer activates nature's life force to produce abundant yields. His gratitude towards the life around him for its generous gifts is like the gratitude one feels towards trusted friends.

If farmers pray to God—with gratitude—for successful harvests of the rice plants they are growing, their sincere attitude will surely be answered by the plants. Since modern science knows nothing about these invisible things, it tends to avoid dealing with them. This is a seriously problematic tendency that science is still adhering to. —*NA*

The Natural Agriculture farmer sees his work as an extension of his spiritual life. The hard work is more than made up for by its many benefits—both physical and spiritual. He is not overly focused on future goals because the gentle art of farming is fulfilling in itself.

In stark contrast to this is the one who works at a job only for the sake of a paycheck at the end of the week. Because he does not enjoy this part of his life, he must seek fulfillment elsewhere. Such perpetual seeking fosters misery no matter where one goes because it creates a habit of dissatisfaction. Tending a garden may offer the perfect antidote to these tendencies. Gardening is both therapeutic and life enriching. Many of our inner conflicts miraculously disappear when we touch the soil and nurture new life. Working with nature helps us to slow down and relax. Nature is innately peaceful, and if we remain open, our gardens can communicate this peacefulness to us. Gardening does not have to be full time. Anyone can practice Natural Agriculture farming during his or her spare time.

Earth laughs in flowers. —Ralph Waldo Emerson

The Spiritual Basis of Natural Agriculture

By having a reverence for life, we enter into a spiritual relation with the world.
—Albert Schweitzer

Spirituality is at the heart of Natural Agriculture. This spirituality operates on three levels; that of perception, feeling, and action.

1. At the level of perception there is the subtle recognition of an invisible, conscious presence that permeates all things.

2. At the level of thought and feeling there is a friendly attitude towards the natural world.

3. At the level of action there is gentle, cooperative interaction with the soil, crops, wildlife, and surrounding environment.

Perception, which is immaterial in nature, can correspond to the spirit of fire. Thoughts and feelings, which affect (and are affected by) both the immaterial and the material, can correspond to the spirit of water, which symbolizes movement and connectedness. Actions, which occur in the material world, can correspond to the spirit of earth, which symbolizes concrete results and physicality. All three levels of spirituality are essential in order to successfully practice Natural Agriculture.

The consciousness within plants, soil, water and air respond well to positive feelings and gentle behavior. Crops thrive when appreciated. Therefore, the farmer is encouraged to cultivate such inner qualities as love, gratitude, reverence, joy, kindness, humility, and serenity.

Spirituality is based on attitudes, perceptions, and behavior. Thus, the farmer is encouraged to always:

- Cultivate feelings of love, gratitude, humility, patience, serenity, joy, and wonder.

- Develop sensitivity to the consciousness within all of nature.

- Recognize that everything in nature is interconnected.

- Strive toward balance and harmony.

- Learn from nature and strive to cooperate with it rather than dominate it.

- Value the profound dignity of life.

- Appreciate the sublime beauty of nature.

- Cherish crops as blessed gifts from nature rather than mere merchandise produced for profit.

- Become familiar with each and every plant in the garden or field.

- Verbally or mentally communicate with the plants, soil, water, weather, insects, and wildlife in the local area. (Crops communicate back to us by their appearance and taste.)

- Act with gentleness and kindness.

- Recognize the mutual interdependence of customers and co-workers.

- Value his or her customers because their purchases financially support the farm.

- Be grateful for the opportunity to offer healthy produce to his or her customers that can bring them both nourishment and pleasure.

Similarly, the buyers of their food are encouraged to eat it with gratitude. Over time, a circle of gratitude is formed by the farmer, the crops, and the consumer. Farming in this way fosters a peaceful mind, a joyful heart, and gentle behavior, which can be viewed as elevated expressions of fire, water, and earth, respectively.

Importance of the Soil

The essential activity within Natural Agriculture is the radiating of compassionate love to our most basic resource for living: the crops we raise for food. This love extends to the soil in which the plants grow, as well as to the entire ecosystem that makes up the farm. Honoring and loving the farmland is not simply idealistic, but is also practical because it creates tangible improvements in the quality of the food grown.

Natural Agriculture places the highest importance on the purity and power of the soil, which is the basic substance of our Mother Earth. Topsoil is not simply "dirt;" rather, it is a complex mixture of minerals, organic material and living organisms. This mix of components is crucial for soil to support productive plant growth.

Healthy soil is inherently alive and full of life force. "Life force" is a mystery beyond science, with its narrow measurement of objective phenomena. Our connection to the earth is obvious; it is the place where our bodies eventually return. The way to draw out the soil's fullest potential is to treat it with kindness. Fertilizers and chemical treatments are never used. Only naturally occurring nutrients enrich the soil, but these are not added deliberately. Mulch and compost are not used to supply nutrients, but to keep the soil soft, moist, and warm (or cool, in very hot climates). Mulch can also help suppress weed growth. Following the example of nature, only locally occurring leaves and grass are used for mulch and compost, not food scraps or animal manure. In addition, we are strongly encouraged to use seeds produced from Natural Agriculture crops in order to maintain purity.

Consider the differences between the agricultural methods I advocate and what others currently practice. Up until now, farmers have used chemical fertilizers and manure, and have achieved some temporarily good results. But over a period of time these fertilizers kill the soil and make it progressively less fertile. The farmers are blinded by the temporary success of the fertilizers and fail to notice the underlying reality until finally the fertilizers poison both the soil and the people. —*It Is Not True that "Honesty Does Not Pay."* ET

The soil is the basis of agriculture, and its profound function is too deep for modern materialistic science to fathom. Meishusama writes, "Soil was made by the Creator in order to produce crops to nourish and sustain humans and animals. Therefore, its essential nature is that of a fertilizer. We could say that it is no less than a great mass of fertilizer. This fact has been unknown before today, and people have mistakenly assumed that fertilizer provides nourishment to crops, and therefore have used all sorts of fertilizers. As a result, the essential nature of the soil has been destroyed. People say that Japanese soil is acidic, and this is due to the process described above." (*A Great Agricultural Revolution. ET*) Based on Meishusama's insights, soil itself can be considered the primary source of nutrition for life.

Modern commercial farming, with its demand for high crop yields, does not recognize the essential power of the soil. Rather, industrialized methods depend on forms of artificial power such as complex machinery, chemical fertilizers, "soil-improvement" chemicals, and animal manure. In the long run, as a result of these heavy doses of artificial power, soil can deteriorate enormously, suffering from manure poisoning, over acidity, mineral imbalances, compactedness, and microorganism destruction. This deterioration destroys the soil's innate power to produce truly nutritious crops. In his book *The Soil and Health*, the British agrarian Sir Albert Howard stated, "The using up of fertility is a transfer of past capital and of future possibilities to enrich a dishonest present: it is banditry pure and simple."

Dead, acidic, and polluted soils tend to produce weeds. Although weeds are often defined as merely plants that are unwanted, they can sometimes be called invasive threats when they take over a large region, such as what the kudzu plant has done in the American Deep South.

In a nutshell, the propagation of our agricultural method can be summarized as a movement to overcome the superstitious belief in fertilizers. —NA

Spiritual Presence in the Soil

Even soil and plants have consciousness. This is an important point that farmers shouldn't neglect. In this sense, it is essential for them to love and respect the soil, and to prevent it from being polluted as much as possible. Since the soil and plants have such nature just as animals do, it is understandable that they would be very upset and resentful if they had human waste or strong poisons poured on the top of their heads. I can imagine that the soil all over Japan is now pretty angry. — NA

Meishusama claims that three universal elements underlie all of physical creation. These are the spirits of fire, water, and earth. The spirit of fire descends from the sun, the spirit of earth rises up from the center of the earth, and the spirit of water, guided by the moon, circulates these two energies. On a chemical level these elements manifest as oxygen, hydrogen, and nitrogen. Although the spirits themselves are unknown to science, nevertheless, it is the spiritual presence within each of these three elements, and their intermingling within various proportional combinations, that enlivens matter and supports the growth and development of all life forms.

The following might be an easier way to understand these three elements: The spirit of fire has the physical attributes of light and heat. The spirit of water has the physical attributes of fluidity and wetness. The spirit of earth has the physical attributes of contraction and density. When all three elements are present and balanced in the soil, the soil becomes warm, moist, and soft.

The energy X that I mentioned earlier is an undetectable power made by the fusion of the spirits of fire, water, and earth. Although this energy [by its mysterious nature] does not allow me to give it an accurate name, I conceive that it is the source of everything in the universe, and that it is a fertilizing element in itself. Soil is a substance made up of a condensed atmosphere of those spiritual elements existing in a well-balanced three-in-one condition. The density of this spiritual atmosphere is changeable; it increases and decreases according to humans' thoughts. If people love and cherish the soil enough, the spiritual density (liveliness) of the soil will increase. This is the real fertilizer. As you see here, this kind of fertilizer is invisible, and it can hardly be considered as an object of modern science. Actually, I would say that science operates more as an obstacle to discovering the true nature of the soil. —NA

The key to creating healthy soil is a deep inner relationship between the spirit of the farmer and the living spirit within the earth. Because the soil is inherently sensitive and intelligent, it is able to respond to the heart of the farmer. When the soil is kept pure and is touched by a sense of love, its spiritual essence becomes thick and powerful. According to Meishusama, this spiritual essence operates in a manner similar to what is attempted through the use of fertilizer. But unlike some fertilizers, which damage the soil, this essence is the true life force that animates all life. As such, it is essential for growth and health. This spiritual principle is the key to understanding Natural Agriculture. The way to know this subtle force is through our hearts.

Respect and love towards the soil helps fully draw its potential power in yielding crops. The key is to keep the soil free from contamination and to purify it. In response to such attitudes and care, the soil, with a sense of gratitude, will rejuvenate and revitalize itself. —NA

Fundamentally, the practice of Natural Agriculture is a spiritual pursuit. When practicing Natural Agriculture, it is important to observe a reverence towards both the soil and its bounty, and to cherish and honor that which gives us nourishment. This requires the spiritual nourishment of the grower, which is the basis of all physical nourishment. Much, therefore, depends on the attitude and commitment of the farmers who choose to pursue Natural Agriculture.

Purification of the Soil

Meishusama has this to say about our attempts to fertilize the soil:

The center of the earth is a huge ball of fire that is constantly radiating heat, that is spirit, to the surface. This takes the form of nitrogen fertilizer given to us by God. It rises up through the surface of the earth and gathers at a certain height in the air, after which it is carried down by rain and soaks into the soil. This natural nitrogen fertilizer falls, as it were, from Heaven, and is of course completely adequate in quantity; it is never too much and never too little.

There is a reason why people started using nitrogen fertilizer instead of allowing it to occur naturally. During the First World War, Germany was faced with severe shortages in its food supplies and had to increase crop production sharply. The Germans discovered how to extract nitrogen from the air and thereby increased production greatly. Since then this technique has spread all over the world, but the good results seen initially cannot be carried on for long. Eventually the soil becomes over-saturated with nitrogen and weakens, causing crop production to fall in quantity. Most people cannot comprehend this basic principle and continue to stick to their mistaken ideas like a drug addict clings to his drug. —A Great Agricultural Revolution. ET

The huge ball of fire at the center of the earth has both a physical and a spiritual aspect. The spiritual aspect is a powerful energetic presence that sustains the entire planet and all that lives on it. The subtle radiations from this ball of fire rise up through the ground and give vitality to the soil, to plants, and to all living creatures. A sensitive person, when exposed to this force, will feel calmly energized. Unfortunately, when chemicals pollute the soil, a dense layer of toxicity is created that short-circuits the flow of energy to the surface. Urban environments, with their asphalt roads and parking lots, and their pervasive use of chemicals and other synthetic materials, are especially devoid of this vital energy. The loss of this energy in our cities is tragic, for its absence leaves us devitalized and increasingly susceptible to stress and illness.

Crops contaminated by chemical fertilizers and insecticides, although seemingly robust, are actually weak. These artificial stimulants force crops to grow faster and larger, but not stronger or healthier. Plants need sufficient time to acquire minerals and covert them into vitamins, enzymes, and other nutritional elements. If plants grow too quickly, this does not happen. And although organic fertilizers and insecticides may seem less harmful, they can also make crops weak. Like a circle without a point in the center, the plants become hollow shells devoid of life force. Lacking inner strength, they become susceptible to damage by insects, disease, and foul weather. Thus the Law of Purification operates to cleanse them of their polluted condition by breaking them down to simpler elements to then be recycled back into nature. Ironically, modern farming's efforts to strengthen crops and eradicate their natural predators actually produce the opposite results over time.

Weeds, on the other hand, do not tend to get disease nor attract so much insect damage. They do not require fertilizers or pesticides to survive in their natural environment, but actually thrive when left alone. Trees in the wild tend to grow large all by themselves, and have been doing so since long before humans arrived on this planet. They also do not require human assistance. How do they do this? The answer can be found in the close study of nature.

Meishusama sees the fundamental cause of human unhappiness as rooted in spiritual clouds. Crops polluted by chemical and natural fertilizers, insecticides, herbicides, fungicides, "soil improvement" chemicals, and other toxic substances during their production process will promote spiritual clouding in those who consume them, thereby contributing to their unhappiness. Meishusama says that fertilizers invite disease and bugs (who eat the fertilizer), and that parasites feed on organic compost, fertilizer, and manure. These parasites often lay eggs, which humans later ingest.

During the first several years after conversion to Natural Agriculture, the soil will continue to be affected by residual chemicals within it, but over time will purify and become rejuvenated. Sometimes, though, when the pollution is excessive, an alternative is to bring in pure soil from another location. Or in more extreme cases, after prolonged use of fertilizer and chemicals, a layer of accumulated toxic residue may be found at a depth of about 30 centimeters beneath the surface of the soil. If a layer of this kind is found, plow the field sufficiently deep in order to completely turn over the soil, allowing it to aerate and break down naturally.

Use of Natural Compost

See how the soil is covered in a deep rich blanket of withered grasses and dead leaves as autumn deepens into winter every year. This blanket is there to make the soil fertile, and this is what we should make the natural compost from. You may think that natural compost supplies nutrition to crops, but this is by no means the case. The essential effect of natural compost is to keep the soil moist, to warm it and keep it from becoming compacted. Thus the soil absorbs heat and water, and does not become hard. —A Great Agricultural Revolution. ET

One might ask how it is possible to revitalize soil that has lost its mineral content, or has become unbalanced from excessive overuse. To answer this question, consider the fact that trees in the forests and jungles have existed for countless millennia without the need for human intervention to improve the soil. Nature has the ability to rejuvenate herself when left alone or treated with sensitivity and respect.

Evidence has accumulated over the centuries indicating that minerals can transform themselves from one chemical element to another through the agency of living organisms. Professor C. Louis Kervran, of the University of Paris, was nominated for the 1975 Nobel Prize in Physiology for his work on the Biological Transmutation of Minerals in human subjects. Dr. Kervran came to the conclusion that, in humans, these transmutations take place in mitochondrion (cellular components that secrete systemic enzymes). Other researchers have found evidence that microorganisms in the soil might be the agency for similar changes in the land. This transformation appears to occur through the addition or subtraction of protons making up mineral elements. In this way, potassium, with nineteen protons, could be combined with hydrogen, containing one proton, to change into calcium, which has twenty protons. Dr. Kervran postulated the presence of living enzyme activities as the primary catalyst for this transformation in humans.

Earthworms are among the most valuable creatures within the soil. In one of Charles Darwin's last published books, *The Formation of Vegetable Mould through the Action of Worms,* he stated that without worms, vegetation could not survive. Earthworms consume and digest enormous amounts of dry earth throughout their short lives, and in the process transform this earth into rich, vital soil. Darwin estimated that in fields with abundant populations of worms, about one inch of new topsoil could be produced every five years.

The point made here is that healthy soil with abundant microorganisms, yeasts, and earthworms has the ability to transform itself and make nutrients available to plants. The correct use of compost and mulch to promote soil that is soft, warm, and moist provides the best conditions for these microorganisms to thrive.

The Mystery within the Seed

Resting within the dark womb of the soil, the small seed lies dormant, conserving its energy for the proper moment to awaken. Suddenly, a tiny sprout emerges out of the seed, driven upwards by powerful inner forces. Following the dictates of an ancient cycle, the seed embarks on a journey from darkness to light, seeking to fulfill its destiny as a fully-grown plant. Soon, if conditions are favorable, it will grow into a tomato plant, a stalk of broccoli, a vine of zucchini squash, or a head of cabbage, and if given enough time, eventually yielding new seeds to produce new generations of plants.

Although science can analyze and classify the various components of a seed—its chemical makeup, cellular structure, and genetic sequencing—it can never comprehend the awesome mystery of life itself. This invisible life force cannot be viewed in a test tube or studied under a microscope. It can only be known from within, not from without. Life is profound and inscrutable. Without life, our planet would be nothing more than an inanimate heap of lonely rocks and aimless dust, circling endlessly through vast empty space.

As a man who has devoted his whole life to the most clear headed science, to the study of matter, I can tell you as a result of my research about atoms this much: There is no matter as such. All matter originates and exists only by virtue of a force which brings the particle of an atom to vibration and holds this most minute solar system of the atom together. We must assume behind this force the existence of a conscious and intelligent mind. This mind is the matrix of all matter. —*Max Planck (Quantum Physicist)*

According to Meishusama, the only way to understand the mystery of a seed is with the inner sensitivity of one's heart, not with the outer scrutiny of one's head. Love connects us with all things, whereas analysis separates us. Love fosters the growth of life, whereas analytical dissection destroys things by taking them apart. This fact is obvious to any frog trapped in a school science lab.

An intelligence dwells within each seed, capable of sensing the optimal conditions for it to emerge as a sprout. The seed germinates when the soil reaches the correct temperature, and there is sufficient water, sunlight, and oxygen. The seed has the inner awareness to interact with the surrounding environment and respond to diverse conditions. This inner awareness cannot be measured, but nonetheless is crucial to growth. Over time, successive generations of seeds grown in the same locality learn how to adapt to their surroundings, thus becoming increasingly vital and strong in the process. This is why "wildcrafted" herbs and spices are considered by many to be superior to those that are cultivated in even the most optimal manner. Because of their accumulated wisdom, these native seeds are the most optimal for use when planting new crops.

Within each seed, limited to its particular species, lays the invisible blueprint for a lush cabbage plant, a tall corn stalk, or giant sequoia tree. Some sequoias are measured to be over 3000 years old and over 300 feet tall, and yet these trees grew from seeds smaller than a vitamin pill and weighing only 5 milligrams. This fact is amazing to contemplate! The blueprint within a seed is more intricate and complex than the largest manmade building, ship, or airplane. These sophisticated human creations seem trivial in comparison. How these intricate patterns within the seed could be created is a profound mystery sealed within the heart of nature.

Seeds are precious, and it is vital that the seeds used in Natural Agriculture be of the highest purity and vitality because collectively they determine the future of all life on this planet. We can experience a future of health and vitality or one of disease and despair depending on how we nurture the seeds we have been entrusted with. We need only to examine the conditions surrounding the humble seed to discover which destiny we are choosing.

Use of Seeds

Seeds are extremely important. Seeds free from the effects of fertilizer are completely different from those that are artificially fertilized. —NA

A seed is a miniature replica of the entire environment from which it emerges. The plant that created the seed is a product of the soil, the air, the water, and the sunlight that nurtured it. Thus, the seed is a reflection of these conditions. Just as no two locations are identical, no two seeds are identical. Any farmer can tell you how much the conditions of a garden can differ from one place to the next —even locations very close to each other. One location may get a lot of water, another a lot of shade. Still another may have many rocks, and another much sand. If we look closely at the birds, the insects, and the flowers, we can see how unique each one is from another. Life is indeed an exuberant expression of diversity; a celebration of individual beauty and intelligence.

Modern farming encourages uniformity and conformity rather than diversity and variety. Unfortunately, with the continuing expansion and dominance of large, corporate monoculture (one type of crop), the diversity of plants, and especially of seeds, is being dangerously reduced. Variety is nature's way of protecting plant species from being destroyed by disease and unfavorable weather conditions because each variety has unique strengths and weaknesses.

Hybrid plants are increasingly dominating modern agriculture, especially grain crops. According to organic gardener Peter Donelan in his book *Growing To Seed*, "Three crops—wheat, rice, and corn (maize)—account for 50 percent of the calories in the human diet." This makes the quality and reproducibility of grain crops extremely important. He continues, "It is believed by some that hybrids are less nutritious, more demanding of soil resources, and more vulnerable to environmental hazards. Others believe that the additional vigor, uniformity, and increased yields of the modern hybrids are essential for feeding a hungry world and for predictable results in your backyard. The uncontroversial advantage of the standard, non-hybrid varieties is that they breed true (maintain a consistency of quality from generation to generation)." Additionally, many hybrid varieties are created by a "male sterility" technique which is dependent on human intervention and, therefore, unnatural.

Genetically modified seeds are those that have had foreign genes implanted into their genetic code. Their inner structure is not in harmony with nature, and so should be avoided. Seeds whose genetic makeup is artificially altered do not have the strength and vitality that seeds native to a particular region have. Because of this, use of these seeds threatens the sustainability of agriculture itself. Indeed, some corporations have used genetic modification to create what are called "terminator seeds" because the crops they produce do not create a second generation of living seeds. Farmers who use these seeds are thus totally dependent upon their suppliers each time they plant new crops, and if they fail to get a new supply, they are left with a barren field. Local sustainability is completely lost with such mercenary practices. Commercial seeds also tend to sprout all at once, leaving the entire crop vulnerable to storms, droughts, floods, and other natural forces. Whereas Natural Agriculture seeds, with their innate wisdom, tend to sprout at varying times, ensuring greater survivability of the crop.

Because of their purity, the most desirable seeds are ones that are obtained from crops grown by the Natural Agriculture method. Seeds from native species and varieties that have been growing in the same area for a long time without human intervention are even better. By developing and adapting to the conditions of a specific locale, they acquire great strength and vitality. Nature is inherently diverse, with each plant and seed differing from the other. So by using local seeds we help to maintain this plant and seed diversity.

The Natural Agriculture farmer is encouraged to allow a certain percentage of his or her crops to go to seed and to collect them and save them for future use. (They should be saved in a cool, dry place.) These heirloom seeds will continue to adapt to the local conditions of the land, and in the process, become increasingly unique to that farm. Beans, peas, lettuce, tomatoes, or other self-pollinating varieties of plants are the easiest to use as seed crops. Individual plants that demonstrate exceptional qualities are the best ones to choose for this purpose because their seeds will likely produce offspring with those same favorable traits. Heirloom seeds can also be shared with other farmers seeking locally grown, pure seeds, with the hope that they too will begin to save their own seeds from their own gardens and farms.

Seeds are part of humanities' collective heritage. They are as important to culture as music, art, and literature. Indeed, the practice of Natural Agriculture brings "culture" back into agri-"culture."

Continuous Cultivation

In the practice of Natural Agriculture, it is best to continuously grow one crop in the same field. Once the soil becomes free from fertilizers, it can fully exhibit its inherent capability to make it suitable to the crop being grown in it. With a single crop, the soil will exhibit its greatest vitality exclusively targeting that crop's needs. However, if another crop is planted on the same spot, the soil has to start over from the beginning, once again working to adjust itself to become suitable to the new plant. This will bring unsuccessful outcomes both to the original and new crops. I hope this explanation is clear enough for you. —NA

Natural Agriculture recognizes the soil's inherent ability to evolve and adapt to the needs of various kinds of plants growing within it. To maximize this natural adaptive ability, Natural Agriculture farmers are encouraged to practice continuous cropping, the practice of growing the same plants in the same spot year after year. This gives the soil the chance to adapt to the plant, and the plant the chance to adapt to the soil. Each exerts a mutually beneficial influence upon the other. According to Meishusama, in the long run, this method helps increase crop yield.

The reason that I recommend continuous cropping is that soil naturally develops certain qualities depending on the plants that are raised in it. The soil's adaptability to a specific plant can be well understood by the following example. People who engage in heavy manual labor develop a muscular body. In comparison, those who engage in intellectual work, such as writers, develop specific functions of the brain. People who continuously change their occupations and domiciles often experience difficulty in becoming successful. A similar thing can be applied to the relationship between crops and soil. Here we come to realize how mistaken conventional agriculture practices are. —NA

Nature is conscious and intelligent. Plants have the ability to sense conditions in the environment and adapt to them. Likewise, soil can sense the plant roots growing within it and create a supportive environment for them. Plants support bacteria, mycelium fungi, yeast, and earthworms within the soil by providing sugars for them to feed on and by holding moisture in the ground. Soil that has been adequately nurtured can provide the correct amount of minerals and microorganisms that the plants need. The more soil, seeds and plants interact with each other, the more they get to know each other. Life is about relationships, and because all of nature is conscious, intelligent and sensitive, these relationships will flourish if given favorable conditions to do so.

However, rotating crops disrupts relationships and interferes with the mutual adaptability of seeds, plants, and soil to each other. Crop rotation, the practice of growing different kinds of crops at different times of the year in the same location, sacrifices long-term success for short-term advantage. Farmers may think they need to rotate crops to prevent the soil from becoming deficient of certain nutrients as can be caused by monocropping. Or they may do so in order to maximize output, especially in temperate or tropical climates that allow for year-round growing seasons. Although this might benefit the farmer at the beginning, over time it creates weak plants that cannot easily survive floods, hurricanes, and droughts. Such food is not as tasty and nutritious as food grown the Natural Agriculture way. Plants, seeds, and soil need time to learn from and adapt to each other. The farmer needs to respect the intelligence of nature if he or she wishes to be successful.

Instead of crop rotation, some farmers balance the soil by growing a mixed variety of companion plants or cover crops alongside their food crops. Other farmers accomplish the same thing by allowing a moderate amount of weeds to grow within their fields.

Monocrops are rare in nature. In fact, the natural world thrives on diversity because this supports ecological balance. The more we study nature, the more we will discover the advantages of non-rotated polycultural farming practices.

Advantages

When the original crops absorb fertilizers, they become extremely weak from the poisoning caused by the absorption of these fertilizers. I have also discovered that this poison provides an attractive diet for pests. Furthermore, as I have already mentioned above, these pests can actually be generated by fertilizers, and then, of course, they eat the crops and multiply. —A Great Agricultural Revolution. ET

The Natural Agriculture method brings a decrease in insect damage, as well as produces crops that are hearty and resilient. Even when these crops are damaged by storms or floods, they soon tend to recover. When harshly beaten, they quickly rejuvenate because of the vitality provided from within. The primary source of this strength is in the roots. "The natural plant has hair roots that are longer and thicker than those of the fertilized plant, and as a consequence is more firmly rooted," writes Meishusama. *(A Great Agricultural Revolution. ET)*

By contrast, conventional farming, by adding fertilizer to the soil, whether chemical or natural, encourages roots to become lazy and less motivated to reach deep into the earth for their nutrients. Consequently, they remain short and shallow, resulting in a weak plant. In contrast, the roots of crops grown by the Natural Agriculture method reach deeper into the ground for their minerals and other nutrients, drawing on the vitality of the earth. These roots are bigger and longer, with a larger spread, providing much greater strength and stamina to the plant. Because of this, the crops are better able to reach their innate potential. The resulting food is safe and rich in nutrition and life force, which greatly contributes to their health-restoring properties. Natural Agriculture is deeply sustainable and regenerative.

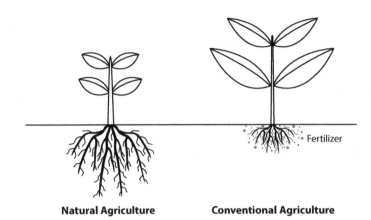

Natural Agriculture　　　　　**Conventional Agriculture**

Comparison between Natural Agriculture and conventionally grown plants

Overall, farming the Natural Agriculture way is simpler, healthier, and safer than conventional and organic methods. It is cheaper because one doesn't have to buy expensive chemical fertilizers and pesticides, and easier because one doesn't have to create organic fertilizer and compost. Also, one doesn't have to buy seeds because one learns to save them from previous crops. Usually there is less digging and turning over of the soil because one learns to allow nature to build the soil gradually without too much human intervention. And as the crops become stronger, they are better able to compete with weeds, especially if mulch is used as a ground cover. Therefore, less time and effort is spent digging and weeding. Furthermore, when one is not exposed to toxic chemicals or manure, one is unlikely to get sick from contamination. The food produced is thus more nutritious and flavorful, which contributes to one's health and enjoyment. Finally, one finds peace and harmony from working with the land. Such value cannot be measured in dollars and cents.

Summary of Methodology

As fostered by Meishusama, the Natural Agriculture approach goes beyond most organic farming methods in its fundamental respect for nature. The farmer demonstrates this respect by:

- Not using compost as fertilizer, but instead to keep the soil soft, warm and moist.

- Not tilling the soil more than a few inches deep so as to protect the microorganisms further down. (This is ideal, although sometimes it may be necessary to go deeper or even to plow.)

- Not using aggressive methods, chemical or natural, to control pests.

- Viewing plant sickness, wind and rain damage, and insect infestation as necessary forms of purification.

- Growing crops well suited for the local environment.

- Using seeds derived from earlier crops grown in the same location.

- Cultivating a loving relationship to the land, crops, weather, insects, and wildlife.

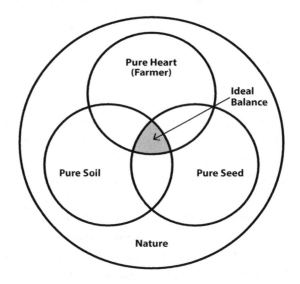

Three Essentials of Natural Agriculture : Pure Soil, Pure Heart, and Pure Seed

Therefore, Natural Agriculture does not attempt to suppress pests or counteract environmental damage with either chemicals or natural remedies. This form of farming is very gentle and non-invasive to the land and that which grows in it. Most significantly, it deeply trusts the natural processes of nature. As a result, it does not add nutrients to the soil, as do most organic methods. In addition, Meishusama stresses the fundamental importance of the farmer cultivating a grateful heart along with a deep respect for nature. These feelings are viewed as the spiritual elements that support healthy, abundant crops.

Farming as Art

Meishusama calls Natural Agriculture the "Art of Agriculture" because the farmer approaches his work with soil and plants in much the same way as an artist approaches canvas or stone. Both the artist and the farmer respond from the heart, not the head. Their inspiration is drawn from what is hidden from the senses but visible to the spirit. Natural Agriculture is not simply a collection of techniques applied to farming, but also a spiritual approach to life.

To Meishusama, the world of nature is God's artwork. Nature never produces an ugly ocean wave or an unattractive cloud formation. Every flower is a gentle song of celebration, and each mountain a cathedral of towering majesty. And it is the job of the Natural Agriculture farmer to support the spirit and integrity of this aesthetic masterpiece.

CHAPTER 12

ART AND BEAUTY

As our eyes pass over the beauties of nature, an inexpressible joy wells up within us. It would be no exaggeration to call our ideal of heaven on earth "the world of art," for it is the world of truth, virtue, and beauty, and it is in art that Beauty finds its true expression. —Religion and Art. ET

The Experience of Beauty

The human soul needs actual beauty more than bread. —D. H. Lawrence

In addition to Jyorei and Natural Agriculture, Meishusama puts great value on the appreciation of art and beauty as a way to elevate people's consciousness and to help transform the world. Visiting an art gallery, a concert hall, or going out for a relaxing walk in nature are all wonderful ways to enjoy and benefit from beauty. Beauty lifts us above our personal problems so we can appreciate and enjoy the simple things in life. By contrast, a life devoid of beauty degenerates into a struggle for survival, devoid of meaning, purpose, or value.

Although Spirit itself cannot be made into a direct object of our experience, qualities that emerge out of Spirit can. Love, peace, innocence, charity, gratitude, joy, and beauty are embodied to varying degrees in people, art, and nature. When experiencing great art forms or communing with nature, the spiritual beauty within us touches the inner beauty of the object perceived. This is not an object-to-object relationship, but rather, a subject-to-subject one wherein the experiencer communes with the inner essence of the work of art. In such experiences, ordinary objectivity is transcended by something higher and more expansive. Various art forms provide us with the opportunity to be thrown into the present moment where we can be more alive and engaged. At its height, beauty is an experience of the inner unity with all things.

In itself, beauty is transcendent. It transcends all phenomena, including the particular medium, culture, or artist that gives it form. Great works of art are vehicles for the expression of beauty, giving it shape, color, and texture in regards to painting, or rhythm, melody, and harmony in regards to music. Neither great art nor great beauty can exist without the other. Art without beauty is devoid of soul, and beauty without art is devoid of substance. Only great art incorporates both in perfect balance.

The ancient Greek Philosopher Aristotle claimed that beauty is the condition where all of the parts are in harmony with each other, where nothing seems to be missing, and nothing needs to be added or changed. This produces satisfaction and contentment in the viewer or experiencer. On the other hand, the three ancient philosophers Pythagoras, Plato, and Plotinus held that beauty was the eternal splendor of "The One" revealing itself through the many, giving meaning and pleasure to all. The former definition is structural and passive, whereas the latter is energetic and active. These two definitions can be viewed as complimentary to each other. Taken together they offer a more complete explanation of what makes something beautiful.

In contrast, within Japanese art there is the aesthetic concept of *wabi-sabi*, the beauty of things imperfect, irregular, impermanent, and incomplete. In popular Western culture this is sometimes called "the Zen flaw" in reference to how a rough or minor imperfection adds beauty and character to a work of art or craft. Sometimes these flaws are the result of a "controlled accident" in which the artist deliberately allows for spontaneous surprises to occur during the creative process. The end result is a work of art that looks uncontrived and rustic. In other words, this is the beauty of nature. Although Meishusama could surely appreciate Western tastes in art, the *wabi-sabi* style was probably closer to his heart.

However, Meishusama's primary concern was not art theory but the alleviation of suffering and the promotion of universal happiness. The experience of beauty, he felt, was central to this goal. Who cannot feel a serene joy when meandering through a beautiful garden, strolling along the seashore at dusk, or wandering down a pristine mountain path? A simple vase of fresh flowers placed in one's home can bring inspiration and pleasure to one's family and guests, as well as promote domestic harmony. Singing, creative writing, playing a musical instrument, painting, and dancing are also excellent ways to connect with beauty. *A beautiful environment is sure to illuminate the hearts of the people who live in it; thus crime and bad behavior will decrease. This phenomenon alone will be one of the means of furthering the realization of Heaven on Earth.*

—Heaven Is a World of Beauty. ET

The Role of the Artist

In the fields of music and art, it is the souls of the artists themselves, as expressed in their various mediums, which most deeply touch the souls of the audience. This is what makes people feel connected through their eyes and ears to works of art. So, if the souls of artists are not spiritually advanced enough, their work will not be truly great. Since artists play an important role by inspiring people through their work, they particularly need to have elevated characters.

—On Being Humble and Flexible. KW

Generally speaking, the modern world regards art as a luxury, not a necessity, because people can survive without art, but not without food and shelter. It may be true that cheap trinkets, shallow television series, and crass advertising art have little value, however art that expresses real beauty does have value. According to Meishusama, beautiful art forms are more than mere decoration or entertainment; they are food for the soul. Beauty is desirable and necessary because it brings meaning and joy to life. Without it, life becomes impoverished. Although individuals may survive without art, cultures cannot.

Meishusama teaches that life has a greater purpose than that of mere existence. Life is short, but the soul endures. From the broader vantage point of the soul, life's only purpose is spiritual growth. One's spiritual level is what most contributes to happiness because it affects one's general mood and outlook, and also influences the type of people and circumstances that one attracts. People with inner beauty attract other people with inner beauty. In these ways, whatever contributes to one's spiritual growth has enduring value, and beautiful art is one of these contributions.

Meishusama felt that a distinction could be made between art that has spiritual value and art that does not. He felt that much of the contemporary art of his day was ugly, depressing, and vulgar, exhibiting no signs of artistic skill or imagination. It had no higher purpose than to gain recognition or money for the artist. Sometimes the only objective was to shock the public by breaking and defying current social standards and artistic conventions. These criteria, Meishusama felt, were not sufficient.

An artist is only one part of the overall structure of society, and can only produce true art by realizing what his or her role is and playing it to the fullest. This, above all, is the duty of an artist.

However, if we think of most of the artists who are active nowadays, we cannot fail to be shocked by their wild and irresponsible behavior. Of course, this is not to deny the existence of a few admirable artists, but for the most part, artists seem not so much to have forgotten their duty as to be incapable of understanding it at all. Moreover, they consider themselves to be special people, and believe that their egotistical and willful behavior is a demonstration of individuality or a manifestation of genius. Due to this way of thinking, they lead completely selfish lives and are shameless in their behavior. This is indeed a terrible state of affairs. Again, society regards artists as superior in some way and gives them favorable treatment, tolerating most of their excesses. The artists, of course, fall deeper into the illusion of the all-importance of their own egos. To avoid this situation, artists must have a character that is far superior to most people.

To put it simply, the mystical power that springs from the artist's soul passes through the written word, through the picture, the musical instrument, the song or dance, and plucks at the strings of the soul of all humankind. This link between the artist's soul and the souls of others is very strong. Because of this, if an artist's character is bad, then all humanity will be debased. And, of course, if an artist's mind is fine and pure, he or she will elevate the characters of everyone else as well. This is the noblest aspect of art, and the artist must so employ his or her art as to become a worthy guide for the rest of humankind. —*The Role of Art. ET*

Psychoanalyst Sigmund Freud also held a dim view of many of the artists of his day. In characteristic fashion, he remarked, "The artist is a neurotic...he is doing what he does for honor, power, riches, fame and the love of women."

With this in mind, we may ask, "What is the duty of society to our artists? How can society responsibly support art?" Society has now become so fascinated by the shadow side of people's character that it often fails to appreciate people who are doing good things. We now find it more entertaining to look at people's flaws than at the good things they produce. We have become cynical about human nature, instead of expecting decent behavior from artists and other public figures. Where can we find individuals to respect and admire?

According to Meishusama, two of the most important factors influencing the creation of great art forms are the purity of the artist's soul, and his or her basic intention. If the artist's character is highly refined and is free from excessive selfishness or ego, then he or she will emit a subtle spiritual influence that will be conveyed to the viewer or listener. Some artists of lesser character can also emit such higher influences if their art is created during peak experiences. In both cases, the artist's experience of beauty, along with the great joy and satisfaction they feel while creating their work of art, is communicated to the viewer or listener through the finished sculpture, painting, architecture, music, literature, dance, or play.

The aim of art is to represent not the outward appearance of things, but their inward significance. —Aristotle

The outer form of art—colors, shapes, textures, sounds, and movements— is not only a vehicle for the artist's inner experience, but also is integral to it. In the best works of art, not a single thing is superfluous or misplaced, and as a whole, there is simplicity of form.

Beauty of style, and harmony and grace and good rhythm, depend on simplicity.
—Plato

The Viewer of Art

Nurture and promote a keen sense of beauty. —Heaven Is a World of Beauty. ET

The world is God's body. It is the outer manifestation of His invisible Spirit. Buildings, cars, trees, and people do not obstruct God; they reveal Him. Those of us who are sufficiently sensitive can experience the divine through an openhearted appreciation of the world around us. This is especially possible in the presence of nature and art because both express beauty. To recognize beauty is to be touched by it, and to be touched by beauty is to be transformed by it. Beauty is a doorway to Eternity.

Heat cannot be separated from fire, nor beauty from the eternal. —Dante
The arts are not meant to merely entertain, they are primarily meant to express. Something from the artist's inner world of feeling and perception is expressed through his or her art that demands a reciprocal response from the person who

encounters it. The arts bring to the surface hidden feelings and values that we may not realize we have. They call forth something profound from deep within us. They reveal the universal in the particular, allowing us to experience the world with greater awareness and insight. Unlike much of the art and music produced by today's entertainment industry, which can be enjoyed in a passive or semi-conscious state, truly expressive art and music require energy and involvement from the viewer or listener for their value to be appreciated.

Viewers of art and listeners of music also have the responsibility to educate themselves about the arts (and society needs to support this education), to cultivate greater sensitivity to beauty, and to refine their own character through spiritual discipline. Otherwise they may fail to appreciate the great beauty that often exists in their ordinary day-to-day lives. Some people can walk through paradise itself but be so consumed by personal suffering that they remain unmoved by the beauty around them. As the American philosopher Ralph Waldo Emerson put it: "Though you may travel the world to find the beautiful, you must have it within you or you will find it not." The communication of beauty is a two-way process between the artist or performer and the viewer or listener, depending as much on the openness and sensitivity of the viewer as on the talent and skill of the artist. Objective beauty mirrors the beauty hidden deep within the viewer's soul. During the experience of beauty, this two-way communication dissolves into a unitary communion where there is no separation between the viewer or listener and the artwork or performance.

About the subjective experience of beauty, the Japanese philosopher, Yasuhiko Genku Kimura, writes,

"Beauty is in the eye of the beholder." This adage is generally understood to mean that beauty is a subjective perception and judgment, different from one person to another, and therefore relative. There is another interpretation: Beauty is precisely in the eye of the beholder because without the [inner] vision that can behold beauty, there can be no experience of beauty. The more we open our [inner] vision for beauty, the more beauty we behold in our eye.

Beauty is a universal quality that is present throughout the universe. Beauty is only subjective in the sense that the kind of beauty that one beholds is determined by the kind of [inner] vision for beauty that one has unfolded. Beauty is only relative in the sense that the degree to which one beholds beauty is proportional to the degree to which one's [inner] vision for beauty is open. (*Beauty as a Path of Peace*)

Therefore, both the artist and the viewer contribute to the experience of beauty—the artist or performer through revealing beauty, and the viewer or listener through his or her sensitivity to and appreciation of that beauty. But this sensitivity and appreciation does not just happen. Beauty, and the recognition of it, must be nurtured. Arts education teaches people how to use their senses. They develop "sense-ability." People are better at problem solving and most everything else when they study the arts.

Beauty opens our hearts and awakens us to higher values, which then allows us to make better decisions in life. In its highest form beauty produces a sense of wonderment in us, like children gazing wide-eyed at the starry heavens. Such innocent wonderment is food for our souls.

People with a heart capable of appreciating art are eligible to live in Heaven.
—Art. MK1

Art Devoid of Spirit

Look about you, look at the literature that plumbs the depths of pornography and cynicism, and look at the paintings that go to the extremes of grotesquerie. Amidst the voices of the artists, the clatter of their music, their plays and films, look deep into your heart and you will know that what I have said is nothing more and nothing less than the truth. —The Role of Art. ET

The essence of art is a mystery. Too specific a definition of art can hamper the creativity that is the essence of art itself. On the other hand, to reject all definitions of art as superfluous concepts, or to dismiss all judgments about art as merely subjective biases, leaves people with no standards to go by. How can people come to a consensus about quality without some form of criteria? Without these, good art cannot be distinguished from bad art, and true talent, when it appears, cannot be recognized or appreciated. This lack of standards is like a ship without a rudder, which is incapable of steering in any particular direction. The end result is an alarming situation in which beauty and refinement are ridiculed, and ugliness and profanity are admired. In our modern era, we need not look too far to find numerous examples of this depressing trend.

A belief popular in today's academic world is that all meaning and values are culturally conditioned, and consequently have no objective validity. From this perspective, what one person may judge as good art, another can justifiably condemn as bad art. If everything is subjective—and therefore relative—then who can say which appraisal is most valid? And if we are left with no standards to go by, then how can we reach any social consensus? Some might question the need for social consensus, and instead assert the greater importance of individual freedom. Although individuality is indeed important, we must also remember that we live in societies, and societies make group decisions based on shared values. It's usually groups of people who choose the types of artwork to put in museums, the shapes of buildings to erect, and the ideas and values to teach in schools; and if they cannot agree on anything, then the person who shouts the loudest will win. If this trend towards cultural relativism continues too far, then soon schools may be teaching that gangster rap music is of equal merit to Beethoven's symphonies or that Shakespeare's plays are no better than urban graffiti. This is not such a wild stretch of the imagination because other forms of rap and hip hop music are already being taught in some of our schools.

In actuality, however, this subjective relativism is not really so unbiased, for it is often used to elevate and promote art, architecture, literature, movies, and music that are disturbing, shocking, or merely clever. This may be because sensationalism draws more attention to itself than does subtlety. In such a distorted cultural environment, beautiful works of art are regularly dismissed as shallow, old fashioned, naïve, or merely commercial, and beauty itself is often scorned.

It is sometimes said that everything is art. But if everything is art, then why bother to put anything in a frame, or perform anything on a stage? The very fact that we do so indicates that we consider that particular art, music, or play to be uniquely valuable. We are obviously putting it in a special place in order to draw attention to it. On the other hand, if everything were equally valuable as art, should we then put the entire universe inside a special frame or concert hall? And if everything were art, then there would be no reason to even use the word *art*, because a word only has meaning when it can be contrasted with its opposite— in this case, *non-art*. Saying that everything is art is like saying that everything is up, or that everything is big. *Up* and *big* have no meaning unless they can be compared with *down* or *small*.

The same can be said about the word *good*. Can all art be good? How can there be good art without the existence of bad art? Value judgments depend on contrast in order to have meaning. And Is it really possible to avoid all value judgments?

How often do we see buildings that seem to defy the laws of gravity or some other functional or aesthetic standard that leaves the average person feeling alienated and uncomfortable? Is there any beauty in these bizarre structures? When music has so much dissonance, atonality, and disjointed structure that it is impossible for the audience to emotionally relate to it, does this strangeness promote the aesthetic experience or uplift the human spirit? And are works of art that appear ugly to the vast majority of people successes, or failures? Of course aesthetic tastes vary from person to person, but everyone has a threshold as to how much dissonance, atonality, asymmetry or chaos they can tolerate. Images and sounds that are repulsive or offensive may serve to catch people's attention for the sake of delivering a particular social message, but in and of themselves they do not feed the soul. If anything, they do the opposite—they poison it. Beauty is as important to the soul as food is to the body. And where else should people go to experience beauty if not to art?

The artist's vocation is to send light into the human heart.
—*George Sand (French Novelist)*

Of course, there have been many instances in the past where a piece of music or a work of art was rejected by the public or the critics but which later became highly acclaimed and popular. Examples include Stravinsky's "Rite of Spring" ballet score, which provoked shock and outrage in the concert hall during its debut performance; Richard Strauss' opera "Salome," which caused a riot when it opened; the artist Picasso's painting "The Ladies of Avignon," which was very controversial at the time; and the works of impressionist painter Cezanne, which gained public recognition only after he died. Such instances of rejection usually occur when the piece introduces dramatically original structures, themes, or patterns. The mind is often disoriented, and the emotions disturbed by that which is new and unusual. People need time to familiarize themselves with anything that seems strange before they can mentally and emotionally connect with it. This type of reaction also occurs in people when confronted by the customs and creations of foreign cultures that they do not understand. On the other hand, most art and music that is popular today will most likely slip into obscurity when current fashions change.

Beauty is the purgation of superfluities. —Michelangelo

Inaccessibility, in and of itself, is of no inherent value. The difference between noise and music depends on the degree of harmony, structure, and meaning it contains. When there is no pleasure in listening to music or viewing art, can it be said to be beautiful? Of course, music, art, or poetry that is shallow or merely pretty is often not very pleasurable, and usually lacks genuine beauty as well. One of the challenges for the arts and the artist is to bring out the hidden beauty buried within dark, painful, or disturbing experiences. This is art's transformative power. The philosopher George Santayana stated, "The subject matter of art is life, life as it actually is; but the function of art is to make life better."

In modern times, the standards for evaluating art have become so confused that often pornography or clever works of cultural criticism are proudly displayed as examples of leading edge art. These works may touch our senses or our minds, but not our souls, for there is no joy in them. It's the Spirit within art that ennobles it, and when communicated effectively, this Spirit also ennobles the viewer or listener.

Art must be full of laughter and joy—a thing full of interest and excitement.
—Religious Pragmatism. ET

Transformative Art

Beauty is not just for one's own personal satisfaction; it brings pleasure to the eye of the beholder, and in this sense is itself an act of virtue. As the level of civilization becomes higher, so do the things in that society become more beautiful. Think about it. —Heaven is a World of Beauty. ET

When an artist's spiritual awareness is highly developed, combined with a great mastery of the techniques of his art, he or she is then capable of both receiving aesthetic inspiration as well as skillfully communicating it. He or she functions as a suitable vessel for Spirit. The result can be the creation of a work of visual, verbal, musical or mixed media art that truly touches a person's soul. Such art appeals to the mind, the senses, and the heart. "Fine art is that in which the hand, the head, and the heart of man go together," wrote John Ruskin, an influential art critic and connoisseur of the Victorian era.

While many artists embody high standards of character that, in turn, are reflected in their work, there are also artists, such as Beethoven, who appear to embody the opposite standards of character, and yet may still produce marvelous works of art. These latter types of artists may suffer from inner torment and depression. Yet during the creative process, while they are painting, composing, singing, or writing, they get absorbed in a higher state of consciousness where everything is experienced as a single flow of ecstatic energy. At this time of pure creativity, the stark division between subject and object is suspended, and they enter into a sublime realm of profound inspiration and inner peace. This is sometimes described as an experience of timeless unity, where everything flows together in wondrous grace and harmony. Unfortunately, this may be the only time when these artists can feel free from their tormented lives. This would explain their compulsion to constantly create; it's their desire to be transfixed into a higher dimension. The higher perception that results from this experience is then communicated through the work of art to the viewer or listener. What is communicated is the energy of the artist's vision, combined with his or her intention, knowledge, skill, and ecstatic joy.

I dream my painting, and then I paint my dream. —Vincent van Gogh

Viewed objectively, all great or transformative art exhibits qualities of clarity, proportion, and symmetry, although not a rigid symmetry but a dynamic one that gives it movement and life. Such art also has integrity, in which all the various elements fit together in a unifying whole. Viewed subjectively, all great or transformative art offers the perceiver a glimpse of reality as seen from a higher perspective—revealing it to be simultaneously extraordinary and ordinary. Through this art, we are given a profound vision of both Heaven touching Earth, and Earth touching Heaven. In other words, this art is divinely inspired. It gives us an experience of eternal Beauty that transcends our mundane sensory perceptions. In this way, art can be a powerful vehicle for spiritual experience. The novelist and essayist, Albert Camus, expressed this idea well: "Beauty is unbearable, drives us to despair, offering us for a minute the glimpse of an eternity that we should like to stretch out over the whole of time."

Profound Beauty has the ability to take our breath away. It awakens our spirit by bringing us a glimpse of the sacred. Through the experience of beauty, our mind stops, and we are transported to a higher realm of radiant splendor. This is one of the most important contributions of art: the ability to bring spiritual perception down into our mundane world while simultaneously lifting our ordinary consciousness up into the divine realm. Beethoven reputedly made this statement about the mystical power of music: "Those who understand [music] must be freed by it from all the miseries which the others drag about with themselves. . . . I am right in saying that music is the one incorporeal entrance into the higher world of knowledge which comprehends mankind but which mankind cannot comprehend."

Nothing is more hallowing than the union of kindred spirits in art. At the moment of meeting, the art lover transcends himself. At once he is and is not. He catches a glimpse of Infinity, but words cannot voice his delight, for the eye has no tongue. Freed from the fetters of matter, his spirit moves in the rhythm of things. It is thus that art becomes akin to religion and ennobles mankind. It is this which makes a masterpiece something sacred. —*Hideo Kishimoto, Mahayana Buddhism and Japanese Thought*

This experience of beauty may occur even though the subject matter may be of a most mundane or even disturbing nature. A painting such as Pablo Picasso's Guernica, about the horrors of the Spanish Civil War, or Henryk Gorecki's Symphony of Sorrowful Songs, about the suffering at the Auschwitz Concentration Camp during World War II, can reveal great beauty and spiritual depth, not in spite of, but because of the subject matter. These two pieces radiate a powerful and universal Light from within their outer darkness. Beauty has the ability to transform a negative experience into something sublime and ennobling that nourishes and deepens the soul. This can be done without denying the objective unpleasantness or even tragedy of the subject matter. Just as spiritual love, by its universal embrace, can heal and transform even the most repulsive of things, so too, does the artist's creative talent reveal the beauty hidden within all things. This inner beauty is the soft breath of God.

Beauty is one of the rare things that does not lead to doubt of God.
                                      —*Jean Anouilh (French Playwright)*

The Purpose of Beauty in Art

I keenly believe that wonderful artworks should not be secluded, but should instead be shown to as many people as possible, to give them enjoyment and elevate their [character]. In this way, fine arts contribute greatly to the development of culture, and this is the true purpose of art.[14] —*Meishusama*

---

14. Meishusama, "The Origins of the Hakone Museum," *Shumei Magazine,* vol. 195 (November 1996).

According to Meishusama, art has two primary purposes: to provide pleasure, and to support spiritual growth. Both the individual and society as a whole can benefit from art that elevates the soul and that promotes Heaven on Earth. So central is art to civilization that it is not an exaggeration to say that there would be no civilization without it. About the significance of art, Meishusama adds, "The progress of culture is demonstrated most clearly in the appreciation of beauty within that culture." *(Heaven Is a World of Beauty. ET)* A civilization that does not value beauty can hardly be called civilized.

Our highest aspirations are given outer expression in the arts. They ennoble humanity through their gifts of great beauty and sensitivity. The aesthetic experience is an entrance to a transcendental unity wherein all separations fall away. Art explores the heights of the sacred while simultaneously embracing the depths of the profane. From its all-encompassing unitary vision, it cannot reject either heaven or earth because it sees them as one integrated whole. Beauty is a seamless fusion of the form and the formless, and of spiritual nourishment and sensual pleasure. It also reconciles both the rational and the feeling parts of human nature. According to composer, Claude Debussy, "Beauty must appeal to the senses, must provide us with immediate enjoyment, must impress us or insinuate itself into us without any effort on our part."

Just as a loving person can inspire us to see the good in others, so too, can great art reveal the hidden beauty that usually escapes our eyes and ears. As the painter Paul Klee states, "Art does not reproduce the visible; rather, it makes visible." In this way, beauty and love are closely related. Both enrich our lives, and both transform the world around us. The Christian mystic Evelyn Underhill writes, "All things are perceived in the light of charity, and hence under the aspect of beauty; for beauty is simply reality seen with the eyes of love."

Enjoyment is the other purpose of art. The simple pleasure that art brings is more than enough justification for its existence. This pleasure is a purposeless purpose because art does not point to a goal outside of itself. Its beauty is its own purpose. Therefore, it is best not to have a purpose in mind when experiencing art, but instead to appreciate art for its own sake, simply because it is beautiful or moving.

The role of art is surely to heighten people's emotions, to enrich their lives, and to give meaning and enjoyment to their existence. —Religion and Art. ET

Living a Life of Beauty

Beauty is a thing that slips in and permeates our souls. —Socrates

Beauty celebrates the joy of living. We can easily bring beauty into our daily lives by the way that we speak, behave, and dress, as well as in the appearance and cleanliness of our homes, cars, and workplaces. Simple things like putting flowers in our home or office can significantly elevate the atmosphere in these locations. Many people grow flowers in their yards or windowsills for this reason. Making an attractive impression on others by our style of dress is another way to incorporate beauty into our daily lives. Listening to music that brings joy and inspiration, or that deepens our capacity for genuine feeling and appreciation, is both convenient and inexpensive. We can also create artwork ourselves. We do not need great skill or talent to do this, although it can help to take art classes to improve our knowledge and skills. Whatever our personal capacities, it is enriching just to sing, paint, dance, sculpt, write, or play musical instruments because creativity can help expand our appreciation of beauty.

When I decorate my room with a camellia from the garden, I feel the pleasure of the world. —Art. MK1

Most important of all is the cultivation of inner beauty, because God lives in a beautiful heart. A warm smile, a cheerful disposition, and actions that are gentle and kind, are all simple ways to express this inner beauty. Such behavior is elegance of the truest kind. Truth tempered by love and elevated by beauty of expression is guaranteed to promote happiness.

Heaven is a world of beauty, and the hearts of those who live there are beautiful as well. —Art. MK1

CHAPTER 13

SHINJI SHUMEIKAI

Our organization, on the other hand, you know, makes "A world without sickness, poverty, or strife—Paradise on Earth" its central slogan, and works for the benefit of all humanity. —A Sense of Justice. ET

Organizational Background

General Information

Shinji Shumeikai, also known as Shumei, is an international spiritual organization dedicated to elevating the quality of life for all of humanity. It is committed to creating an ideal state of health, happiness, and harmony by applying the wisdom and spiritual insights of Meishusama to a variety of human activities. Since the founding of the organization, Shumei has been best portrayed as a fellowship that places the highest value on cultivating a grateful heart and praying for the happiness of others. These values are essential to the teachings of Meishusama. Helping others was Meishusama's primary concern, and a feeling of gratitude and love were at the core of his dream of creating a Paradise on Earth.

Growing primarily out of Meishusama's spiritual revelations, Shumei also has some roots in the Shinto tradition of Japan. Shinto is an integral part of the cultural heritage of Japan, and to this day influences many of its attitudes and customs. Shumei shares Shinto's deep reverence for nature, and it incorporates some of Shinto's ritual practices and chants in its various religious services. Although Shumei has some religious traits, its principle mission is not otherworldly; it seeks to help build an ideal world here on earth. It is in harmony with all religious traditions that promote peace and happiness. In other words, it is a comprehensive, practical approach to bringing spiritual growth and overall happiness to people.

Many members find that their association with Shumei enhances and deepens their current religious beliefs and spiritual practices.

Today, there are over 500,000 members of Shumei worldwide, with centers in over a hundred cities throughout Japan, as well as in North and South America, Europe, Australia, and other parts of Asia. Under the leadership of Ms Hiroko Koyama (whose formal title is Kaicho-Sensei), Shumei has expanded its global work for world peace through its three main activities: Jyorei, Natural Agriculture, and the arts. In recent years, believing that the twenty-first century offers critical opportunities to realize the Founder's vision of global peace and world citizenship, the organization has taken a more active role in international activities. Shumei's goal is not only to raise the individual to a more enlightened level of consciousness, but also to create a world of peace, health, and prosperity.

Historical Background

Shumei was originally formed under Meishusama's guidance in 1949 in Kyoto, Japan, by one of his foremost students, Mihoko Koyama, whom Shumei members respectfully refer to as Kaishusama (meaning "the organizational founder" or "most revered leader").

Mihoko Koyama was raised in a family with a pious faith in Kannon, the Buddhist deity of wisdom and compassion, and was also deeply inspired by Christian educators in her latter school days. During this time, she acquired both the spirit of humanism and a faith in God. Her first encounter with Meishusama was in 1941, about a year after her initial experience of Jyorei through a student of his. In those days, Jyorei was called the Okada Style Spiritual Acupressure Treatment. This initial experience occurred during World War II, while her husband was overseas fighting at the front lines. During those years she had to take care of her three little children all by herself.

Under those difficult circumstances, Kaishusama felt fortunate to have been introduced to Jyorei and its healing powers. Putting her full faith in Meishusama, she decided to devote her entire life to serving God and to helping others. As she became active in sharing Jyorei, demonstrating its great effectiveness, and caring for others with love and affection, more and more people were drawn to her. Gradually, a group formed, consisting of those who were attracted by Kaishusama's selfless dedication to helping others and by her loyal devotion to Meishusama. With a sincere heart, and Meishusama's guidance, she worked passionately to create the foundations of Shumei. This name *Shumei*, meaning "Supreme Light," was the name given by Meishusama to her group in April of 1949.

After World War II, Meishusama established the Japan Kannon Society *(Nihon Kannon Kyodan)* in 1947, and then created the Japan Miroku Society *(Nihon Miroku Kai)* in 1948. Until those two organizations became united under the name of Sekai Kyuseikyo[15] in 1950, Shumei belonged to the Japan Miroku Society. The creation of Sekai Kyuseikyo involved the integration of approximately eighty groups of Meishusama's disciples in various parts of Japan. The groups were of differing sizes, but all shared a self-sustaining power and independence from their mother organization. However, after Meishusama's passing in 1955, Sekai Kyuseikyo began moving toward more standardized policies and centralized direction. As a result, some of the original groups broke away.

From the earliest days of Sekai Kyuseikyo, Shumei, under Kaishusama's leadership, took an active role in sharing Meishusama's teachings with others and contributed significantly to the organization. As a result of this, in 1967, Kaishusama attained an important administrative position in the organization. However, this new, deeper involvement in the central functions of the Sekai Kyuseikyo soon put her in a difficult situation. She began to witness things that made her feel that the organization was deviating from Meishusama's spirit and was becoming corrupted by greed and power. Included in her concerns, at this time, was the beginning of an aggressive restructuring of the organization into greater centralization of power. After painful deliberation, she decided, in February of 1970, to separate her Shumei group from Sekai Kyuseikyo along with her original group. She felt this action was necessary to maintain the purity of Shumei. Recollecting the day that she decided to leave the organization created by Meishusama, Kaishusama commented, "It was the longest day in my entire life."

Shumei's withdrawal from Sekai Kyuseikyo was unexpected and shocking to both its affiliated members and to the headquarters of the mother organization. Consequently, it was inevitable for Shumei to face bitter conflicts and turmoil, both among its own members, and with those of Sekai Kyuseikyo. In this whirlwind of chaos, Kaishusama and her first son, Sokichi Koyama, respectfully known as Mikotosama, soon returned to using of some of the ritual-related items put aside by Sekai Kyuseikyo after Meishusama's passing. These included the Zengen-sanji prayer, the Kannon Screen, and the Daikokusama statue (each explained in the following pages). Most importantly, Kaishusama and Mikotosama resumed

15. Sekai Kyuseikyo was originally called Sekai Meshiyakyo.

using Meishusama's original calligraphies as their holy scrolls. At that time, they tirelessly endeavored to console and unite the hearts of members who might have been confused or upset. Although most of Shumei's members had sufficient trust in Kaishusama to willingly follow her in the new direction, others needed time to be persuaded and convinced.

The 1970 break with Sekai Kyuseikyo was one of the most traumatic struggles for Shumei. In accordance with Meishusama's teachings, these struggles were viewed as a purification process rather than a meaningless or unfortunate hardship. During these dark and painful times, Kaishusama and Mikotosama reaffirmed the spirit of Meishusama, and firmly resolved to stand on their conviction that the Founder's spirit was still alive and well among them. Three months after giving initial notification of independence from Sekai Kyuseikyo, Shumei gained legal independence as an organization. Thus, Shumei was born again, and began to further Meishusama's legacy with even greater dedication. (The word *Shinji*, which means Divine Love, was added to the name *Shumei* at the end of 1970.)

In order to bring Shumei's members back to the original spirit of Meishusama's teachings, Kaishusama and Mikotosama strongly encouraged them to actively introduce Jyorei to the people of the world. Soon, members began going door-to-door, offering Jyorei to people in their homes. Others stood in public places, including parks, train stations, and college and university campuses, inviting passers-by to receive Jyorei. The members exhibited a great deal of passion and dedication at this time, and the membership continued to grow rapidly. In particular, many young people became involved with Shumei, drawn by all the excitement and powerful spiritual experiences so many of them were having.

For those who followed Kaishusama's and Mikotosama's spiritual guidance, it was obvious that the power of Jyorei, instead of weakening, as claimed by some, had become much more potent. Various miraculous events occurred through Jyorei. Shumei members interpreted these abundant miracles as a divine message, indicating their strong connection with the spirit of Meishusama.

Blessed by the Divine Light of Jyorei, Shumei recovered its vigorous momentum, and in 1972 purchased the vast, forested land in the Shigaraki Mountains, east of Kyoto, which was later transformed into their primary sanctuary, called Misono. With great courage and determination, Mikotosama inspired members to support the construction of Misono, which he personally directed during the final ten years of his life. The most magnificent building in Misono is Meishusama Hall, where members attend regular services (sampais) to chant and exchange Jyorei. Its creation in 1983 was a truly remarkable achievement. In July of the next year, at the age of forty-eight, Mikotosama left this world. But his spirit lives on and still touches the hearts of everyone who visits there.

After his passing, under the spiritual guidance of Kaishusama, the seeds of faith Mikotosama had sowed and cultivated, particularly in young members, blossomed into new leaders who continued to share Meishusama's teachings with the world. Consequently, the membership steadily increased and, in addition to the centers in Hong Kong and the United States, new centers were later opened in many other countries. Hiroko Koyama, Mikotosama's younger sister and his successor, began to work closely with Kaishusama in supervising the entire Shumei community. In 1992, Kaishusama began promoting Natural Agriculture as well as planning the construction of the Miho Museum. In 1994 Hiroko Koyama became the third president of Shinji Shumeikai, and was given the formal title of Kaicho-Sensei.

Beginning in 1997, after years of intense activity focused on bringing Jyorei to people's homes and to public places, Shumei decided it was time to redirect its efforts toward promoting greater balance within individuals as well as throughout the organization. It was felt that in order to better help others, Shumei needed to focus more on self-cultivation, Natural Agriculture, and art.

Following the opening of the Miho Museum in late 1997, Shumei began to establish a public presence that continues to this day with lectures and seminars, interfaith activities, and performances of taiko drumming. In 2002, with the opening of Shumei International Institute in the state of Colorado, USA, Shumei's three sacred sites were completed (the other two being Misono, high in the Shigaraki Mountains, and the Center on Kishima Island, in the midst of the Seto Inland Sea, to the west of Osaka, Japan). In 2003, the Shumei Natural Agriculture Network was established to bring the principles and techniques of Natural Agriculture to the general public. In 2004, Shumei International acquired consultative status as a Non-Governmental Organization (NGO) with the United Nations.

After a long and meaningful life dedicated to Meishusama and his vision of universal enlightenment, Kaishusama left this world in November of 2003. Her enormous achievement, in the face of formidable obstacles, of creating Shinji Shumeikai and vastly expanding its membership, is a living testament to the greatness of her character. Her love, inspiration, and guidance are constantly felt and appreciated by many throughout Shumei.

We wish to bring harmony to all humankind and to make the whole world into one family. Since we believe in this kind of pacifism, we recognize all religions as our colleagues and link hands with them in mutual amity as we continue onwards.
—Citizens of the World. ET

Three Sacred Grounds

In line with Meishusama's teachings concerning the significance of the three spiritual elements, Shumei has constructed centers at three special locations: Misono, representing fire; Kishima, representing water; and Crestone, representing earth. The centers serve as sacred pilgrimage sites where visitors can commune with the unique spiritual energies found at each location.

Misono

Shumei's international headquarters moved from Kyoto in 1983, and assumed permanent residence in Misono in the Shigaraki Mountains east of Kyoto. Misono, meaning "Sacred Garden," was created to serve as an archetype of the heavenly world that Meishusama envisioned. The site on which Misono stands has been considered sacred since ancient times, when five Shinto shrines occupied the area and protected its serenity. The foremost architects, artists, engineers, and craftsmen collaborated in creating this sanctuary of beauty and spirituality. At Misono, nature, art, science, and technology come together to form an archetypal prayer for peace, prosperity, and beauty for mankind and the world.

In the beautiful surroundings of Misono, one of the most outstanding pieces of architecture is Meishusama Hall. Completed in 1983, it was designed by Minoru Yamasaki (1912-1986), who also designed the World Trade Center's Twin Towers in New York City (lost in 2001). Resembling the shape of Mount Fuji, the structure is supported, amazingly, by just four curved buttresses. The structure is sixty meters in width, ninety meters in length, and fifty meters in height. This masterpiece by Yamasaki was realized with the aid of his engineering partner, Yoshikatsu Tsuboi (1907-1990), a leading authority on structural dynamics. It stands as a symbol of peace, happiness, and well-being for all mankind.

Entering the sanctuary of Meishusama Hall, you will see a vast, light-filled space. The structure enclosing this space is supported by four gracefully arching buttresses that rise to a height of fifty meters. Nature's beauty is forever a presence within the Hall as the glass walls that encircle most of the interior allow one to enjoy the surrounding gardens and mountains. Both man-made and natural beauty are entwined in the ambiance of this great building.[16]

Misono functions as Shumei's primary spiritual center; a sacred pilgrimage site; the organization's international administrative headquarters; and a spiritual training facility for young *hoshishas* (volunteer workers who learn how to selflessly dedicate their lives to God and Meishusama). One of the major events that Misono periodically hosts is a spiritual gathering referred to as the Monthly Sampai. At these events, and others, Misono welcomes members and guests from all over the world. Members from different countries visit Misono to celebrate the legacy of Meishusama and the birth of Shumei, especially during the Grand Sampai in early May.

16. Hiroko Koyama, "Shumei's Three Sacred Places," *Shumei Magazine*, vol. 255 (Jan./Feb. 2005).

Because Misono is located high up in the mountains—where the spiritual Light is most intensely focused—it is generally regarded as an embodiment of the element of fire. Fire is warm and bright, with its flames rising upward to the heavens. It burns impurities in order to create new beginnings. Fire is sacred because its light illuminates our daily existence.

Kishima Island

Located in a designated nature preserve in the midst of Seto Inland Sea, west of Osaka, Japan, Kishima Island is blessed with abundant scenic beauty. Shumei originally acquired a part of the island in 1962 as a place where children and young people could cultivate their inner nature by getting in touch with nature.

The construction of Shumei's first Center on the island began soon thereafter. It was built by volunteers who hand-carried the construction material to the highest point on the Island. In 1989 a new center sanctuary was built to replace the original structure. The exterior of this sanctuary is shaped like a seashell in acknowledgment of the sea that surrounds it. The interior of the sanctuary is unique in that it is constructed of concrete, stainless steel, and glass. Through the large windows you can see the vast expanse of the sea, including a spectacular view of the evening sunset. After the sanctuary's completion, Kaishusama said, "Kishima Island is surrounded by the sea, and the sea is what connects us to the whole world." She envisioned the island as a base from which Shumei's message would spread over land and sea so that one day all people could benefit from the values and ideals that Meishusama promoted.

Since Shumei's purchase of the island, it has also been devoted to the research and practice of Natural Agriculture. Fields of crops can be seen throughout the island, demonstrating the wonderful variety and wholesome quality of the food naturally produced there.

There are two camping villages on the island. A series of camping trips for children, including one for the physically and mentally challenged, are held each summer. Young Shumei members experience the natural splendor of

Kishima by attending summer camp on the island, and by learning the art of Natural Agriculture throughout the year. Kishima is also being developed into an environmental research center that will host conferences on conservation and the promotion of an environment free of industrial chemicals. Increasingly, Kishima is serving as a spiritual retreat center, hosting various workshops on communication, personal growth, and spiritual development.

As a place surrounded by water, Kishima Island is generally regarded as an embodiment of the spiritual element of water which flows laterally and accepts all things by permeating and dissolving them into itself. Water is sacred because it is the source of all life.

Crestone

The town of Crestone, Colorado, in the United States, is the home of Shumei International Institute (SII), a non-profit organization that was established in 2002. SII is located on a thirty-five acre site, 8,300 feet above sea level, in the Sangre de Christo Mountains of the San Luis Valley. Shumei was drawn to this location by its natural beauty and spiritual energy. Other spiritual and religious groups from various parts of the world also have felt this special place's allure and built ashrams, monasteries, and retreat centers here.

Crestone is a place where many religious and spiritual centers have sprung up; among them are Christian, Buddhist, and Hindu sanctuaries. Each tradition represented there has its own goals and activities. Yet, despite their differences, these diverse people in Crestone have become friends and live in harmony with one another. They do not close themselves off from the practices and values of others. They truly engage in interfaith activities.[17]

Inspired by the teachings of Meishusama, SII helps people of the world realize that they are world citizens able to act for the common good. The Institute's headquarters, which are also used as the Shumei Crestone Center, provides an environment for spiritual growth through interfaith activities, the practice of Jyorei and Natural Agriculture, as well as art, environmental, and cultural events. It offers programs for training young people in leadership skills, caring for our precious natural environment, and respecting the diversity of cultures and people.

Because SII is located in the largest high-altitude valley on earth, and is dedicated to the ecological concerns of the environment, SII is generally regarded as an embodiment of the element of Earth. In line with this symbolism, it was built using the best available regenerative technologies to sustain the earth and to show respect for the surrounding environment. Earth is heavy, dense, and solid, and therefore provides the physical matter from which all material things are created. It is sacred because it supports and sustains our manifest existence.

With the completion of SII in Crestone, Shumei's three sacred sites were established embodying the elements of fire (Misono), water (Kishima), and earth (Crestone). According to Meishusama, when all three of these elements are

---

17. Ibid.

harmoniously combined, a dynamic, creative energy is unleashed. Since the establishment of this third sacred site, many have noticed an increased level of Light within Shumei, as well as a trend towards greater openness and creativity. The opening of SII was thus a significant milestone in Shumei's ongoing mission to disseminate Meishusama's message and to create an ideal world here on earth.

The Miho Museum

For someone who has knowledge of art and literature, to gaze at the flowers of spring, the autumn leaves, or a view of the mountains or sea, is delightful.
—Religion and Art. ET

Shumei's commitment to encouraging the arts led to the creation of the Miho Museum in 1997. Meishusama wanted everyone to experience art, not only for its spiritual benefits, but also for its pure pleasure and enjoyment. He taught that, "A museum is a symbol of an ideal world."

Inspired by Meishusama's ideals, Kaishusama initiated the planning and construction of the museum, guiding the process every step of the way. She received enormous support from her daughter, Hiroko Koyama, who oversaw all the practical details of the project. The word "Miho," in Japanese, means "excellence in beauty," and it is also the first two syllables of Mihoko Koyama's (Kaishusama's) first name. Thus the word serves two purposes: to honor the creator of the museum, and to highlight its key theme.

Located in the Shigaraki Mountains an hour and a half drive from Kyoto and less than a mile from Misono, the Miho is a stunning achievement of design and engineering. In addition to Kaishusama's private collection of traditional Japanese art (now housed in the North Wing), the museum's collection has expanded to include thousands of ancient masterpieces from throughout Eurasia and Egypt (located in the South Wing). It is now considered one of the most impressive art collections in Japan. A visitor here has the combined benefit of viewing an outstanding array of traditional art, a building of dramatic yet elegant beauty, and an exquisite natural setting of mountains, trees, and sky. Not only does the surrounding landscape add to the beauty of the museum, but it also contributes to its spiritual influence. Meishusama called the world of nature "God's Art."

Designed by one of the world's greatest architects I.M. Pei, the Miho Museum evokes the image of a traditional Japanese temple while embracing the aesthetics of modern design. Of significance is the quantity of light that floods into the building through the glass walls and skylights, which are supported by large metal beams arrayed in strikingly geometric patterns. Through the abundance of glass, the building seems to expand to the outside surrounding landscape, allowing the art of nature to contribute to the collection.

With eighty percent of the structure contained within the mountain slope, the Miho Museum is not intrusive, but instead blends harmoniously with the surrounding landscape. This consideration for the inherent beauty of the land is a reflection of Meishusama's love and respect for nature. This unity and harmony with nature is a source of inspiration for visitors who come to the Miho Museum.

In addition to welcoming visitors from around the world, the museum holds special exhibits, symposiums, seminars and lectures for children and adults. The Miho promotes art and beauty as a transformative experience for humanity's spiritual advancement.

A visit to the Miho might call to mind a spiritual pilgrimage, in which a traveler seeks out a remote place to find contemplative peace and spiritual guidance. Here, both transcendence and aesthetic enjoyment come together in a seamless harmony that is heavenly as well as down to earth.

Waterfall in Misono

The primary source of Jyorei, as described in earlier chapters, is the spirit of fire, which is one of the three fundamental spiritual elements in the universe. Jyorei dispels spiritual clouds accumulated in our spiritual body just as fire burns combustible material. In line with this, Jyorei is often referred to as purification by fire.

In addition to the healing of Jyorei, Shumei offers another distinctive form of healing, one that clearly symbolizes the power of the spirit of water. Water has been commonly used as an important medium for purification in religious communities throughout the world, including the two main religious traditions in Japan: Shinto and Buddhism. In both of these traditions, people who come to visit their temples or shrines are customarily advised to rinse their mouths and wash their hands before entering the sacred area. Water is used to purify the defilements of people, which they accrue during their daily life, and to help them prepare for moving into the sacred dimension.

In Shumei, water also has this value, and it is also used for the same purpose as mentioned above. There is usually a stone water fountain or spring at each Shumei center to use in a simple purification ritual of rinsing the mouth and washing the hands.

Such places where water purification occurs are called Mitarashi. Among the many places where it is practiced, the Shumei Kyoto center (former international center) and Misono (present and permanent international center), in particular, are quite noteworthy because of the remarkable healing properties found in the water.

The healing by water first appeared in the Kyoto Center's Mitarashi, a stone fountain designed in the shape of a five-petalled plum flower. It was around the beginning of 1975 that the first report of its healing effects first came to light, and since then a number of healing incidents have been reported, among which are healing from brain tumors, gastric ulcers, lung cancers, skin diseases, impaired hearing, toothaches, rheumatism, and burn injuries.

When Shumei's headquarters was transferred from Kyoto to Misono in 1983, Misono's Mitarashi, called "The Cascade" (Kumo Ga Taki), began showing similar healing properties, and its water is now regarded as highly sacred.

It seems natural for one to compare this miraculous water of the Cascade with that of Lourdes in France. Interestingly, the healing effects of Mitarashi at the Kyoto center emerged after a group of Shumei members led by Kaishusama visited Lourdes, following which Kaishusama had an audience with Pope Paul VI in May of 1974.

Although we have no explanation as to why and how such "miracles" started, the effect of healing is undeniable, and members of Shumei take it as a divine gift from God and Meishusama.

Shumei's Symbol of Light and Power

The history of the world, up until today, has been characterized by two different cultural traditions: Eastern culture, which leans towards spirituality, and Western culture, which leans towards materialism. And, since both cultures veer toward extremes and are not integrated with each other, nothing goes well for them. This situation does not bring any real solutions to humankind's suffering and the unstable condition of the world never seems to end. Observing this, I believe that the creation of an ideal world culture is not possible without the harmonious union of the vertical and the horizontal. So what concerns us is when, if ever, these two aspects will be united, and to your surprise, that very moment is now. Our mission is to assist this important event, which is perfectly symbolized by the design of our organization's emblem. — Vertical and Horizontal. KW

Shumei's official symbol is a circular form with four curved shapes extending outward from a central circle. The horizontal axis of these shapes represents water, the element that flows and spreads horizontally, and the perpendicular axis represents fire, the element that burns vertically. Fire represents shojo (inwardly uniting with God), and water represents daijo (outwardly embracing others). The small circle in the middle represents the spirit of Izunome, the balance and harmony between these two opposite principles. This relates to Meishusama's analogy of the point within the circle, indicating spirit within matter—that which animates all living things.

Official Symbol of Shinji Shumeikai

About the spiritual significance of this central point, Meishusama writes, "Symbolized by the design of our organizational emblem, we should be in a position where daijo and shojo cross each other. This crossed point is Izunome. In the dimension of Izunome, there is no vertical or horizontal. If daijo and shojo are perfectly crossed, it creates a circle leaving no trace of either vertical or horizontal. The true meaning of faith is to seek this state. And to realize this, I think, is enlightenment." (*Daijo and Divine Wisdom. KW*)

These two elements of water and fire, the one extending horizontally and the other vertically, combine to produce Light, which radiates outwardly from the spiritual presence located within the center of the circle. This spiritual presence is the Light of Jyorei.

The four curved shapes indicate movement, and symbolize spirit in motion. The overall form is bending clockwise, symbolizing the power to establish truth, virtue, and beauty in the world. This is the divine power of God manifesting in the realm of time and space.

We will start a civilization that revolves clockwise. Our task is to establish a completely civilized world, a world of Light. —Creating the World of Light. KW

The Shumei Taiko Ensemble

Taiko are Japanese percussion instruments used on various occasions and in settings such as local festivals, religious rituals, and traditional Japanese plays. They were also used to summon the combative spirit of samurai warriors in battle fields with their dynamic vibrating sounds.

Shumei often uses taiko drumming during Sampai to strengthen and amplify chanting through the agency of their powerful vibrations. The dynamic rhythms and invigorating sounds of the taiko clears the mind, bringing awareness back into the present moment. This heightened presence allows for greater receptivity to the spiritual influences of chanting and Jyorei. The brisk, sharp sounds of the taiko heighten the contrast between sound and silence, while simultaneously joining them together through the experience of pure beauty.

The performances of the Shumei Taiko Ensemble are non-verbal prayers for world peace and harmonious relationship with nature. For the performers, taiko drums are not merely tools for entertaining their audience, but sacred instruments, whose sounds can purify the atmosphere and bring healing to the world. For them, beating drums is a spiritual practice involving rigorous training and discipline. It follows then, the purpose of the sounds they create is to uplift and refine the souls of the listeners.

The listeners often experience a synchronization of the taiko vibrations with their own heartbeat, and some discover an inexplicable feeling of deep serenity amidst the booming intensity of the drumming.

Many local Shumei centers have formed taiko groups of their own. These groups have been especially popular amongst youth members. Beyond the obvious aesthetic experience, involvement in these groups also helps promote character development, stressing self-discipline, reliability, and cooperation.

Since the Shumei Taiko Ensemble was founded in 1982, it has come to occupy an eminent place in the world of Japanese performing arts. Acclaimed for its mastery of traditional taiko technique, the Ensemble has built upon these techniques to create a pure, strong, and exhilarating form of taiko performance that is both modern and original.

In recent years, the Ensemble has been organizing the annual summer concert tour, during which they give concerts in several locations throughout Japan.

The Ensemble has performed not only in Japan, but also in other countries at events such as the Parliament of World Religions in Cape Town, South Africa (1999) and Barcelona, Spain (2004), and the World Peace Summit for Religious and Spiritual Leaders at the United Nations headquarters in New York City (2001). While they were in Cape Town in 1999, the Ensemble also performed at the first World Festival of Sacred Music, which was initiated by His Holiness the Dalai Lama to mark the approaching millennium with a message of peace, cultural understanding, and spirituality.

The Shumei Taiko Ensemble continues to pursue its mission of uniting the hearts of people around the world through the captivating sound of taiko.

CHAPTER 14

SHUMEI'S RITUALS

The Purpose of Rituals

Rituals highlight important public gatherings such as victory celebrations, inaugurations and award presentations. These rituals order and structure human behavior in predetermined ways. Yet some question whether rituals have any relevance to this modern, scientifically oriented age. However, most people would surely be disappointed if they attended a birthday party where no one sang "Happy Birthday" and the honored person did not blow out the candles. They would also probably be dismayed if they attended a wedding or funeral devoid of formality and ritual. Such ceremonies serve the purpose of publicly acknowledging significant events, deeds, and activities in life, and the various rituals they contain channel people's emotions in meaningful ways, providing them with feelings of satisfaction and completion. Collective activity of this sort also reinforces a sense of group solidarity.

The purpose of sacred rituals is to deepen our relationship to the Divine and to support spiritual cultivation. Within Shumei, bowing at the entrance of the sanctuary reminds us that we are entering sacred space. During the ceremony, bowing, clapping, and chanting express reverence and appreciation to God and Meishusama. Over time, these attitudes get reinforced through repetition. In other words, the more we do something, the more it becomes ingrained in our consciousness. Through repetition, rituals promote character development.

Sacred rituals also harness the power of symbolism to communicate higher truths to the subconscious mind and to induce spiritual experience.

Lastly, sacred rituals generate refined energy fields that uplift the atmosphere of the locations where they take place. The effect can be felt as serenity, joy, and clarity.

Scroll of Light

Since humans, by nature, long for Light, if a Center is full of Light, more people will naturally be drawn to it. —Warm Hearts Attract People. KW

Located in the altar area within each Shumei Center is a Scroll of Light containing a reproduction of calligraphy by Meishusama. The scroll at most Centers has two Chinese characters inscribed on it: one signifying 'Bright' and the other signifying 'Divine Light.' Centers that are regional headquarters each have scrolls containing three characters that indicate "Great Bright Light." As an embodiment of Divine Light, the Scroll of Light is an object of deep veneration, although what is actually focused on during Sampai is the energy and ideas behind these symbols rather than the visible characters, themselves.

It is customary for the scroll to be enshrined behind a screen that is only opened during Sampai. In Misono, an original scroll created by Meishusama is located behind Meishusama Hall, housed in a special eight-sided annex called "The Octagonal Shrine" (Shinden).

Usually, there is a floral arrangement to the side of the scroll, affirming Shumei's belief that beauty is a form of spiritual nourishment, and a picture of Meishusama, in honor of his role as the "Bringer of Light." Beneath the scroll is an offering table with a pair of candles and flowers arrangement. An extra table is often used for daily offerings of gratitude consisting of water, rice, and salt. These humblest of foods constitute the essence of nourishment, and it is this essence that is offered to God, whose spiritual presence is intensified in the altar area.

Sampai

Sampai means "going to a higher, purer place for spiritual purposes." Specifically, sampai is a form of ritual that, through its structure, provides a sense of order and serenity. In Shumei, a sampai can be conducted either individually or collectively, and will include sharing Jyorei when more than one person is present. Each Shumei Center has its own scheduled Daily Sampai gatherings, with at least one in the morning and evening. In addition, every month a larger group gathering, called the Monthly Sampai, is held at each Center during which a sensei (teacher) gives Jyorei en masse to those attending.

Sampai is, in essence, a precious moment of communion with the Divine, and a process of purification through prayer, chanting, and Jyorei. The more often one comes to sampai, the more one's spiritual cords connecting to God and Meishusama will be strengthened. Receiving Jyorei during a Sampai heightens the power of spiritual energy, thereby increasing healing and spiritual growth.

Collective Sampais, such as the Monthly Sampai, are especially significant because the more people who attend, the greater the energy. The monthly gathering is meant to readjust and improve one's relationship with God and Meishusama, and to function as a joyous celebration. Even though the Monthly Sampai is designed with a large group in mind, it is usually maintained as a simple ceremony.

Many members of Shumei also conduct Monthly Sampais in their homes. These members have enshrined, above a small altar, a Scroll of Light that is similar to the larger scrolls enshrined at official Shumei Centers. Many believe that these home scrolls radiate divine Light not only to one's family, but also the surrounding neighborhood. Having a scroll enshrined in one's home entails a good deal of responsibility on the part of the recipient. It is both an honor and a mark of dedication to Shumei's ideals.

Also, in many homes there are altars with Kannon Screens dedicated to deceased family members and ancestors. The Kannon figure on the screen is a copy of a painting by Meishusama. Maintaining a Kannon Screen is an act of reverence for our departed loved ones who exist in the spiritual realm and who often help us. The positive energy that we send to our ancestors by honoring them with gratitude and sacred chants before this special altar helps purify and uplift their consciousness. Many believe this benefits us as well as them, because the higher their spiritual level, the greater their capacity to help us in times of need.

In your house, you should perform respectful services of enshrinement in front of the altar, which insures the purification of the entire household's spiritual form. To protect your house, you should enshrine the Scroll of Light and honor it daily, which will purify the entire household's spiritual atmosphere. —Fire and Jyorei. ET

Otamagushi

Otamagushi is a financial offering given before attending a Sampai. The word means 'pure human heart (or intentions) aligned with the heart of God.' An alternate meaning is 'a pure human soul and God's Spirit joined as one.' Offering Otamagushi is an essential part of the Sampai, as is washing the hands and rinsing one's mouth, and it helps prepare one's mind for contemplation and prayer. Whether small or large, what is put in an envelope to offer is important only if it comes with gratitude for all of God's blessings. If one does not have the financial means to give Otamagushi, then an act of hoshi at the Center, such as washing the sink, sweeping the grounds, or mopping the floor, is an appropriate substitute. Both are good ways to demonstrate the sincerity of one's gratitude. The intent behind Otamagushi is to give back to God a portion of what has been given to us. One whose heart is full of gratitude comes to realize that all things are gifts from God.

Shumei Chants

Kototama

According to Meishusama, the universe is filled with invisible ether through which inaudible sounds frequencies are carried. Many ancient cultures believed that the world was created by these sound frequencies. Meishusama explains that there are seventy-five primal sounds in the universe in continual vibratory motion. In addition, there are five root syllables that are essential conveyors of spiritual power. When these five sounds are out of harmony, the universe is thrown into disarray.

The three sacred chants that Meishusama promoted—the Amatsunorito, Kamigoto and Zengensanji—incorporate all five syllables throughout their length. When chanted with the correct pronunciation, tone and rhythm, and with pure intent, balance and harmony are restored in the world.

The power of chanting is based on the principle of Kototama, the concept that every word has a spiritual power inherent in its sound, irrespective of its actual meaning. The idea of certain root sounds having special power is similar to the Eastern concepts of *bija* syllables and mantras, which are used for meditation and inner transformation.

Amatsunorito

The Amatsunorito, with its unique combination of sounds, is used to purify the spiritual world, the condition of which affects the physical world. Meishusama believed that this chant was a particularly powerful means of purification. In accord with the principles of Kototama as well as his own spiritual insights, Meishusama slightly refined this ancient prayer to make it more potent.

The Amatsunorito, which means "heavenly prayer," is the basic chant recited during Sampai. Amatsunorito is comprised of two words, "amatsu" and "norito." "Amatsu" means "heavenly," and "norito" refers to a type of ancient Japanese ritual-prayer that stems from the Shinto tradition.

The origin of the "Heavenly Prayer" is ancient and obscure, the author or authors are unknown. Its language is archaic, and most modern Japanese cannot comprehend the words. This is comparable to a modern English speaker attempting to understand the original text of the Beowulf epic, which roughly dates to the same time as the Amatsunorito. To understand the Amatsunorito's literal meaning, the following background in Japanese myth is helpful.

The demigod or kami, Izanagi, defiled himself by entering the underworld to bring his dead wife, Izanami, back to the world of the living so they could continue to create the land in which they and their descendants were to live. When he found her on the other side of the gates of the palace of the dead, she told him with deep regret that he had come too late. For she had already eaten the fruits of the underworld—literally from the ovens of hell—and could not return to the land of the living without permission. She made him promise to wait for her and not follow or even look at her until she safely returned to him. She left Izanagi and went to plead with the rulers of the underworld to release her. A very long time passed as Izanagi waited. Finally, impatient, he broke his pledge and entered the netherworld to find his wife. When he did, he looked at her and saw that her flesh was putrefied and consumed by maggots, and the sounds of every kind of thunder emitted from her head and limbs. She cursed him for his betrayal and sent hoards of demons to pursue him. He picked up three peaches, imbued with divine power, and threw these at the demons, chasing them away. Once he reached the realm of the living again, his wife appeared one final time on the other side of death's gates. So, man and wife, Izanagi and Izanami, stood at opposite sides of the border between life and death, she respectfully threatening to kill all his descendants, he with due courtesy pledging to produce more progeny than she could ever manage to kill. Finally, done with her, he rolled a boulder over the maw of Hades and left.

Although escaping death, entering the kingdom of the dead had left him impure, and so he washed himself in the waters near the small mouth of a river surrounded by a field of evergreens at Himuka Tacibana (Tachihana) in Tsukushi. And as Izanagi bathed, from the river waters sprang the newly born spirits of purification.

The story is, of course, fantastic. Yet, it has universal implications that echo in legends and myths throughout the world. Westerners might recognize similarities in Izanagi's story with that of the primal father Adam and his first wife Lilith, or that of Orpheus following Eurydice into Hades. All these stories are meant more to entertain and fill the listener with wonder than to be literally believed. Yet, as legends and metaphors they express more than a little truth. As all Izanagi's children eventually would stand on one side or the other of the portals of life and death, so do all humanity's children. And we all are capable of breaking pledges, going against the natural order of things (as Izanagi did by venturing into the realm of the dead while still alive), or being tainted by circumstances beyond our control. And we all need purification from time to time. As such, chanting this prayer is a great means of being made clean.

The poem opens with an image related to its meaning: Kamurogi and Kamuromi on the heavenly plane. Shinto scholars have often identified "Kamurogi" and "Kamuromi" as collective nouns representing male and female ancestral deities. Both can be thought of as universal principals, rather like yin and yang, or as universal forces that constantly purify the world.

A loose translation of this prayer follows:

Prayer of Heaven

On the highest planes of heaven

Primeval Kamurogi and Kamuromi live.

And in accord with them, Izanagi,

In a grove of pine at Tsukushi,

Bathed at a river's clear mouth.

As he bathed, purifying spirits were born.

Of them we ask that all fault,

Baseness, and filth be washed away.

Humbly, we plead that they be dispelled

And we be made pure.

Please, divine spirits,

Legions of heaven and earth,

Answer our plea.

And just as the dappled horses of heaven

Perk their ears at the slightest rustle,

Hear our meek prayer.

The exact meaning of the chant is not as significant as its overall intent. In general, the Amatsunorito is a supplication to God and Meishusama to dispel all our negativity and wrong actions, which are the main causes of misfortune and suffering. It asks for protection as well as blessings for supreme happiness and spiritual growth.

Chanting the Amatsunorito aligns us with the purpose, power, and rhythm of the universe. It is one of the principal means for bringing us into harmony with God and nature. Just as a musician tunes an instrument before playing it, so too, does chanting tune the instrument of the self by harmonizing one's individual vibratory expression.

The purity of the individual reciting the Amatsunorito chant greatly affects the degree of power emitted by the words. The higher a person's spiritual level, the greater their ability to affect the world. Words spoken with virtuous intent emit high vibrations and dispel spiritual clouds, whereas words spoken harshly or with lack of awareness do the opposite.

Kamigoto

Kamigoto, like the Amatsunorito, came from the Shinto tradition, and it means "words of Kami," or "divine words." This chant has the great capacity to purify spiritual clouds, rejuvenate our spiritual energies, and align us with higher truth. Chanting either of these prayers generates a strong sound vibration that purifies the atmosphere in the area and prepares one to receive Light.

Although the Kamigoto sounds similar to the Amatsunorito, it can be regarded as a longer version of the latter. Unlike the Amatsunorito, it is generally chanted only on special occasions. While the Amatsunorito is chanted during all daily Sampais, the Kamigoto prayer is typically chanted only three times a year, on February 3, June 30, and December 31, as well as when purifying one's Ohikari.

Individual members may recite the Kamigoto when they need a special purification, or as a means to make a resolution in response to some regrettable situation they may have caused. Everyone makes mistakes occasionally, and unfortunately, sometimes these mistakes hurt others. At such times, it is only natural to feel remorse for one's thoughts, words, or actions. Chanting Kamigoto, with sincerity, helps one to maintain an open heart by dissipating some of the spiritual clouds generated by wrong actions. In cases where we have hurt or offended someone, we should, as a demonstration of our sincerity, apologize to them, as well as chant Kamigoto. It is always important to understand the reason for chanting, and to take full responsibility for our actions. This is the true test of our sincerity. When we chant with such sincerity, and with correct resolution, the solution to our problems sometimes will come to us spontaneously. This is because the sound of Kamigoto naturally purifies the mind so we can see things more clearly.

The Kamigoto chant has a loose story-like narrative that relates a request for divine intervention to purify the land, the body, and the spirit because of some major indiscretion. The poem calls on kami-deities to come in and dissipate the resultant spiritual negativity. The various kami-deities then intervene to dissipate the spiritual pollution, which is carried by the wind, rivers, and ocean, until finally it is flushed down into the underworld, where it is purified and transformed.

In the final refrains of the Kamigoto, both Miroku Omikami (the Ultimate God of Divine Light) and Meishusama are called upon to cleanse the chanters' bodies, minds, and spirits of the world's pollution, and to protect and bless them with happiness and spiritual growth.

Zengensanji

Zengensanji literally means "The Good Words of Praise." In contrast to the Amatsunorito and the Kamigoto, both of which originated from the Shinto tradition, the Zengensanji is based on a specific chapter of the Lotus Sutra, one of the most influential of all the sacred scriptures of Mahayana Buddhism.

Just prior to the official commencement of the Japan Kannon Society in 1935, Meishusama asked one of his students to bring him a copy of chapter twenty-five of the Lotus Sutra, entitled "The Universal Door of the Bodhisattva Who Listens to the Sounds of All the World." This is popularly called the Kannon Sutra. Following a series of profound mystical experiences with Kannon, Meishusama was led to this sutra, from which he drew inspiration and borrowed some key terms based on their spiritual power.

Kannon is a Buddhist name referring to one of the most important Bodhisattvas of the Mahayana tradition. A Bodhisattva is a being, either super-natural or human, who seeks Buddhahood, but who, upon attaining perfect virtue, renounces entry into the final state of Nirvana until all other beings are saved first. Kannon Bodhisattva is said to be "One Who Hears the Outcries of the World." She has been worshiped and revered for many centuries for the qualities of compassion and wisdom that she is felt to embody. It is popularly believed that these divine qualities of Kannon manifest in the world as a power that can rescue people from their sufferings.

The Kannon Sutra presents a scene in which the Buddha, responding to a question about the name "'Kannon Bodhisattva,'" describes in detail, as well as allegorically, Kannon's divine nature. The beautiful description of Kannon, along with the power of salvation believed to be embedded in the text, has inspired the creation of a variety of paintings and sculptures of this deity which are widely revered as both sacred symbols and beautiful artworks.

Meishusama describes Kannon in one of his poems: "From infinite love and compassion God becomes Kannon Bodhisattva in order to rescue the world." (*Kannon Bodhisattva. MK1*) Kannon is an aspect of God's compassionate love, made manifest for the salvation of the world. For Meishusama, the salvation of the world is identical with the construction of a paradise on earth. Kannon, with her wisdom, compassionate love, and divine power, is the active agent that helps humanity bring about this ideal state. Furthermore, Kannon also represents infinite adaptability. Meishusama writes, "This also points to the significance of Kannon, who transforms Herself from moment to moment in myriad forms according to the eternal flux of the universe. Kannon is sometimes known as Ojin Maitreya, and this indicates exactly this function, for *"Ojin"* has the meaning "to adapt oneself." In other words, Kannon is capable of infinite adaptation and transformation in terms of things temporal and physical." *(Henri Bergson. ET)*

The Zengensanji does not directly share the same depicted scenes and tones as the Kannon Sutra. While Sutras in Japan have been traditionally written in

Chinese, and chanted with Chinese sounds, the Zengensanji is a mixture of both Chinese characters and Japanese. It is not chanted with the same rhythm as Sutra chanting. In this sense, the Zengensanji, rather than being categorized as a Sutra, can more accurately be viewed as a norito prayer about the paradise that Meishusama perceived during his divine revelation.

The Zengensanji emits a powerful vibration by its words, and is therefore considered to have the same kind of effect as the Amatsunorito and Kamigoto prayers. However, in contrast with those prayers, when chanting the Zengensanji it is important to understand the core meaning of the prayer, the gist of which is the creation of an ideal world, and to form an image or feeling about that world.

Meishusama stresses the importance of the power of will. If we do not have sufficient will power, or if our will to approach an ideal world is weak, then how can we make real progress? The Zengensanji is a prayer that describes the ultimate state of the world, and chanting it helps to strengthen the prayer by evoking vivid images. Chanting it is a way to align ourselves with Kannon's wisdom, compassionate love, and divine power, as well as to manifest God's Intentions on earth.

Yet, if visualizing scenes of world redemption is difficult, there is no need to struggle, because as long as we idealize and yearn for the living reality of a paradise on earth, that feeling is sufficient to hold when chanting the Zengensanji. What is most important is one's intention to join with God in helping to create an ideal world here on earth. With this altruistic attitude, one receives great benefit from the Zengensanji.

Bowing and Clapping

Within Shumei, it is customary to bow and clap both before and after chanting. Before the chant, one bows three times. The first bow is shallow and acknowledges one's open-hearted presence before God. The second and third bows are deep and express respect and gratitude. Bowing is followed by three handclaps, symbolizing the divine world, the spiritual world, and the physical world, respectively. They also signify the unity of body, mind, and spirit. The abrupt, brisk sound from the clapping clears the mind, bringing us into the present moment, and makes us more receptive to God's blessings.

Chanting usually concludes with a deep bow and three handclaps. If one is chanting before one of Shumei's Scrolls, this bow is directed toward the Scroll.

Daikokusama

It was 1933, and I had been in debt for some time and was becoming a little dispirited. A bank employee who sometimes visited me had an ancient figure of Daikoku that he offered to give me. I accepted it gratefully and placed it in front of my hanging scroll which has a painted image of Kannon on it. From that month on, my financial problems ended and money began to roll in.

—Daikoku, the God of Prosperity. ET

Meishusama attributed the dramatic turnaround in his financial problems to the acquisition of a statue of the Japanese folk deity, Daikokusama. Thus began an inner relationship with this deity that lasted to the end of his life. As Meishusama began collecting statues of Daikokusama, his financial situation continued to improve.

All Shumei centers now have a statue or picture of Daikokusama within their premises. At the headquarters in Misono, there is a special shrine dedicated to him located on the edge of the Great Plaza outside of Meishusama Hall. He appears as a chubby, elderly man with a gentle smile on his face, holding a small mallet in one hand, and carrying a large bag of rice over his shoulder. Historically, Daikokusama symbolized financial wealth, health, longevity, and wisdom. Meishusama advised people to keep a statue or picture of this deity in their homes to promote wealth and abundance. In order to enhance the blessings, he volunteered to strengthen the spiritual presence within each of their statues. Some Shumei members honor this deity by chanting a modified version of the Amatsunorito in front of this statue or picture, which they keep in their homes.

CHAPTER 15

CONCLUSION

The Spiritual Significance of Meishusama

When asked to explain just who Meishusama was, we can reply that he was a healer, mystic, prophet, humanitarian, visionary, saint, and more. We can also say that he was a unique manifestation of God. But it is difficult to label Meishusama because to those who knew and loved him, he did not easily fit into any single classification. Many would say that to some degree he exhibited all of these traits because his talents and range of interests were so vast. Those who knew him well could also say that because the deepest truths of God's being are beyond the reach of the mind, our ability to understand Meishusama's true identity must also be limited. Therefore, to really understand Meishusama, we would need to get inside the man.

On a purely biological level, he was simply a man. The outer man was an author, healer, artist, businessman, farmer, art connoisseur, and husband. He was successful in these and many other roles, but this was merely the outer man, not the inner man.

To simplify things, we can identify three distinct identities in Meishusama. First, there was the human who loved his friends and family, and who had personal feelings and interests. Second, there was the man who was subject to the cultural influences of the time and place where he lived, which was Japan during the first half of the twentieth century. And third, there was the universal, spiritual dimension of his identity, which transcends time and space. Concerning these three aspects of his being, Meishusama himself writes, "When I think about myself, I see that I am a man but not a man, God but not God." *(Meishusama II. MK2)*

*Despite his elevated spiritual status, and despite the global scope of his universal philosophy, Meishusama was still a Japanese man who spoke Japanese and acted Japanese. And although often quite critical of Japanese society, he nevertheless embraced the people around him with great love and affection. Meishusama's life story was a living demonstration of the power to heal and grow through spiritual purification. He lived and breathed the principles that he taught, which gave his teachings enormous authority.

Meishusama never lost sight of the distant stars that beckoned him onward despite all the rocks encountered along the road. Each person's health and spiritual needs were cared for to the best of his ability, and each business or organizational problem was attended to as effectively as possible. Yet, despite all the day-to-day concerns, he always remained true to his grand vision of the spiritual transformation of the world and to his deepening inner relationship with the Absolute. In this way, it can be said that Meishusama's life exemplified the ideals of Kannon's Way, the way of dynamic balance.

To understand the spiritual dimension of Meishusama's identity, we need to explore the nature of Spirit and its relationship to the world of nature. Miroku Omikami is the idea that God's Spirit is everywhere and within everything. This means that God resides within all people as their divine spirit. The direct perception and inner realization of this fact is the goal of evolution and spiritual growth. But because of the clouding of our spiritual vision, we see only separation and limitation everywhere, and therefore cannot perceive the underlying unity and perfection of all creation. This blindness to reality cuts us off from the Divine.

We can assess the wisdom in a person by the way he or she treats others. The more spiritually evolved a person is, the more that person exhibits such refined qualities as honesty, love, kindness, wisdom, and integrity in his or her behavior. These attributes come from Spirit, and reveal the degree to which a person has purified his or her soul from the inner clouds of darkness. Meishusama exhibited all of these positive characteristics. He surrendered his life to a Higher Will. He was inspired to work for the salvation of humanity, and despite tremendous obstacles and suffering, went on to accomplish great things.

Having conquered physical attachments, I see not a cloud in the sky of my heart.
—Meishusama VI. MK1

God works through everyone because we all have God's Spirit within us. For most of us, though, this divine influence is blocked by the presence of spiritual clouds. But the more we clear these clouds, the more receptive we become to this divine guidance. Then eventually, after the sky of our heart becomes cloudless and clear, our individual intentions shall perfectly align with God's Intentions.

I am but God's vessel, navigating in accordance with Divine Will.
                                                    —*Meishusama II. MK2*

Meishusama was just such an inspired individual. The Light of God shone brightly through him, and could actually be seen and felt by others. Because of this Light, and its tremendous impact on people's lives, many considered him a living embodiment of God. In Meishusama, this Spirit was not only inner, but also outer. In him, Spirit emerged to the surface and influenced everything he thought, said, and did. Indeed, he confessed that there was no longer any separation between God and himself—the two were fused together completely. Thus, many felt that to approach Meishusama was to see the Divine in action.

Like a drop of water merging with the ocean, Meishusama merged with God. Inwardly the two became One. However, this does not mean that they were exactly equal. The ocean contains the drop, but the drop does not contain the ocean. In other words, Miroku Omikami is always greater than the limited consciousness of humans. It is all-knowing, all-powerful, and equally present everywhere, whereas humans are still limited by time and space. Although Meishusama was One with God, it is also true that he could not speak Latin, move mountains, nor be in millions of places simultaneously (at least as far as we know). Nonetheless, through his spiritual awakening he partook of Divinity and was inwardly free and complete. He became part of the Divine, but not the totality of it. Yet, this part had no boundaries separating it from the whole, just as a drop of water has no boundaries separating it from the ocean that surrounds it.

Although the Divine is essentially formless, it can manifest in the world through Kannon, the deity of compassion, and act through a spiritually transformed individual such as Meishusama. The Divine Light of God radiates through such great souls for the spiritual benefit of humanity. Kannon was often seen standing and moving near Meishusama. He claimed that she made use of his body to serve others. Within his abdomen She placed a bright orb of golden light, which became the source of his healing and blessing power.

Through Kannon's mysterious power filling my body, transformation is here for all people. —Meishusama I. MK1

Meishusama had a deep and profound relationship with Kannon. She literally entered into him and took over his body, and then used it for the healing and upliftment of all who came into contact with him. About this relationship, Meishusama writes:

I later realized with a shock that the spirit of Kannon had begun to associate closely with me. Along with this, miraculous events connected with Her began to occur. (I will write about the details of these things as time goes by.) Finally, I came to realize that the spirit of Kannon is but one of the many manifestations of God. This divine being has transfigured Herself in order to help the world for a certain period of time, and then when the proper time comes, She will revert to Her original undivided union with God.

Since the year 1926, I have been continuously physically possessed by the spirit of Kannon. She has told me many things and given me many orders. Indeed, Kannon has used my body with perfect freedom as a physical vehicle to aid all sentient beings.

As I have previously said, I did not attain my present state through faith in Kannon. Quite the reverse, it was Kannon who approached me to use me as Her instrument. I am, one could say, a physical embodiment of Her. I am used completely as Kannon thinks fit and do not have the freedom of an ordinary person, but I do have a freedom that the ordinary person lacks. This spiritual state is very difficult to explain, as it is beyond normal comprehension. —*My Testament. ET*

Deities such as Kannon are manifestations of God's Power. Each deity tends to manifest a particular spiritual quality, such as compassion, truth, wisdom, peace, or joy. All deities are inwardly One with God, yet separate in terms of outer appearance. If one were to think of God as an invisible person, then deities could be viewed as the clothes that God wears in order for people to see Her. Because deities have a discernable form, it is easier for many to feel closer to them than to something as incomprehensible as Miroku Omikami.

Both little children and valiant men adore and yearn for Kannon's merciful eyes.
                                                    —*Infinite Compassion. MK1*

Kannon, in particular, is known in different countries by different names: in China she is called Kwan Yin, in Tibet she appears as a male deity named Chenrezig, and in India she is also regarded as a male deity named Avalokitesvara. In Japan, Kannon is sometimes perceived as female, while at other times male. This reflects the fact that God, as Miroku Omikami, is beyond gender.

Although Spirit transcends duality, it supports the manifestation of all dualities and qualities within the realm of time and space, much like a prism refracts light to create various colors and shapes. The soul is also, in its essence, neither male nor female, although it takes on these gender specific roles from one lifetime to another during the long course of its evolution.

At a certain point in the soul's evolution, it will begin to identify less with the conventional personality and more with the spiritual presence at the core of its being. When this happens, the individual becomes truly humble and selfless. Its former identity is transcended and is replaced by deep inner silence and peace. Although the personality still remains, it now operates more like a superficial mask rather than as one's true identity. The divine spirit, on the other hand, no longer feels separate from anyone or anything and now recognizes its undivided Oneness with all things.

Beyond this, if the soul continues to evolve further, it may discover that various spiritual qualities and powers begin to manifest through it. Kannon is one of these powers, and the more a soul surrenders to God the more Kannon or another divine form will operate through it to serve others. In Meishusama, this surrender appeared complete, which resulted in his soul merging completely with Kannon Bodhisattva.

Kannon descends from heaven in a cloud of golden light.
—The Descending of Kannon. MK1

Thus is revealed the great mystery of God in human form: a paradox of the human and divine, and of the physical and the spiritual. In truth, there is only one, undivided reality—not two—and all of creation partakes of this divine unity. Few, however, have the ability to clearly perceive this absolute reality. Meishusama was one who did so, and it was his sacred mission to open our eyes to greater truths and to help manifest the "World of Light."

The Light of Miroku Omikami softens and appears in the world as Kannon.
—Kannon Bodhisattva. MK1

The Mysticism of Three

Every tension of opposites culminates in a release, out of which comes the "third." In the third, the tension is resolved and the lost unity is restored. —Carl Jung

A common pattern one discovers in Meishusama's teachings is the constant reference to groups of three. Here are some examples: Currently we live in a world of sickness, poverty, and strife, but—through the cultivation of love, gratitude, and makoto—we can help usher in a world of truth, virtue, and beauty. Through the three spiritual practices of Jyorei, Natural Agriculture, and Art, we can transform our body, mind, and spirit, as reflected in our thoughts, words, and deeds. His universal philosophy embraces both the subjective realm of thoughts, feelings, and intention, as well as the objective realms of science, religion, and art, to bring us into harmony with the divine world, the spiritual world, and the physical world. All of these trinities manifest through the symbolic substances of fire, water, and earth. And finally, the spiritual development of our soul is dependent on its relationship with the three spirits: the divine spirit, the instinctive spirit, and the guardian spirit.

On a mundane level, the number three includes the following triads: length, width, and height as dimensions of space; melody, harmony, and rhythm as properties of music; solid, liquid, and gas as levels of density; past, present, and future as aspects of time; birth, life, and death as key phases of our lives; and good, better, and best as qualities of value. These triads and others form the world of our ordinary experience. On the mundane level, three represents wholeness and completion.

This emphasis on 'three' reflects Meishusama's intention to reconcile humankind's history of dualistic conflict. The number two is the basis for opposition and conflict. Most of Western Philosophy is based on the dialectics of opposites. Not only is good at war with evil, but also, fate contradicts free will. Faith is at odds with doubt, and reason struggles with emotion. Like a computer, our minds use binary logic. Everywhere, we see opposites. The direction 'up' opposes 'down', the location 'in' differs from 'out', the temperature 'hot' contrasts with 'cold.'

Meishusama draws on a third factor, a spiritual principle, to bring mediation, reconciliation, and harmony to the world of opposites. A two-legged table is unstable and can easily fall down, whereas a three-legged table is stable and, therefore, remains upright. The third leg adds width to the directions of length and height, resulting in a volume of space in the middle. This space is the principle of awareness. Introducing an impartial third observer into a conflict situation often produces a peaceful resolution because of the extra awareness that person brings.

The number three has long played a significant role in the mythologies and theologies of the world. Christians believe in the mystery of the Trinity made up of the Father, the Son, and the Holy Spirit (which can be interpreted as God the transcendental Spirit; the Son as the embodiment of Spirit; and the Holy Spirit as the love and energy that permeates the universe). Buddhism emphasizes the importance of the three jewels of the Buddha, the Dharma, and the Sangha (the teacher, the teachings, and the spiritual community). Hindus worship the deities Brahma, Vishnu, and Shiva, who perpetually create, preserve, and destroy the universe. The ancient Egyptians revered the gods Osiris, Isis, and Horus who symbolized the conscious, unconscious and superconscious aspects of the mind, respectively. Taoists cultivate Jing, Chi, and Shen, the three qualities of universal energy.

According to Pythagorean numerology, the number one symbolizes pure unity, unpolarized energy, and the transcendent cause of all things. The number two symbolizes polarized energy, dichotomy, and opposition. When the absolute unity of God separates into duality in order to become conscious of Itself, the One simultaneously becomes two and three. The objective world is the number two, and the process of the One becoming conscious of Itself is the number three. Two people in a room are not in relationship until they get to know each other. To establish a relationship, first they must communicate with each other. Number three is thus the principles of communication, relationship, mutual understanding, and love. It combines the perceiver, the perceived, and the act of perceiving into a unified process. The number three is objective awareness. As Carl Jung stated, "Three is an unfolding of the One to a condition where it can be known—unity becomes recognizable."

It is clear that Meishusama puts great value on the number three because of the spiritual principle that it introduces. The Age of Night was trapped in the conflict of opposites, and was a world of strife. With the dawning of the Age of Day, it is time to transcend conflicts through love and understanding, which are qualities of the number three. This is more than just abstract symbolism, for it has the higher purpose of reintegrating the sacred dimension back into our ordinary, day-to-day lives.

Happiness

While passing through this transient world, create the happiness of eternal life.
—Life and Death. MK1

Many people have asked, "What is the connection between the three main practices of Shumei? What do Jyorei, Natural Agriculture and Art have in common?" The single principle that ties these three together is the universal pursuit of happiness. Meishusama had great sympathy and concern for people's suffering. Very simply, he wanted, with all his heart, for people to be peaceful and happy. Happiness, to be complete, depends upon both inner and outer harmony. Inner peace contributes to outer harmony, and outer harmony contributes to inner peace. They are mutually supportive.

More than countless riches, happiness is living in safety and health.
—Gratitude. MK2

Even a saint would probably not be very happy living in a ruthless, totalitarian country that frequently violates human rights and practices genocide. His happiness would also probably be even more diminished if he was sick and in terrible pain. Although ultimate happiness comes from Spirit, even great saints have bodies capable of feeling physical pain and minds capable of experiencing emotional suffering. To experience complete happiness on all levels of body, mind, and spirit, not only do we need inner peace, but we also need our outer social and physical environment to be peaceful and healthy.

Conversely, a person living in a utopian environment would not be very happy if he was inwardly full of anger, fear, or sorrow. How often have we ignored the beauty around us because of a problem on our mind? Inner peace is essential for us to enjoy the world around us. As we grow in consciousness we become more sensitive—not less—and therefore, our preference for a harmonious environment increases. The alternative to sensitivity, which would be to deaden ourselves to feeling, is not the solution to pain because, in the process, we also dull our ability to experience joy and excitement. Thus, pain medications and psychiatric drugs do not produce happiness either.

Happiness largely depends on both subjective and objective factors. Subjectively, we feel happiest when we are relaxed in the body, quiet in the mind, and peaceful in the heart. In the objective environment, we feel happiest when we have access to good food and decent shelter, as well as a peaceful and loving environment full of beauty and comfort. Wanting to help people at all levels of spiritual development, Meishusama understood the importance of both our inner and outer worlds for fostering a balanced happiness. He wanted to help the average person in very immediate, practical ways. Thus, he avoided the trap of overly ascetic spiritual traditions that deny the importance of physical necessities while at the same time recognizing the superficiality of most utopian dreams of worldly fulfillment. This middle path was an expression of Kannon's Way—a balanced approach that avoids the extremes of asceticism and hedonism.

All three of Meishusama's prescribed activities affect both the inner and outer worlds. Through practicing Natural Agriculture, the farmer begins to develop a spiritual relationship with nature, and begins to feel a profound inner peace and contentment. Outwardly, Natural Agriculture helps to rejuvenate the ecosystem through its avoidance of toxic chemicals, and through its respect for the land. It also provides people with pure food that promotes increased levels of health and vitality.

Inwardly, beauty calms the mind, opens the heart, and uplifts the spirit. Outwardly, beautiful environments uplift society and promote social harmony by making the world an enjoyable place. In contrast to this, ugly slum dwellings promote crime, violence, and despair. The best in people and society is brought out by exposure to beautiful art, music, and architecture, whereas the worst is brought out by ugliness, noisy music, and unaesthetic, monotonous or dilapidated buildings.

Jyorei transforms the subjective dimension of experience (thoughts, feelings, and perceptions) as well as the objective dimension of experience (relationships, finances, and health). The inner leads the outer and the invisible precedes the visible. Initially, one may be like a dirty window covered by layers of grime, but over time, through Jyorei, the window becomes clean and transparent, allowing more light to shine through. As one's spiritual clouds begin to disappear, physical health is revitalized, emotional balance is restored, mental tranquility returns, and most importantly, spiritual freedom is attained. Meishusama writes: "Jyorei is usually given with the purpose of healing sickness, but it really has significance far greater than that. This significance is, in short, that Jyorei is a way to create happiness." *(Jyorei and Happiness. ET)*

Everything exists within Eternity, while, paradoxically, also moving closer toward it. Thus, the closer we get to the Divine, the more we recognize it's constant presence everywhere. We discover the absolute Unity that has always been here. Additionally, the more we are able to see the perfection around us, the more we can relax and enjoy life. The main objective is to bring about, through the purifying process of Jyorei—as well as through selfless service to others—a dramatic acceleration in our spiritual development. By doing this, we also contribute to the spiritual evolution of the world.

The way to liberate humanity lies in guiding people to the path of eternal life.
—*Meishusama III. MK1*

In this way, Jyorei, Natural Agriculture, and art and beauty, contribute to both inner and outer happiness. However, happiness primarily comes from within. Happiness comes from inner purity and love, as well as from the satisfaction gained from helping others to be happy. It comes from realizing our essential unity with the world, in which we do not see ourselves as separate from the people, places, and things around us. Feeling love for others, along with the desire to be of service, transcends mere healing—they are expressions of spiritual maturity. Love and service are also the basis for peace on earth.

However, healing the body is not enough. What most needs healing is the soul. And for the world to become a better place, society needs to be healed.

Meishusama's primary objective is the creation of a Paradise on Earth, which he describes as a world of truth, virtue, and beauty. These values and qualities will be the true foundation for world transformation. True Paradise on Earth will come from universal peace and love, not from political revolutions, social campaigns, or financial reforms. Although quite necessary, these efforts toward change must be based on peace and love, not conflict and hate. Therefore, the primary goal and activity of Shumei is soul evolution, which spiritual healing supports and is the secondary to this goal.

What Jyorei, Natural Agriculture, and art and beauty have in common is that they all promote human happiness, both on a relative level and on a spiritual level. On a mundane level, happiness tends to increase when the outer conditions in our lives improve. But on a higher level, happiness comes from inner peace and harmony, which require spiritual transformation. Jyorei promotes spiritual growth, beauty elevates the soul, and Natural Agriculture fosters love and respect for all things. Together, they contribute to a better world by bringing Light into it.

After thousands of years of waiting, a bright, shining age now draws near.
—*World of Light. MK1*

Epilogue

Meishusama is still with us in the invisible spiritual world. Many people feel his divine guidance and support as a constant influence in their lives. The three main activities that he promoted continue to expand throughout the world. Jyorei, as a spiritual practice, has spread to the four corners of the world; Natural Agriculture is replacing chemically-based farming in many areas of Japan, and interest in this approach to farming is spreading from one country to the next; while the Miho Museum is continuing to gain greater international attention.

With these activities, we hope more people may benefit from personal healing and spiritual awakening. The road to increased happiness begins when one embarks upon a program of purifying one's body and soul, and most importantly, when one takes the major step of serving God by serving others. This decision is no small matter, but is crucial for leading a truly spiritual life.

Since receiving a new life, his eyes have become gentle, his face radiant and bright.
—*Faith. MK1*

It is a paradox that the more self-serving we are, the more miserable we become, whereas the more we serve others, the happier we become. True happiness comes from expanding our sense of self to include the world around us. By serving others we also serve God. We should not, however, exclude ourselves from this greater unity, because we can also serve God by taking care of our own needs, which, in turn, enables us to better serve others. After all, how can we help others be happy if we, ourselves, are miserable? How can we aid others financially if we are destitute? How can we feed others if we cannot feed ourselves?

God's presence can be found both within and without because that which is beyond boundaries cannot be divided or confined to any specific area. God is everywhere, including the space between atoms, the vastness between planets, and the gap between our thoughts. With our limited imagination, we tend to categorize reality, putting everything into mental boxes. This creates divisions where there is really only unity. Love blossoms from seeing Spirit everywhere. God's Spirit is in the trees, the water and the sky; in the animals that roam the earth; in the fish that swim in the sea; and in the birds that soar through the heavens. Both our friends and our enemies are equally God's children. All have God's presence within them.

By serving others, we find that we are actually serving our own selves, since all of us have the same Spirit within us. Service to others purifies our motives, opens our heart, clarifies our mind, and allows God's Power to work through us. It was Meishusama's heartfelt desire to see everyone happy and fulfilled, free of the three maladies of poverty, sickness, and strife. Our sacred task is to help transform the world with love and Light into the fulfillment of his dream of Heaven on Earth.

Just as Meishusama was inspired by Kannon's infinite compassion, may each of us also be so inspired. May we also come to realize that love and gratitude are their own reward.

Thinking of the happiness that my transformation has brought me, how can I refrain from giving myself, body and soul, to returning what I have received?
—Gratitude. MK1

Glossary

Amatsunorito: Ancient chant, derived from the Shinto tradition in Japan, for divine blessings and purification. It literally means the "Heavenly Prayer."

Ancestor Spirit: Spirit of one's deceased ancestor, also referred to as *the Guardian Spirit.*

Aura: A spiritual radiation that reflects the condition of the soul.

Bodhisattva: One who dedicates himself to the salvation of others.

Daijo: A term of Buddhist origins adapted by Meishusama. It is horizontal in nature and represents a spiritual expression that is tolerant, adaptable, and inclusive.

Daikokusama: A demigod of financial wealth, health, longevity, and wisdom.

Divine Light: Spiritual radiance. *Jyorei.*

Divine Spirit: The eternal, formless, unchanging, divine spark located within individual.

Divine World: The highest level of the spiritual world. Also referred to as the World of Ultimate Mystery.

Guardian Spirit: An *Ancestor Spirit* selected to watch over and assist a person from within the *spiritual world.*

Hoshi: Selfless service to others, while dedicating the results to God.

Hoshisha: Members of Shumei who perform *hoshi* on behalf of Shumei's mission to promote the betterment of humankind.

Instinctive Spirit: A non-physical being who activates our basic desires and instincts for our survival and propagation.

Izunome: The perfect harmony and balance between *Daijo* and *Shojo.* It also represents the spiritual essence of *Kannon's Way.*

305

Jyorei: A spiritual healing method for purification and spiritual growth introduced by *Meishusama*, also referred to as *Divine Light*. The word *Jyorei* literally means "purification of the spirit."

Kaicho-Sensei: Current president of Shinji Shumeikai, Ms Hiroko Koyama.

Kaishusama: Organizational founder and the first president of Shinji Shumeikai, Ms Mihoko Koyama.

Kamigoto: Chant for atonement and purification.

Kannon: Buddhist deity of compassion and wisdom. *(See the footnote on page 8.)*

Kannon's Way: A flexible, moderate, and balanced approach to life that includes patience and tolerance, and brings harmony to one's life. *(See Izunome.)*

Karma: What we do always comes back to us in equal manner either sooner or later.

Kototama: A spiritual power inherent in the correctly pronounced sounds of words.

Makoto: A fundamental character trait that includes such higher qualities as honesty, integrity, altruism, and sincerity. A person has makoto when his actions are in alignment with his words and ideals. Essential to the practice of makoto is the consideration of others and the greater good of all.

Meishusama: A spiritual teacher who introduced *Jyorei* and *Natural Agriculture* to the world. "*Meishusama*" is an honorific, meaning "Master of Light," commonly used by Shumei members when referring to *Mokichi Okada*.

Miho Museum: A museum dedicated to Meishusama's vision of beauty.

Mikotosama: The second president of *Shinji Shumeikai*, Mr. Sokichi Koyama.

Misono: Shumei's International Center located in the mountains in Shiga prefecture, Japan.

Mokichi Okada: The birth name of *Meishusama*.

Miroku Omikami: All-encompassing presence of God.

Natural Agriculture: A spiritually based form of farming. The essence of this practice is having reverence for nature and cultivating the food crops in a manner close to how plants thrive in a natural setting.

Ohikari: Silk amulet worn when transmitting Jyorei. It consists of a small parchment bearing calligraphy by *Meishusama*.

Otamagushi: Monetary offering given in gratitude prior to *Sampai*. *(See page 285.)*

Possessing Animal Spirit: Evil spirit of discarnate animals which like to put people under their control, and can possess human bodies.

Primary Guardian Spirit: *(See Guardian Spirit.)*

Proactive Purification: Purification through positive actions such as eating healthy food, helping others, and receiving Jyorei.

Purification: A natural mechanism and process to cleanse the *spiritual clouds* accumulated in one's spiritual body. Depending upon the degree and type of *spiritual clouds*, it can appear in various forms and intensities.

Reactive Purification: Purification through pain and suffering.

Reincarnation: The individual soul's rebirth again and again on its evolutionary journey toward God.

Sampai: In Shumei, it means 'coming to a Shumei center to chant and receive *Jyorei*.'

Secondary Guardian Spirit: *(See Animal Spirit.)*

Sensei: A Japanese word meaning "teacher." It is a title given to those who have achieved a certain degree of skill and knowledge in a certain field of endeavor. Shumei's senseis are authorized by the organization to teach, counsel, give spiritual guidance, perform rituals, and oversee administrative work.

Shinji Shumeikai: Spiritual fellowship following Meishusama's teachings. It is often referred to as *Shumei*.

Shojo: A term of Buddhist origins adapted by *Meishusama*. Shojo is vertical in nature and represents a spiritual expression that is principled, restrictive, narrow, and disciplined. It is conservative, introspective. It is the complementary principle of *daijo*. *Meishusama* taught that both horizontal *daijo* and vertical *shojo* must be in harmony for a spiritual pursuit to succeed. The symbol of such harmony is the equilateral cross.

Shumei: *(See Shinji Shumeikai.)*

Soul: That which carries a person's deepest individual characteristics from lifetime, and is capable of evolving spirituality.

Spirit: The innermost essence and source of all things. Within individuals it is referred to as *Divine Spirit*. *(See Divine Spirit.)*

Spiritual Body: The immaterial body that influences the mind and affects the physical body.

Spiritual Clouds: Impurities caused by one's negative thoughts, words, and deeds that obscure our spirit and darken our soul. They are the source of all human misery.

Spiritual Cords: Invisible, spiritual bonds between people, places, and things.

Spiritual World: The invisible, spiritual dimension of existence that exerts a profound influence on the physical world. It is also referred to as the world of deceased spirits.

Toku Energy: The spiritual wealth gained by doing good works and making others happy. Not only does one profit from the accumulation of this energy, but it also benefits one's friends and family as well. Although good always comes from amassing *toku energy*, its specific benefits ultimately are in the hands of God. *Toku Energy* is sometimes referred to as "Grace."

The World of the Ultimate Mystery: The highest level of the spiritual world. Also referred to as *the Divine World*.

Zengensanji: Special chant composed by Meishusama for envisioning an ideal world.

Bibliography

Appleton, Nancy. *The Curse of Louis Pasteur*. Santa Monica, CA: Choice Publishing, 1999.

Braden, Gregg. *Awakening to Zero Point: The Collective Initiation*. Belleview, WA: Radio Bookstore Press, 1997.

Combs, Allan. *The Radiance of Being: Understanding the Grand Integral Vision; Living the Integral Life, 2nd ed.* St. Paul, MN: Paragon, 2002.

Dauncey, Guy. *"Ten Reasons Why Organic Food is Better,"* Common Group Magazine. August 2002.

De Chardin, Teilhard. *The Phenomenon of Man*. Translated by Bernard Wall. New York: Harper & Row 1959.

Deguchi, Kyotaro. *The Great Onisaburo Deguchi*. Translated by Charles Rowe. Tokyo: Aiki News, 1998.

Donelan, Peter. *Growing To Seed*. Willits, CA: Ecology Action, 1999.

Enby, Erik, Peter Gosch, and Michael Sheehan. *Hidden Killers: The Revolutionary Medical Discoveries of Professor Guenther Enderlein*. Austin, TX: Sheehan Communications, 1990.

Francis, Raymond, with Kester Cotton. *Never Be Sick Again: Health Is a Choice, Learn How to Choose It*. Deerfield Beach, FL: Health Communications, Inc., 2002.

Frederick, Perls S.. *The Gestalt Approach & Eye Witness to Therapy*. Palo Alto, CA: Science and Behavior Books, 1973.

Fromm, Erich. *The Art of Loving*. New York: Harper & Rowe Publishers, 1956.

Fukuoka, Masanobu. *The One-Straw Revolution: An Introduction to Natural Farming*. Emmaus, PA: Rodale Press, 1978.

Goble, Frank G. *The Third Force: The Psychology of Abraham Maslow*. New York: Simon & Schuster, 1970.

Hall, Edward T. and Mildred Reed. *Hidden Differences: Doing Business with the Japanese*. New York: Anchor Books/Doubleday, 1987.

Hamilton, Lisa H. *Farming to Create Heaven on Earth*. Shigaraki, Japan: Shumei International Press, 2007.

Harman, Willis W. and Elisabet Sahtouris. *Biology Revisioned*. Berkeley, CA: North Atlantic Books, 1998.

Hawkins, David R. *Power vs. Force: The Hidden Determinants of Human Behavior*. Sedona, AZ: Veritas Publishers, 1995.

The Holy Bible, New Kings James Version. Nashville, TN: Thomas Nelson Inc, 1982.

Isaacs, Nathan. *A Brief Introduction to Piaget*. New York: Schocken Books, 1974.

Iwao, Takahashi. *Okada Mokichi ni okeru Shukyo to Geijutsu (Spirituality and Art in the Philosophy of Mokichi Okada).* Japan: Kazeno Bara, 1984.

Jerkins, Diana. *Spirit of The Land: Shumei Natural Agriculture Philosopy and Practice.* Shigaraki, Japan: Shumei International Press, 2012.

Jodidio, Philip. *Heaven on Earth.* Shigaraki, Japan: Shinji Shumeikai Press, 2014.

Johrei Fellowship. *Reminiscences About Meishu-sama: A Collection of Stories and Anecdotes.* Torrance, CA: Johrei Fellowship, 1996.

Kasulis, Thomas. P. *Shinto: The Way Home.* Honolulu: University of Hawaii Press, 2004.

Kimura, Genku Yasuhiko. *"Beauty as a Path of Peace," The Journal of Integral Thinking for Visionary Action.* Anaheim, CA: Vision in Action™

Kishimoto, Hideo. *"Mahayana Buddhism and Japanese Thought," Philosophy East and West.* University of Hawaii Press. October, 1954.

———. (translation) *Lao Tzu: The Book of Balance: Lao Tzu's Tao Teh Ching.* University of Science and Philosophy, 2002.

Koren, Leonard. *Wabi-Sabi for Artists, Designers, Poets & Philosophers.* Berkeley, CA: Stone Bridge Press, 1994.

Kropotkin, Petr. *Mutual Aid: A Factor in Evolution.* London: Freedom Press, 1998.

Lipton, Bruce. *The Biology of Belief: Unleashing the Power of Consciousness, Matter and Miracles.* Santa Rosa, CA: Mountain of Love/Elite Books, 2005.

Lovejoy, Arthur. *The Great Chain of Being.* Cambridge, MA: Harvard University Press, 1936.

May, Rollo. *My Quest for Beauty.* Dallas, TX: Saybrook Publishing Co. 1985.

McIntosh, Steve. *Evolution's Purpose.* New York, NY: SelectBooks, 2012.

McIntosh, Steve. *Integral Consciousness and the Future of Evolution.* St. Paul, MN: Paragon House, 2007

Mitchell, Stephen. (Translation) *Tao Te Ching.* New York, NY: Harper and Row, 1988.

Naka, Masao. *Michi Hitosuji:Shinji Shumeikai no Ayumi (Going Straight into a Path of Faith: Development of Shinji Shumeikai).* Tokyo: Time Life Books, 1983.

MOA Publications. *The Light from the East: Mokichi Okada, Volume two.* Atami, Japan: MOA Publications, 1986.

Okada, Mokichi. *A Hundred Teachings of Meishusama 1st ed.* Japan: Shinji Shumeikai, 2001.

———. *Foundation of Paradise.* Torrance, CA: Johrei Fellowship, 1984.

———. *Fragments From the Teachings of Meishu-sama.* Torrance, CA: Johrei Fellowship, 1998.

———. Gokowaroku *(The Guiding Light: A Collection of Oral Teaching by Meishu-sama Vol. 1).*Translated by Henry Ajiki, Tuson, AZ: Johrei Fellowship, 2003.

———. *Health and the New Civilization.* Torrance, CA: Johrei Fellowship, 1998.

———. *Johrei: Divine Light of Salvation.* Translated by Ichiro Nakamura, Kyoto, Japan: The Society of Johrei,1984.

———. *Kannon Gyō (Kannon's Way).* Shigaraki, Japan: Shinji Shumeikai, 2004.

———. *Meishusama Shizen-nōhō Goronbun-shyu (Natural Agriculture Teachings of Meishusama).* Shigaraki,Japan: Shinji Shumeikai, 2005.

———. *Miakarishu: A Collection of Light.* Pasadena, CA: Shinji Shumeikai of America, 1992.

———. *The Teachings of Meishusama.* Pasadena, CA: Shinji Shumeikai of America, 1990.

Oxford University Press. *The Dhammapada: The Sayings of the Buddha.* New York: Oxford University Press, 2000.

———. *Gestalt Therapy Verbatim.* Moab, Utah: Real People Press, 1969.

Picken, Stuart D. B. *Shinto: Meditations for Reversing the Earth.* Berkeley, CA: Stone Bridge Press, 2002.

Philippi, Donald. *Norito: A Translation of the Ancient Japanese Ritual Prayers.* Princeton, NJ: Princeton University Press, 1990.

Prabhavananda, Swami, and Christopher Isherwood. *The Song of God: Bhagavad-Gita.* Hollywood, CA: The Vedanta Society of Southern California, 1951.

Rohlfing, Gerard. *Sincerity and Truth: The Life Story of Meishusama.* Pasadena, CA: Shumei America Publications, 2005.

Sahtouris, Elisabet. "*A Tentative Model of a Living Universe, Part 1 & 2,*" *The Journal of Integral Thinking for Visionary Action.* Anaheim, CA: Vision in Action™

Schumacher, E.F. *A Guide for the Perplexed.* New York, NY: Harper & Row, Publishers, Inc., 1977.

Scott, Graham G. *The Complete Idiot's Guide to Shamanism.* Indianapolis, IN: Alpha Books, 2002.

Sheldrake, Rupert. *A New Science of Life: The Hypothesis Formative Causation.* Toronto, Canada: Saunders of Toronto Ltd., 1981.

Shumei America. *Shumei's Chants: The Amatsunorito, Zengensanji, and Kamigoto.* Pasadena, CA: Shumei America, 2004.

Smith, Huston. *The Forgotten Truth: The Common Vision of the World's Religions.* New York: Harper & Row, 1976.

———. *The World's Religions: Our Great Wisdom Traditions.* New York: Harper Collins, 1991.

Stafford-Clark, David. *What Freud Really Said.* New York: Schocken Books, 1971.

Stiskin, Nahum. *The Looking-Glass God: Shinto, Yin-Yang, and a Cosmology for Today.* Brookline, MA: Autumn Press, 1972.

Suzuki, David. "*Organic Farming is Realistic, Science Matters*" *Common Ground Magazine.* Vancouver, Canada: Common Ground Publishing Corp, August 2002.

Talbot, Michael. *The Holographic Universe.* New York: HarperCollins, 1991.

Tielhard de Chardin, Pierre. *The Phenomenon of Man.* New York: Harper & Rowe, 1959.

Timms, Moira. *Beyond Prophecies and Predictions: Everyone's Guide to the Coming Changes.* New York: Random House, 1994.

Tolle, Eckhart. *The Power of Now: A Guide to Spiritual Enlightenment.* Novato, CA: New World Library, 1999.

Tompkins, Peter, and Christopher Bird. *The Secret Life of Plants: A Fascinating Account of the Physical, Emotional, and Spiritual Relations between Plants and Man.* New York: Harper and Row, 1973.

———. *The Secrets of the Soil: New Solutions for Restoring our Planet.* New York: Harper and Row, 1998.

Vedavyas, Dr. *Hinduism in the Space Age.* Hyderabad – Bangalore, India: Vedavyasa Bharathi', University of Vedic Sciences, 1995

Wa'na'nee'che (Renault, Dennis), and Timothy Freke. *Principles of Native American Spirituality (Thorsons Principles Series).* London: HarperCollins Publishers, 1996.

Waters, Owen, *The Shift: The Revolution in Human Consciousness.* Delaware: Infinite Being Publishing LLC, 2006.

Watson, Burton. (Translation) *The Lotus Sutra.* New York: Columbia University Press, 1993.

Watts, Alan. *The Book: On the Taboo Against Knowing Who You Are.* New York: Pantheon Books, 1966.

———. *Tao: The Watercourse Way.* New York: Pantheon Books, 1975.

———. *The Way of Zen.* New York: Pantheon Books, 1957.

West, John Anthony. *Serpent in the Sky: The High Wisdom of Ancient Egypt.* New York: Harper & Row, 1979.

Wilbur, Ken. *The Marriage of Sense and Soul: Integrating Science and Religion.* New York: Random House, 1998.

Williams, George. *Shinto,* Philadelphia: Chelsea House, 2005.

Yu, Chun–Fang. *Kuan-Yin: The Chinese Transformation of Avalokitesvara.* New York: Columbia University Press, 2001.

Illustrations

Diagrams

Drawings

Photographs

(All of the photographs listed below were originally in color.)

Index

117, 155, 156, 182, 196, 198, 199,
268, 294, 297, 298, 305, 307
Divine World 65-67, 292, 298
Donelan, Peter 243
Dynamic Balance 160, 186

E

Eckhart, Meister 46
Edison, Thomas 230
Einstein, Albert 115, 128, 178, 227, 232
Emerson, Ralph W. 36, 88, 233, 255

F

Fairness 187
Farming 12, 224, 230, 234, 249, 309
Flexibility 173, 187
Francis, Raymond 96, 98
Freud, Sigmund 37, 170, 189, 253
Fukuoka, Masanobu 230, 309

G

Genetically Engineered Organism (*also*
GMO) 87, 227
Gentleness 122, 187
Gibran, Kahlil 213
Gorecki, Henryk 261
Gratitude 10, 21, 37, 44-48, 55, 62, 109,
151, 160, 206, 210, 232, 234, 265,
283-285, 304, 306
Grof, Stanislav 221
Guardian Spirit 74, 305, 307

H

Happiness 1, 5, 9, 15 15, 20, 21, 26, 41,
42, 44, 47, 52, 55, 58, 109, 111,
112, 117, 123, 132, 139-142, 144,
148, 151, 153, 172, 185, 195, 198,

199, 203, 210, 212, 239, 252, 265,
288, 289, 300-304
Hasidic proverb 195
Hippocrates 105
Holistic 22, 186
Hopi 126
Hoshi 148, 150-152, 285, 305
Howard, Albert 236
Humility 181, 183, 188
Humor 183-185, 188

I

Inclusiveness 187
Instinctive Spirit 72, 305
Interconnectivity 29
Izunome 50, 122, 141, 149, 189, 305

J

Jesus 70, 122, 140, 150, 153, 203
Jung, Carl 190, 298, 299
Jyorei xii, xiii, 17, 26, 34, 38-41, 60, 65,
81, 89, 93, 95, 104, 125, 139, 192,
194-218, 250, 266, 268, 269, 274,
277, 279, 280, 284, 301, 302, 306

K

Kaicho-Sensei (*also* Hiroko Koyama)
xiv, 266, 269, 306
Kaishusama (*also* Mihoko Koyama) 17,
266-269, 272, 275, 278, 306
Kali Yuga 126
Kamigoto 286, 289, 290, 291, 306, 311
Kannon 8, 11, 19, 22, 61, 62, 152, 157,
160, 162, 186, 191,192, 206, 216,
267, 284, 290, 292, 295-297, 304,
306
Kannon Society of Japan 11

Made in the USA
Middletown, DE
08 April 2021